PLAYS

BY

BJÖRNSTJERNE BJÖRNSON

PLAYS

BY

BJÖRNSTJERNE BJÖRNSON

THE GAUNTLET (EN HANSKE)
BEYOND OUR POWER (OVER EVNE)
THE NEW SYSTEM (DET NY SYSTEM)

TRANSLATED FROM THE NORWEGIAN WITH AN INTRODUCTION BY

EDWIN BJÖRKMAN

LONDON
DUCKWORTH & CO.
1913

CONTENTS

INTRODUCTION

INTRODUCTION

BJÖRNSTJERNE BJÖRNSON was born December 8, 1832, in a solitary rectory, lost among the mountains of northern Norway. His father was then the spiritual head of the smallest parish in the whole country. There the boy spent the first years of his life, seeing more of nature than of man. When he was six the family removed to the Romsdal district, on the Atlantic coast, which is one of the most beautiful and also most characteristic parts of Norway. In 1843 the boy was sent to school in the little fishing-town of Molde, not far from his parental home, and at eighteen he went to Christiania to study at the same school where the young Ibsen was then preparing himself for entrance into the national university.

He was only twenty when he wrote his first play—historical, of course, with a theme from the Sagas. It was accepted by the Christiania Theatre, but before it reached a performance the young author realised its shortcomings and withdrew it. His public career began as dramatic critic on a daily newspaper, and in this capacity he made history by leading the opposition against the Danish influence, which had until then prevailed on the national stage. From the very first he spoke with the assurance and authority of a born chieftain, and however frequently challenged, his leadership was never surrendered or lost. Toward the Norway with which the world is familiar to-day—a nation having a culture marvellously disproportionate to its physical and economical conditions—no one man has contributed more than Björnson,

3

and to understand his spirit is to understand the country itself.

His first dramatic work of lasting value was produced in 1856, after a visit to the Swedish city of Upsala, where students from the three Scandinavian countries had met for the promotion of mutual sympathy. It was a brief historic play named "Between the Battles," which, because of its novelty of form, exercised an unmistakable influence both on Ibsen and Strindberg. Its terse prose was that of the old Sagas. The next year Björnson produced and published his first peasant tale, "Synnöve Solbakken" (Synnöve Sunnyside). Henrik Jäger, the literary historian of Norway, says that two things assured the success of that tale and those that followed: their style, at once picturesque and simple; and their author's discovery that mental reserve and laconic expression are characteristic traits of the Norwegian peasant.

To this discovery and to his own charming application of it, Björnson was led by a double study: of the old Sagas and of the peasants themselves. Always and everywhere he strove to recognise the unbroken connection between the life of the past and the life still led by the people around him. The result of his effort was that he forestalled Maeterlinck in effective use of commonplace, almost meaningless words.

In 1857 he succeeded Ibsen as leader of the theatre started at Bergen by Ole Bull, and during the eighteen months he remained in that place he married a young actress, Caroline Reimers, whose devotion and loving comprehension of his genius served him as a valuable support to the very end of his life. On the whole, the fate of Björnson was always fortunate, and not the least so in regard to his marriage. It resulted in a relationship that coloured his art, and made him logically what he later became: a champion of the new womanhood. And few have done more than he to assert and defend the essential equality of the two sexes.

After his return to Christiania in 1859, he wrote a number of charming lyrics, many of which were set to music by Halfdan Kjerulf, who was then Norway's greatest composer. He wrote also several patriotic songs, and one of these, "Yea, We Love the Land that Bore Us," caught the popular taste to such an extent that it rapidly won acceptance as the national hymn.

Björnson was the first man in Norway to receive an annual pension from the government. This happened in 1863, when he was only thirty-one years old, and in the same year he delivered the first of those public lectures which came to form such an important part of his activity, bringing him into a personal contact with the people that a man like Ibsen could never attain. As a speaker he exercised a magnetism that has rarely been equalled either in his own country or outside of it. Yet his words were simple enough, though at times he could rise to the highest poetic flights even when speaking impromptu. But what really secured his hold on his listeners was his transparent sincerity, his earnestness, and his insistence on telling them not what they liked to hear, but what he believed to be right and true. Add to this that he possessed an almost uncanny perception of what was going on in the mind of the people, and that he knew well how to reckon with what he thus perceived, although often enough his task was to lead his countrymen to a position diametrically opposed to the one previously held by them.

In 1862 Björnson wrote his first really significant play, the trilogy "Sigurd the Bad," which two years later was followed by another fine, although not epoch-making piece of work, the historical drama "Mary Stuart in Scotland." When, in 1865, he broke new ground at last, the medium he used for the purpose was slight enough: a two-act play named "The Newly Married Couple." But it was a prose play dealing with the everyday life of his own time and place. It displayed no violent passions, and was in no way sensational. All it did was to portray "the soul processes taking place within a young woman as she leaves her parents' home to follow her husband—that is, as she ceases to be primarily a daughter, in order to become primarily a wife."

In spite of its unmistakable shortcomings, the play exercised a wide influence, and not the least so on Ibsen, who a few years later produced "The League of Youth." The relationship between Ibsen and Björnson, which always remained one of mutual give and take even when they were emotionally estranged, has often been represented as one of a smaller mind to a greater. The truth is that Björnson was as great as Ibsen, but in a different way. The latter specialised in the drama, while the former was always tempted to embrace the entire field of literary endeavour; nay, the whole vast realm of human life in all its varied manifestations.

Ibsen became in the end one of the world's great dramatists, and one of the corner-stones of the new drama which is only now coming into existence. If we restrict the comparison between them to this field alone, Björnson must necessarily suffer, but even then a closer analysis will prove him to have rendered much greater service than is generally admitted. The constant exchange of impulses and ideas between him and Ibsen constitutes one of the most interesting phenomena recorded in literary history, and, strange as it may seem, in this mutual exchange it was Björnson who gave the most. As a rule it seems as if the seeds of the forms still to be developed sprang into being within his richer and more enthusiastic mind, to be later nursed into perfection within the colder but more persistent mind of Ibsen. The evolution of the man who wrote "Rosmersholm" may be characterised as a process of slow and painful elimination, while the onward march of Björnson was one of triumphant discovery. Three times, in particular, the latter seems to have furnished the "clue" needed by Ibsen in his tormenting pursuit of self-knowledge. This Björnson did through two of the plays already mentioned, "Between the Battles" and "The Newly Married Couple," and through a third one that followed in 1875, "A Business Failure."

Nor does this reflected importance of Björnson, derived from his influence on the development of his more famous rival, dispose of his significance in the annals of the modern drama. Some of his plays belong to the greatest produced during the last century, and will undoubtedly live for a long time to come. They are less universal in their application than those of Ibsen, but they are also more human, better adapted to that side of man which forbids his living up to his highest possibilities at each single moment of his life. I do not mean to say that Björnson's dramatic art administers to the weaknesses of man, as do so many plays of ephemeral attraction; it simply reckons with them. Somebody said once that whenever Björnson had thundered for a while, he had to smile a little—and his smile was not grim like that of Ibsen. In other words, his work is more emotional than that of Ibsen, and for this very reason it should exert an increasing appeal on the generation that is now arriving at maturity.

"The Editor," a drama picturing the demoralising effect exercised by an influential press under the leadership of selfish and unscrupulous men, preceded "A Business Failure," but though belonging to the new order, it was still too uncertain in form, and too polemical in spirit, to achieve the revolution resulting from the later play. "A Business Failure " was not only the first wholly successful specimen of the modern prose play produced in the Scandinavian North, but it served also to introduce money and business into Scandinavian literature, and thence into the literature of Germany. In this respect it went beyond what had already been achieved by Augier and the younger Dumas in France. To them love was always the supreme theme; to Björnson it was only one strand out of many that are woven into the rope of life. For this very reason, perhaps, "A Business Failure" achieved an additional distinction, which by many critics has been declared its greatest: namely that of being the first true stage picture of a Norwegian home. And this quality of domestic realism goes far to explain why it became at once, and has always remained, a great favourite in Germany, while to this day it has failed to win approval in France.

In 1877 Björnson published his first novel, "Magnhild," which, while an exquisite piece of work, was rendered significant chiefly by the new view of marriage voiced in it. If not based on love, Björnson dared to assert—and the assertion was a very radical one in those days—marriage was as immoral as any illegitimate relationship, if not worse, and the breaking of it must be held not only permissible, but a duty. In other ways, too, the novel was a forerunner of the play, "The Gauntlet," by which, a few years later, Björnson furnished one of the main impulses for the Scandinavian feminist movement.

Of "The New System," completed in 1879, Björnson said himself that its interest was psychological rather than dramatic. For this very reason, however, it should be germane to the present time. And it derives still further interest from being the main dramatic expression of the principle which had gradually become Björnson's final formulation of man's foremost duty to himself, to others, and to life in its entirety.

The cry uttered by Ibsen in "Brand" as the utmost wisdom to be distilled out of life was: "Be yourself!" The cry of Björnson, uttered first in an address to the students of Christiania University, and later made the ever-present undercurrent in "The New System," was "Live in Truth!" What he meant was that no appearances matter in the end; that nothing really counts but what we *are;* and that, consequently, the way to perfection lies through a frank acknowledgment of our innermost natures. And this demand for truthfulness he extended to the state as well as to the individual. In these days, when the best men all over the civilised world seem agreed that the most effective remedy for social evils and mistakes lies in publicity, "The New System" has a timeliness almost equalling that of a political platform.

The electoral campaign of 1879, which placed the Radical party, known as the "Left," in control of the government, marked a turning point in the country's history as well as one of the first definite steps toward the dissolution of the union with Sweden. Björnson was the soul of the movement which carried that campaign to victory, thus extending his leadership also to the field of politics. How powerful that leadership was may be judged from the nickname given him of "Norway's uncrowned king." Both in Sweden and among his opponents in Norway, it was often asserted that he used his position in a manner meant to enhance his own fame and power. But although, like all strong and farseeing men, he was arbitrary in his self-assertion, yet his motives remained always pure and his purposes raised far above those of men usually classed as politicians. And in all he did to guide his country to self-consciousness and spiritual as well as political independence, there seems to have been little, if anything, of hatred toward those that stood in the way.

It was for those that made life small and mean and ugly that his actual hatred was reserved, and it never was more likely to break into open flame than when anybody repeated the time-honoured belief that life was impelled by desires rather than by duties. The presence and power of such desires, especially those connected with man's sexual life, he admitted readily, and he was always prepared to take them into practical account. But that any desire must needs be stronger than the man within whom it makes itself felt, he neither could nor would admit. Out of this feeling on his part sprang "The Gauntlet" first of all, and later the novel "The House of the Kurts." The main objective of his attack was the so-called double standard of morality, by which a separate code of sexual ethics was provided for each of the two sexes. It was by no means the first time that standard had been attacked, but until then its enemies had almost invariably been satisfied to demand for woman the liberties accorded to man by time-honoured custom. Björnson was probably the first one to assert—and undoubtedly the very first one to do so in a work of high artistic quality—that men must be as chaste as women if they are to retain that precious stamp of social approval known as "respectability." Other writers had defended the woman "with a past"; Björnson dared to attack the man with a similar past—and for a time, at least, he did so with undoubted success. Whether his position will finally be assumed by the race in this matter remains yet to be seen, but as long as the race continues the discussion of that matter, with all its ramifications among human institutions and ideas, Björnson's play must be counted a contribution that cannot be overlooked by any seeker after truth.

Before he was led to take this extreme attitude in questions of sexual relationship, his spiritual position had in other ways undergone a marked and far-reaching change. From his parents he had inherited not only a strong religious feeling, but a view of Christianity that rendered it a satisfactory outlet for a typical Scandinavian tendency, designated by one of the younger Swedish writers as "the passion for the infinite." During the seventies Björnson drifted more and more away from his inherited attitude, led principally by the evolutionary re-interpretations of scientific truths. In 1880–81 he made a lecture trip to the United States, which seems also to have, in many ways, furthered and hastened this broadening of his spirit. Shortly after his return he published a story named "Dust," in which his new attitude of mind found its first artistic expression. It was his "Ghosts"; but the inheritance from which he saw men suffering was spiritual rather than physical.

This change within him found its clearest and yet fairest utterance in the first part of "Beyond Our Power," published the same year as "The Gauntlet." In "Dust" he had taken issue against outgrown religious ideas. In the play he turned once for all against man's craving to escape from life's realities by building up around himself a supernatural sham-existence. He had come to feel that the belief in miracles lay at the bottom of the Christian faith, its most typical characteristic, and he had also come to feel that this belief implied an unrealisable hope of a special setting aside of universal laws for the benefit of the individual who did not dare to face the consequences of his own acts.

In a second play, named also "Beyond Our Power"—which is a sequel to the earlier one, but written in such a manner that the two plays remain mutually independent—there appears a character named *Johan Sverd*, and a blind man might see that he is none but Björnson himself. In his mouth Björnson has laid a passage that explains not only what moved

him to write the two parts of "Beyond Our Power," but
also the spirit that informed his entire subsequent artistic
activity.

"But I tell you," says *Johan Sverd*, "that the day will come
when mankind must discover that there lies more greatness
and poetry in what is natural and possible—however insignifi-
cant it may frequently appear—than in the world's whole
store of supernaturalism, from the first sun-myth down to
the latest sermon preached about it."

In his later development, Björnson was almost Greek in his
aversion to what pretended to exceed human measures while
still having its roots within man himself. "Is there anything
more gruesome," cries another character in the play just
mentioned, "than that force within ourselves which goads
us on to what our whole nature resists? And can happiness
be possible on this earth until our reason becomes so completely a part of our nature, that nothing retains the power
of using us in that way?"

Björnson never wrote more than one novel of the length to
which American and English readers have been accustomed.
It appeared in 1884, and the name of it, literally translated,
is "The Flags Are Flying." In English it is generally
known as "The House of the Kurts." The problem which
its author set for himself in this story was that of heredity
vs. education—and it was strictly in keeping with his life-long
optimism that he found a verdict for education, by which he
believed it possible to overcome the tendencies implanted in
the organism at birth. At the same time, however, Björnson
returned in this book once more to the question of sexual
morality, but less with a view to stating what it ought to
imply, than with a hope of outlining a road for the attain-
ment of it. Here as elsewhere, his plea was for knowledge
as the one firm basis on which life may be safely rested. For

the innocence that is based on ignorance he showed not only contempt but actual hostility.

His greatest novel was undoubtedly "In the Ways of God," printed in 1889. There science and religion, knowledge and faith, the natural and the supernatural stand face to face in the persons of a physician and a clergyman. The entire book, from the first line to the last, is a sermon against intolerance, but clothed in exquisitely artistic form. Life comes first, religion and everything else in the second place, is its lesson. God is still supreme in this new world of Björnson's, but it is a God of law and evolution, not of lawless miracles. And what the author has to say against the superstitions and the dogmas commonly masquerading under the name of religion may as well be said against the dead and stiffened dogmas of a science believing itself to have said the final word on life and its limitless possibilities.

The second part of "Beyond Our Power," published in 1895, did for social superstition what the earlier play had done for that element in religion which Björnson had come to regard as lying "beyond the limits of man." It is one of the most powerful portrayals of the modern struggle between capital and labour which western literature has produced so far. At the same time, it presents a rarely beautiful picture of love between brother and sister.

From 1898 to 1904 Björnson produced four plays, notable both in spirit and form. All but one of them dealt with the relationship between the coming and the going generations, between parents and children. With sympathy for both, and understanding of the new as well as the old, Björnson, as a rule, took sides against the Nietzschean tendencies of the younger generations. The last of those plays, "Dayland," was his "Fathers and Sons," but unlike Turgeniev's work, it brings the two warring elements to a mutual understanding, based on the fact that age, if willing to see, may recognise its own youth in the children, while these, as they grow older, tend to revert to the position still held by their elders. This play was dedicated to the Swedish Academy, from which Björnson in 1903 had received the Nobel prize for literature.

During his later years much of his time was devoted to efforts on behalf of two ideas in which he believed the future happiness of mankind principally involved. Those were the ideas of universal peace, and of the gradual federation of related races which, in the course of time, had become broken up into hostile nationalities. Dealing first of all with his own race, he advocated a Pan-Germanic ideal, based not on conquest, but on voluntary combination. At the same time he was tireless in his pleas for justice to oppressed racial groups, like those of the Poles and the Finlanders, the Danes of Schleswig-Holstein, and the Austrian Slovaks.

In 1909, within less than a year of his death, he brought out a final play, "When the Young Wine Blossoms," which proved an astounding revelation of powers retained to the very verge of the grave. In this last work, as in almost all its predecessors, Björnson displayed a good humour that literally sparkled. Reformer and prophet that he was, he was nevertheless a man who saw more of life's pleasant than of its unpleasant sides. And most of the time there was a merry twinkle in his eye that sometimes expanded into an abandon more Gallic than Scandinavian. But his laughter was always as innocent as it was whole-hearted.

As the presentiment of approaching death seized him at last, he made a final endeavour to preserve the life he liked so well. Leaving his beloved homestead, Aulestad, he made his way to Paris, and there he lingered, now hopeful and now resigned, until the end came in 1910. First of all, and from first to last, he was a great personality—a man who towered so high that even his own work looks small in comparison with what he *was*. Clean, strong, fiery, gifted with a wonderful magnetic power, he seemed throughout his long life a giant among ordinary men. Rarely, if ever, has a private individual to such an extent been able to stamp himself on the life and fate of a nation. Still more rarely has such an individual so completely refrained from using his exceptional position for the promotion of his private interests. And it must be held rarest of all that a man thus favoured preserved to the end the simple virtues that are generally associated only with those lowly ones whose position removes them beyond the reach of temptation.

A CHRONOLOGICAL LIST OF PLAYS BY BJÖRNSTJERNE BJÖRNSON

THE GAUNTLET
(EN HANSKE)
1883

CHARACTERS

RIIS
MRS. RIIS
SVAVA, *their daughter*
CHRISTENSEN
MRS. CHRISTENSEN
ALF, *their son*
DR. NORDAN
KARL HOFF
MARGIT, *maid at the Riises'*
THOMAS, *the man-servant of Dr. Nordan*

THE GAUNTLET

(EN HANSKE)

ACT I

A room with double doors in the middle of the rear wall. The doors are open and show a park, through the trees of which may be seen glimpses of the sea. There are windows on both sides of the doorway. Both side walls also have doors. Between the door on the right and the nearest window toward the park stands a piano. Against the opposite wall stands a cabinet. On either side, nearest the audience, there is a sofa with a small table, easy-chairs and other chairs in front of it.

FIRST SCENE

MRS. RIIS. DR. NORDAN.

MRS. RIIS is seated on the left-hand sofa. DR. NORDAN is sitting on a chair right between the tables. His head is covered with a straw hat which he has pushed far back on his head. A large handkerchief lies across one knee. He is leaning forward over his hands, which are resting on the top of his walking stick.

MRS. RIIS. Why, you are not listening to me at all.

NORDAN. What was it you asked?

MRS. RIIS. About the suit against Mrs. North—what else could it have been?

MRS. RIIS. But, dear doctor, don't you believe with all of us, that this will turn out a happy marriage?

NORDAN. He is a fine fellow. But nevertheless—I have been fooled so often— Uh, huh!

MRS. RIIS. But she was happy. And so she is to-day.

NORDAN. Well, it's too bad I can't see her. Good morning, madam.

MRS. RIIS. Good morning, my dear doctor. So you are going away now?

NORDAN. I have to have a breathing spell.

MRS. RIIS. Yes, you need it. Well, good luck to you— and I thank you with all my heart!

NORDAN. And I thank you, Mrs. Riis! [*As he walks out*] Too bad I couldn't say good-bye to Svava!

SECOND SCENE

MRS. RIIS. *Later* RIIS.

> MRS. RIIS *takes a foreign periodical from the table at the left and makes herself comfortable on the sofa in such a position that she faces the park. During the next two scenes she reads as often as she has a chance.*

RIIS. [*Comes from the right; he is in his shirt sleeves and busily occupied with his collar*] Good morning!—Was that Nordan who left?

MRS. RIIS. Yes.

> RIIS *goes toward the door on the left, turns and disappears through the door on the right; then he comes in again and performs the same manœuvre; all the time he is struggling with his collar.*

MRS. RIIS. Is there anything I can help you with?

RIIS. Thanks just the same! These modern shirts are a nuisance. I bought a few in Paris.

MRS. RIIS. I think you brought home a whole dozen?

RIIS. And a half! [*He goes into the room on the right, comes out again, makes the same excursion to the left as before, accompanied by the same struggle with the collar as before*] Otherwise I am speculating on something.

MRS. RIIS. It must be some very intricate question.

RIIS. So it is.—So it is.—Indeed!—Well, if this collar isn't— There! At last! [*He disappears and returns again, but now with the collar in his hand*] I am thinking of—thinking of— of what our dear daughter is made up.

MRS. RIIS. Of what she is made up?

RIIS. Yes—how much of you, and how much of me, and so on.—That is, what she has from your family, and what from mine, and so on.—Svava is a remarkable girl.

MRS. RIIS. She is, indeed.

RIIS. As a whole, she is neither you nor me—nor the two of us together.

MRS. RIIS. Svava is something more.

RIIS. And something considerably more at that. [*He disappears once more, whereupon he reappears with his coat on and engaged in brushing it off*] What did you say?

MRS. RIIS. Nothing.—For that matter, Svava takes more after my mother than after anybody else.

RIIS. Well, I declare! Svava, with her quiet, graceful ways—what are you thinking of?

MRS. RIIS. Svava can be passionate, too.

RIIS. Svava never neglects the outward forms as your mother did.

MRS. RIIS. You never understood my mother. But, of course, I admit that they differ in many things also.

Riis. Tremendously!—Can you see now, that I was right when I began to talk all sorts of languages to her while she was still a mere slip of a girl? Do you see now? You used to object.

Mrs. Riis. I was against having her bothered with it all the time—and also against your constant jumping from one thing to another.

Riis. But the results, my dear—the results?

[*Humming to himself.*

Mrs. Riis. I hope you don't mean to say that it is the languages that have made her what she is?

Riis. [*As he disappears again*] Not the languages, but— [*From the other room*] The languages have done a lot. Did you notice her last night? She has *savoir vivre*, hasn't she?

[*Coming out again.*

Mrs. Riis. That isn't what one cares most for in Svava.

Riis. Oh, no.—On board the steamer somebody asked me if I were related to the Miss Riis who had started the kindergarten movement in this city. I replied that I had the honour of being her father. Then you should have seen the man. Why, it actually gave me a lump in the throat.

Mrs. Riis. Yes, the kindergartens have been a success from the very first.

Riis. And I suppose they brought about her engagement also—did they?

Mrs. Riis. You had better ask her.

Riis. But you don't notice my clothes at all.

Mrs. Riis. Oh, yes, I do.

Riis. And not so much as a teeny-weeny gasp of admiration? At such a general effect—such a combination of colours —down to the very shoes—the handkerchief even? What do you say?

Mrs. Riis. How old are you, dear?

Riis. Oh, keep quiet! But for that matter—how old do you think I am taken for?

Mrs. Riis. About forty, of course.

Riis. "Of course,"—how genuine that sounds from your lips! But this dress is a sort of triumphal overture, composed at Cologne on receipt of the telegram about Svava's engagement. Think only: at Cologne, a mere ten-hour ride from Paris. But I couldn't wait ten hours—to such an extent was my sense of personal elegance increased by the thought of becoming related by marriage to the richest family in the country.

Mrs. Riis. And did it stop at that one suit?

Riis. What a question! Wait only till my trunks come out of the custom-house.

Mrs. Riis. Yes, then we are in for it, I suppose.

Riis. Are you in for it? Why, think of it—an overjoyed papa who, at the crucial moment, happens to find himself at Paris——

Mrs. Riis. And what did you think then of the party yesterday?

Riis. I thought it a fortunate chance that the steamer was delayed so that I was dropped down, as if by magic, right in the midst of a *fête champêtre*. And one given in honour of the dear daughter, at that, where, of course, papa found himself more than welcome!

Mrs. Riis. What time did you get home last night?

Riis. Do you think we could escape playing cards even yesterday? It was impossible to refuse, for I was asked to sit at table with Abraham, Isaac, and Jacob—that is, with our host, the Prime Minister, and old man Holk. It was an immense honour to be permitted to lose one's money to such bigwigs. And I lose always, as you know.—I came home about three, I should say.—What is it you are reading?

Mrs. Riis. The *Fortnightly.*

Riis. Has there been anything good in it while I was away?
[*He begins to hum a melody.*]

Mrs. Riis. Ye-es.—Here is something about heredity now, that you ought to read. It fits in with what we started to talk of.

Riis. Do you know that melody? [*He hurries over to the piano*] It's all the go just now.   I heard it all over Germany. [*Begins to play and sing, but breaks off abruptly*] Let me get the music, while I have it in mind!

> *He goes into the room at the right and returns with a sheet of music; sits down at the piano again and begins to sing and play as before.*

THIRD SCENE

> Mrs. Riis.   Riis.   Svava *enters through the door on the left.*

Riis. [*Looks around, stops, and jumps up*] Good morning, my dear! Good morning! I have hardly had a chance to speak to you yet. At the party last night everybody was taking you away from me.

> [*He kisses her and leads her down the stage.*]

Svava. Well, why were you so slow in coming home?

Riis. Why didn't some people give notice when they intended to become engaged?

Svava. Because those people didn't know anything about it until it had already happened. Good morning again, mother dear!   [*She kneels down beside her mother.*]

Mrs. Riis. Oh, what a smell of out of doors there is about you! Have you been walking in the woods after your bath?

Svava. [*Rising to her feet*] Yes, and just as I was coming

home, Alf passed by and waved a greeting up to me. He will be here in a minute.

Rɪɪs. To tell the truth—and one should always tell the truth—I had quite given up the hope of seeing our old maid so happy.

Svava. Yes, indeed! I had quite lost hope myself.

Rɪɪs. Until the prince arrived.

Svava. Until the prince arrived—who had taken his time in coming.

Rɪɪs. And for whom you had been waiting for ever and a day?

Svava. Not at all. I had never even given him a thought.

Rɪɪs. This is becoming mysterious.

Svava. It is a mystery how two people who have known each other since childhood without ever giving a thought to each other, all of a sudden—for that's the way it happened. Beginning with a certain given moment he became in my eyes quite a different man.

Rɪɪs. While in the eyes of all the rest he remained the same as before.

Svava. I hope so!

Rɪɪs. At least he has become a little less solemn—in my eyes.

Svava. Yes, I saw you two laughing together last night. What was it about?

Rɪɪs. We were talking of the best manner of making one's way through this world of ours. And I presented him with my renowned three principles of life.

Mrs. Rɪɪs and Svava. Already!

Rɪɪs. They made quite a hit with him. Do you recall them, irreverent child that you are?

Svava. No. 1: never disgrace yourself.

Rɪɪs. No. 2: never incommode anybody else.

SVAVA. No. 3: always be in fashion.—They are not *very* difficult to recall, seeing that they are neither deep nor dark.

RIIS. But all the harder to put into practice! And that's just the merit of all such principles.—Accept my compliments on your new morning dress. Everything considered, it is really "sweet."

SVAVA. Everything considered—that means, considering that you did not help to select it.

RIIS. Yes, for *I* should never have chosen those trimmings for it—but "everything considered," it might be worse. And the cut—hm—yes?—Well, now you just wait till my trunks get here.

SVAVA. Surprises?

RIIS. Great ones!—And I have something for you at once.

[*Goes out.*

SVAVA. I think he is more restless than ever, mamma.

MRS. RIIS. It's the joy of it, girl!

SVAVA. And yet there is always something suppressed about papa's restlessness. He is— [RIIS *returns from the right*] Do you know what the Prime Minister said of you yesterday?

RIIS. Oh, well, a gentleman of that kind has always got to say something.

SVAVA. "Your father, Miss Riis, remains always our man of fashion *par excellence.*"

RIIS. Ah, *il a bien dit Son Excellence!* No, then I have something better to tell. You are getting your father knighted.

SVAVA. Am I?

RIIS. Yes, who else? Of course, the government has had some little use for me now and then in connection with various commercial treaties. But this time, as related by marriage to our great man, I become a knight of the Order of St. Olav.

SVAVA. Permit me to congratulate you!

RIIS. You know: when it rains on the parson, it drips on the sexton.

SVAVA. You are most uncommonly modest in your new grandeur.

RIIS. Yes, am I not? And now I am to appear in the modest part of an exhibitor of elegant costumes, or rather designs for costumes—which is still more modest—to be used in the new play at the *Théâtre Français*.

SVAVA. Oh, no, papa! Not just now!

MRS. RIIS. That will have to wait till the afternoon.

RIIS. Really, one might think I was the only lady in the family! Well, as you please—*you* rule the world! But then I have another proposition, in two parts. First: that we sit down!

SVAVA. We are sitting down! [*She and her father take seats.*

RIIS. Then you tell your home-coming papa just how this whole thing happened. All that thing about the "mystery," you know.

SVAVA. Oh, that!—Well, you must excuse me, but it cannot be told.

RIIS. Not in all its charming details! Heaven defend! Nobody would be such a barbarian as to ask for a thing like that during the first honeymoon of the engagement. No, I mean only what was the actual *mobile* back of the whole matter.

SVAVA. Oh, I see. Well, *that* I can tell you, for to know it is merely to become really acquainted with Alf.

RIIS. For instance: how did you come to talk with him at all?

SVAVA. Oh, I think it was about our blessed old kinder-gartens——

RIIS. Oh-h!—You mean *your* blessed old kindergartens?

NORDAN. The suit against Mrs. North! I had a talk with Christensen a few moments ago. He has advanced the money and will try to get the banks to stop the suit. But this I have told you before. What more do you want?

MRS. RIIS. The gossip, my dear friend, the gossip.

NORDAN. Oh, we men don't tell tales on each other as a rule.—Isn't it about time to let *him* know about it? [*Nodding toward the door on the right*] He's in there now, isn't he?

MRS. RIIS. Let us wait.

NORDAN. For Christensen must have his money back, of course. I have promised him that.

MRS. RIIS. Of course. I hope you never imagined anything else?

NORDAN. [*Rising*] Well, I am going away for a little rest, and now Christensen will have to look after that matter.—I suppose it was a grand affair last night?

MRS. RIIS. No pomp of any kind.

NORDAN. No, the Christensens never indulge in ostentation. But numbers made up for it, I suppose.

MRS. RIIS. I have never seen so many people at a private affair.

NORDAN. Is Svava up?

MRS. RIIS. She is out for a bath.

NORDAN. Already? Did you get home that early?

MRS. RIIS. Oh, about twelve, I think. Svava wanted to get home. Mr. Riis stayed much longer, I believe.

NORDAN. Hm—the card-tables!—She was radiant, I suppose?

MRS. RIIS. Why didn't you come?

NORDAN. I never attend engagement or wedding feasts. Never. The sacrificing of those wreathed and veiled victims —oh!

Svava. When there are more than two hundred of us girls——

Riis. Well, let it go at that! So he contributed?

Svava. He contributed, and more than once——

Riis. Oh-h!

Svava. And once we fell to talking about luxury. That it was better to use money in such ways than for mere luxuries.

Riis. Well, what is to be called "luxury"?

Svava. We didn't say anything about that, but I said that I thought luxury immoral.

Riis. Immo—? Luxury?

Svava. Yes, I know that is not your opinion. But it is mine.

Riis. Your mother's, you mean, and your grandmother's.

Svava. Of course; but my own also—if you permit me?

Riis. Oh, the Lord preserve us!

Svava. I told of an incident which mother and you and I witnessed in America—do you remember? At that temperance meeting where we saw ladies who were to support the cause drive up in their carriages—ladies—well, we didn't have any exact figures as to their fortunes, but as they appeared, with their carriages, horses, dresses, jewelry—and especially jewelry—they must have been worth—oh, say——

Riis. Let us say many, many thousand dollars apiece— that would be true!

Svava. It *is* true. And in its way such a thing is as much of an excess as drinking.

Riis. Oh, well——

Svava. Yes, shrug your shoulders! But Alf didn't. He told me what he had seen—in the big cities. It was dreadful!

Riis. *What* was dreadful?

Svava. The chasm yawning between rich and poor—the boundless and reckless display of luxury on one side——

RIIS. Oh, so!—I thought— Well, go on!

SVAVA. He didn't play the indifferent and keep on polishing his nails——

RIIS. I beg pardon!

SVAVA. Please, don't stop!—No, he foretold a great social revolution, and he became quite excited about it—and then it came out how he thought wealth should be used.—It was a complete surprise to me—and much of it was new to me in every way. You should have seen how handsome he looked then!

RIIS. Well—handsome?

SVAVA. Isn't *he* handsome? That's what *I* think, at least! And mamma also——?

MRS. RIIS. [*Without looking up from her periodical*] And mamma also.

RIIS. Mothers always fall in love with their daughters' lovers. But becoming mothers-in-law generally cures them.

SVAVA. Is that *your* experience?

RIIS. That's *my* experience. So Alf Christensen has grown handsome? Well, we'll have to bear with it.

SVAVA. As he was standing before me, he seemed so sure of himself, and so clear in his mind, and so—so chaste—and that is something I demand also.

RIIS. What do you mean by "chaste," my girl?

SVAVA. Just what's in the word.

RIIS. And I am just asking what you put into that word.

SVAVA. The same meaning I should put into it if I were speaking of myself.

RIIS. That is, you put the same meaning into it whether it be applied to a man or a woman?

SVAVA. Of course.

RIIS. And you think that the son of Christensen——

SVAVA. [*Rising*] Papa, now you are offending me!

RIIS. Can it offend you that he is his father's son?

SVAVA. In this respect he is not.   It is no longer possible for me to make mistakes in such matters.

MRS. RIIS. I have just been reading about hereditary tendencies—and his heritage need not necessarily have come from his father.

RIIS. Oh, well, as you please!   But I am a little fearful on behalf of your superterrestrial theories.   I don't think you can get very far with them.

SVAVA. What do you mean—?   Mother, what does he mean?

MRS. RIIS. I suppose he means that men are not as you want them to be.   And it is no use hoping that they ever will be.

SVAVA. No, you cannot mean that?

RIIS. But why so violent about it?   Come and sit down! And besides, how can you know anything about it?

SVAVA. Know?—What *do* you mean?

RIIS. About any individual case——

SVAVA. If the man standing before me, or passing me, is an unclean, repulsive beast—or a man?

RIIS. Etc., etc.!   Well, you may be mistaken, my dear Svava.

SVAVA. No, no more than I can be mistaken about you, papa, when you begin to tease me again with those dreadful principles of yours.   For in spite of them, you are the finest and cleanest man I know.

MRS. RIIS. [*Putting away the periodical*] Are you going to keep that morning dress on, my dear?   Don't you think you had better change before Alf comes?

SVAVA. No, mamma, you can't get me away from this!— For I have had to see more than one of my girl friends nestle

close to "the prince of her heart," as the old ballad says, only
to wake up in the arms of a beast.—I want none of that.
And I am not going to make the same mistake.

MRS. RIIS. There is no reason, dear, to take it so to heart.
Alf is an honest young man.

SVAVA. So he is. But I have had to witness one revolting
experience after another. And now, only a month ago, the
case of Helga. And then I myself—I can tell you all about
it now, for now I feel happy and secure—and now I can tell
you of the time I once had to go through. There was a long
time when I did not dare to trust my own judgment. For I
came near letting myself be deceived also.

BOTH PARENTS. [Rising] You, Svava?

SVAVA. I was very, very young then. Like most young
girls, I was looking for an ideal, and I found it in a brilliant
young man—what's the use of naming him? He had—oh,
his principles were noble, and his aims of the highest—in this
respect he was the complete opposite of papa. It would not
be enough to say that I loved him! I worshipped him. But
then—oh, I cannot tell you what I discovered, or how I discovered it—but that was the time when all of you feared
that I had become——

MRS. RIIS. Consumptive? Is it possible, dear? Was it
that time?

SVAVA. Yes, that time— Nobody can endure such de-
ception—nobody can forgive it!

MRS. RIIS. And you told me nothing?

SVAVA. One who has not fallen into the same mistake
cannot know what it is to be ashamed of oneself.—Well, it is
all over, now. But one thing is sure: that nobody who has
had a first experience of such a kind will ever make the same
mistake again.

RIIS *has in the meantime left the room.*

Mrs. Riis. Perhaps it was for the best.

Svava. I am sure it was— Oh, well, it's over and done with now. But I was not quite done with it until I found Alf.—What became of papa?

Mrs. Riis. Of your father? Why, there he is coming now.

Riis. [*Comes from the right, with hat on, and busily pulling at one of his gloves*] Listen, children! I simply have to get my trunks out of the custom-house. I am now going down to the station to telegraph about it. You must get yourself ready, too, for the king will soon be coming this way, as you know—and then!—Good-bye, my sweet little girl! [*Kissing her*] You have really made us very, very happy. Otherwise you have some ideas that—oh, well! [*Going toward the door*] Good-bye!

Mrs. Riis. Good-bye!

Riis. [*Pulling off his glove again*] Did you notice the melody I was playing when you came in? [*Sits down at the piano*] I heard it all over Germany. [*Plays and sings; then breaks off suddenly*] But, good gracious, here is the music, and you can sing and play it yourself. [*Goes out humming.*

Svava. Isn't he funny! There is really something innocent about him. Did you notice him last night? He just glittered "with a hundred facets," as they say.

Mrs. Riis. Apparently you couldn't see yourself.

Svava. Oh—was I like that?

Mrs. Riis. Your father's daughter—completely.

Svava. Yes, mamma, it's no use denying that however great our happiness be, it is made still greater by other people's goodwill. This morning, as I walked along, I was recalling all that had given me pleasure last night, and I found —oh, I can't put it into words. [*She clings closely to her mother.*

Mrs. Riis. My happy little girl!—But now I must look after the house a little.

SVAVA. Do you want me to help you?

MRS. RIIS. By no means.

[*They walk together toward the background.*

SVAVA. Then I'll run through papa's new melody a couple
of times—and soon Alf will be here.

MRS. RIIS *goes out to the left.* SVAVA *sits down at the
piano.*

FOURTH SCENE

SVAVA. ALF, *from the left.*

ALF. [*Comes in noiselessly and bends down over* SVAVA *so that
his face almost touches hers*] What a day that was—yesterday!

SVAVA. [*Rising quickly*] Alf!—But I didn't hear you ring?

ALF. The music—which was beautiful also.

SVAVA. And yesterday—how can I thank you?

[*They move down the stage together.*

ALF. I don't think you have any idea of what a hit you
made?

SVAVA. Some, perhaps. But you had better say nothing
about it as—it isn't held proper to be aware of it.

ALF. People had to tell me about it, of course, and my father
and mother. And to-day everybody is very happy at home.

SVAVA. And here, too!—What is that you are holding in
your hand? A letter?

ALF. A letter. The maid who opened the door handed it
to me. Some bright wit has figured out that I should probably appear here in the course of the day.

SVAVA. It wasn't very hard to figure out, do you think?

ALF. Not very. It's from Edward Hansen.

SVAVA. Oh, you can take a short cut to his place right
through our park. [*Pointing toward the right.*

ALF. I know. He says it's important, with "important"
underlined——

SVAVA. You can take my key—here it is. [*Gives him the key.*

ALF. Thank you, very much!

SVAVA. Oh, it is pure selfishness. I shall have you here
again the sooner.

ALF. I'll stay here until dinner-time.

SVAVA. You'll have to stay here longer than that, I tell
you, for we have such a lot of things to talk of. About
yesterday——

ALF. Yes, I think so, too.

SVAVA. And many other things also.

ALF. I have a very important problem to submit to you.

SVAVA. You have?

ALF. Perhaps you can solve it for me before I return?

SVAVA. Then it cannot be so very knotty.

ALF. Oh, it is. But you have inspirations at times.

SVAVA. Well, what is it?

ALF. Why couldn't we have discovered each other several
years ago?

SVAVA. We were not yet ready for each other, of course.

ALF. How can you tell?

SVAVA. From the fact that I myself was not the same then
as I am now.

ALF. But there is a natural kinship between those who love
each other. I feel it. And it must have existed then as well
as now.

SVAVA. Such a natural kinship does not assert itself while
you are developing along different lines.

ALF. And so we have been doing—and yet——

SVAVA. And yet we are in love with each other. Because
it does not matter how far the roads diverge when, in the end,
they meet again.

ALF. In the same way of thinking, you mean?

SVAVA. In such a communion as ours is.

ALF. So very close together?

SVAVA. So very close together!

ALF. But it is just then—when I hold you in my arms as now—that I ask myself over and over again: why have I not done this before?

SVAVA. And I don't give a thought to it—not the least thought. This is the safest place in all the world: that's what I think!

ALF. And without those by-gone years it might not have been so.

SVAVA. What do you mean?

ALF. I mean—oh, I suppose, at bottom, I mean the same as you: that I have not always been what I am now.—But I have to hurry. The letter says I must.

[*They move up the stage.*

SVAVA. It isn't a question of minutes, is it? For there is something I want to tell you first.

ALF. What is it?   [*Stands still.*

SVAVA. When I saw you among all the others, it was at first as if I didn't know you at all. You appeared in a new aspect, as if you had taken on something from the others—in fact, you *were* different.

ALF. Of course! One always is among strangers. When you moved among the other women, it was as if I had never really noticed you before. And, you know, there are certain measures that cannot be taken except when others are present. Only then did I learn whether you were tall or short. Only then did I become aware of a way you have of bending to one side—oh, just a wee bit—as you greet somebody. And your colour—I had seen nothing before——

SVAVA. Now will you stop and give me a chance?

ALF. I will not—oh, here we are again, and I simply *must* leave!   [*They go up the stage again.*

SVAVA. Only a word. You didn't let me finish. When I saw you standing among the other men, it was at first as if I had not recognised you. But just then your glance caught mine, and you nodded to me. I don't know what kind of transformation took place in you or in myself, but I blushed until my face burned. And it was some time before I dared to look at you again.

ALF. And do you know what happened to me? Every time somebody was going to dance with you, I begrudged him the chance of doing so. I didn't seem able to bear it. By heavens, I can't bear that anybody else so much as touches you! [*They embrace*] And yet I have not mentioned the best of all!

SVAVA. And what is that?

ALF. It is this—that when I see you among others—when I catch a glimpse of your arm, for instance—then I say to myself: that arm has been lying around my neck, and there is nobody else in the whole world who can say the same thing. She belongs to me, that girl over there, and to nobody, nobody, nobody else!—That, you see, is the best of all!—But now we are back again in the same spot—it is as if we were bewitched. —Now I *must* go! [*Goes up the stage*] Good-bye! [*Leaves* SVAVA *only to seize hold of her again the next moment*] Why couldn't I have had all this happiness long ago?—Good-bye!

SVAVA. I think I'll go with you.

ALF. Yes, do!

SVAVA. Oh, no, I remember now. I must practise that new song before papa returns. For if I don't do it now, I am sure you will give me no chance later.

[*A ring at the door-bell is heard.*

ALF. Somebody is coming! For heaven's sake, let me get out first!

> *He runs out to the right.* SVAVA *stands looking after him and waving her handkerchief. She is about to return to the piano, when* MARGIT *appears.*

FIFTH SCENE

SVAVA. MARGIT. *Later* HOFF.

MARGIT. There is a gentleman here who wants to——

SVAVA. A gentleman? Don't you know him?

MARGIT. No.

SVAVA. What sort of a gentleman?

MARGIT. Oh, sort of—a little bit——

SVAVA. Suspicious looking?

MARGIT. Oh, no—he's a very nice man.

SVAVA. Tell him that my father is not at home. He has gone down to the station.

MARGIT. I told him so. But it's you, Miss Svava, he wants to speak to.

SVAVA. Ask my mother to come in—oh, well, what's the need of that?—Let him come in.

> [MARGIT *goes out;* HOFF *enters.*

HOFF. It's Miss Riis I am having the honour to— Yes, I see it is. My name is—Hoff—Karl Hoff. I travel in iron.

SVAVA. But what have I to do with that?

HOFF. Oh, yes—for had I been an ordinary, home-staying fellow, there might have been a lot—that never happened.

SVAVA. What might not have happened?

HOFF. [*Pulls out a large pocket-book and takes from it a tiny letter*] Will you please—would you read this—or perhaps you would rather not?

SVAVA. Well, how can I tell?

HOFF. No, that's so—you must first—if I may?

SVAVA. [*Reading*] "To-night between ten and eleven; that is to say, if the old fool doesn't come home before. Oh, I love you, I love you so much— Put a light in the hall window."

HOFF. "The old fool"—that's me.

SVAVA. But I don't see——

HOFF. Here's another.

SVAVA. "I am suffering from bad conscience. Your cough scares me. And now when you are expecting—" But what in the world have I to do with all this?

HOFF. [*After some hesitation*] Well, what do you think?

SVAVA. Is there anybody who needs my help?

HOFF. No, poor thing, she needs no more helping. She's dead.

SVAVA. Dead? She was your wife?

HOFF. That's it. She was my wife.—I found these and some other things in—in a box. The papers were furthest down—there's more of them—and then some cotton on top of them. Then there were ear-rings and such things which she had got from her mother. And then—these bracelets. I guess they cost too much to come from her mother.

SVAVA. She must have died suddenly then, as she hadn't time——

HOFF. Oh, I don't know. Consumptives never think they're going to die.—She was such a weak, delicate thing.— Do you mind if I sit down?

SVAVA. Not at all! Are there any children?

HOFF. [*After some hesitation*] I don't think so.

SVAVA. You don't think—? The reason I ask was that I thought our kindergarten society— Frankly, this is painful to me!

HOFF. I thought it would be—yes, I thought it would—
and really I don't know if— Oh, *you* can't understand all
this, can you?

SVAVA. No, I cannot.

HOFF. No, of course, you can't— I have heard so many
fine things said of you these last years—and my wife used to
speak that way of you, too.

SVAVA. Did she know me?

HOFF. Maren Tang—she that was lady companion to——

SVAVA. ——to Mrs. Christensen, who is to be my mother-
in-law? Oh, it was she? That very quiet, refined woman—
Don't you think you are mistaken? A couple of notes without any name—without a date even? Don't you——?

HOFF. Could you recognise the handwriting?

SVAVA. I?—No.—And it looked as if it had been disguised.

HOFF. Well—but not so very much.

SVAVA. But you must have had some definite purpose in
calling on me?

HOFF. So I had.—But I guess I won't bother about it.
You don't understand this kind of thing, I can see.—Maybe
you just think me a little off?—And maybe we might let it
go at that?

SVAVA. But there was *something* you wanted?

HOFF. Yes, that's so. You see, these kindergartens——

SVAVA. So it was the kindergartens after all?

HOFF. No, that wasn't it. But on account of them I kind
of thought a lot of you, you see. And if you don't mind my
saying it: young ladies of the better class who do something
useful—well, I had never heard of it before. Never before.—
I am nothing but a poor fellow who's failed in his own business and now has to travel for others—not much good for
anything, I dare say—and maybe I deserved what I got.—
But just the same I wanted to see *you* kept out of it. I kind

of thought it was my duty—nothing less than my duty—
But now, when I see you sitting like that before me—then it
makes me unhappy all through. And so I don't want to say
anything to you at all. [*Rising*] Nothing at all!

SVAVA. This is something I cannot understand.

HOFF. Now, don't you pay any attention to me at all.
All I ask you is to excuse me—excuse me very much!—No,
please don't give yourself any trouble! Not at all! It's just
as if I hadn't been here. That's all.

> *He goes toward the door, where he meets* ALF; *seeing that*
> SVAVA *is watching them, he hurries out.*

SIXTH SCENE

SVAVA. ALF. *Later* RIIS.

SVAVA. [*As she watches the two men meeting, she gives vent to
a subdued cry. Then she goes quickly toward* ALF. *But when
she stands face to face with him, she seems to be seized with terror.
He approaches her in order to support her, but she cries out*]
Don't touch me! [*She tries to reach the door on the left, but
seems for a moment unable to find it. Then she hurries out and
is heard locking the door from within. Shortly afterward the
sound of violent crying is heard, but rendered faint by distance.
It lasts only a moment. Then somebody on the outside is heard
singing the melody already familiar to the audience, and a few
moments later* RIIS *appears on the stage*]

Curtain.

ACT II

The same room as in the previous act.

FIRST SCENE

Svava. Mrs. Riis.

Svava *is reclining on the right-hand sofa so that she rests on one arm and has her face turned toward the park.* Mrs. Riis *is sitting beside the sofa, facing her daughter.*

Mrs. Riis. These sudden decisions, Svava, are in reality no decisions at all. For there is always so much that comes after.—Take time to think! I believe him to be a pretty fine man. Give him time to show it. Don't break off at once.

Svava. Why are you constantly telling me this?

Mrs. Riis. But, dear girl, I have really had no chance to tell you anything at all until now.

Svava. But all your remarks have been set to the same tune.

Mrs. Riis. And what tune would you prefer?

Svava. The old one—your own—which is quite different.

Mrs. Riis. It is one thing to teach one's child how to choose among life's offerings——

Svava. And another to stick to one's own teachings?

Mrs. Riis. Another thing it is to live. Then it is sometimes necessary to make allowances, especially when two are to live together.

Svava. In minor matters this is all right.

Mrs. Riis. Only in minor matters——?

Svava. Yes, in regard to peculiarities and such things that

44

are mere accidentals. But not when it is a question of essential development.

MRS. RIIS. Then, too.

SVAVA. Then, too? But we marry only to develop ourselves. Why should we otherwise marry at all?

MRS. RIIS. You'll find out.

SVAVA. No, I won't. For I am not going to marry.

MRS. RIIS. You should have said that before. Now it is too late.

SVAVA. [*Half rising from the sofa*] Too late? Had I been married twenty years, I should be doing exactly the same thing.
[*Lies down again.*

MRS. RIIS. Oh, Lord preserve us!—You don't know—no, you don't know at all into what kind of net you have stumbled. But you'll discover it the moment you try in earnest to tear yourself loose.—Or do you really want your father to throw away everything we have built up here? Do you want us to start all over again in a strange country? For he has repeatedly declared during the last few days, that the disgrace of a breach is something which he cannot face. He means to leave, and if he does, I shall have to go with him.— Yes, now you are twisting and turning in the net! And think of the others! It is a little dangerous to be made so much of as you were at the engagement party. It is as if you had been lifted up on a platform supported by all the others. Take care lest they push you down again! And you may be sure they will, if you violate their ideas of propriety.

SVAVA. And is this their idea of propriety?

MRS. RIIS. Not exactly. But that no scandal be caused is inevitably one of those ideas, and perhaps the first of all.— Nobody takes kindly to a disgraceful exposure. Particularly those that are most powerful. And least of all do people like to see their children disgraced.

Svava. [*Half rising*] But, good Lord, am *I* disgracing *him?*

Mrs. Riis. No, I suppose he is doing it himself——

Svava. Well! [*Drops back again.*

Mrs. Riis. But you will never make them see it that way. —No, you won't.—As long as only the family and a few close friends are whispering about what has happened, they don't regard it as any disgrace at all. For the same thing is happening in too many other places. It is only when it becomes known to all the world that they look upon it as a disgrace. And if there should be a breach, and the cause of it become known—that the eldest son of the Christensens had been ignominiously jilted on account of his past—then they would regard this as the worst scandal that could ever befall them.— And we should have to suffer for it. We, and every one dependent on us. And you know, they are not a few. You have taken them under your care, especially the children. But then you would have to let all those go that you have helped. For you would have to follow us. And I am sure that your father is in earnest about leaving.

Svava. O-oh!

Mrs. Riis. I wish I could tell you why I am so sure of it. But I cannot—not just now, at least— No, you mustn't ask me to do so— There is your father now. Take time to think, Svava. No breach! No scandal!

SECOND SCENE

Svava. Mrs. Riis. Riis *comes from the outside with an open letter in his hand.*

Riis. Oh, lying down a little, are you? [*Goes into his room to deposit hat and stick, and then returns*] Nothing serious, I hope?

MRS. RIIS. No, but——

RIIS. Well, here is a letter from the Christensens now. As you don't want to see Alf, or even receive letters from him, you have to be prepared for the interference of his family. There's an end to everything, of course. [*Reads*] "My wife, my son and I will have the honour of calling on you between eleven and twelve."—It's a wonder that this hasn't happened long before. They have shown a great deal of patience, I think.

MRS. RIIS. We, on our side, haven't got any further than we were before.

RIIS. But what are you thinking of, Svava? Can't you see where *this* kind of thing must lead to? You have a heart in you, I know, and I am sure you don't want to ruin all of us? Really, it seems to me, Svava, that you have shown all the firmness that could possibly be needful in this case. Their self-assurance has been shaken down to its very roots —you can depend on it. What more do you want? Or do you actually want to push the matter still farther? Well, name your conditions. In all likelihood they will be accepted.

SVAVA. Oh, faugh!

RIIS. [*In despair*] Well, it just won't do to take it that way!

MRS. RIIS. No, it won't, Svava! You should rather try to meet them half-way.

RIIS. And, really, you should deign to consider what you are throwing away. One of the richest families in the country, and also one of the most honourable, I dare say. I have never heard of any indiscretions on their part. Yes, that's what I say. No indiscretions, I say. There may have been a lapse—or more than one—but then—good Lord!

SVAVA. Yes, bring Him in, too!

RIIS. Yes, that's just what I mean to do. For the matter

is serious enow⸗... Even if there has been a lapse of some kind,
I say, the poor young fellow has been punished hard enough
for it.   And, after all, we have to be a little reasonable, and
forgive. We *have* to forgive. And more than that. We
have to help those that err—we have to raise up those that
fall—we have to set them on the right path— Yes, set them
on the right path! And that's a thing *you* can do so beautifully.   You are just made for it.—As you probably know,
my dear, it doesn't happen very often that I talk morality or
that sort of thing. Frankly speaking, it isn't becoming to
me, and I feel it perfectly. But on this occasion I simply
cannot refrain.—Begin by forgiving, my child—that's what
you should begin with! And besides, can you imagine a
continued life together without some—without some—well,
without *that?*

SVAVA. But there is no question here about any continued
life together—or about forgiving either. Because I don't
want to have anything more to do with him.

RIIS. But this passes all limits!—Because he has dared to
love somebody else before you——?

SVAVA. Somebody?

RIIS. Yes, no more than that, so far as I am aware of.—
No, not a thing more! And it beats the deuce, the way people
run around with slander and gossip. But what I say is this:
because he dared to look at somebody else before he looked
at you, or before he ever *thought* of you, that's no reason why
he should be eternally condemned. How many could then
get married, I might venture to ask. Everybody declares
him to be such a fine and honest young fellow that the proud-
est girl in the world could trust him with her faith—yes, and
that's just what you said yourself a while ago! Don't deny
it! But now he is all of a sudden to be utterly spurned because *you* don't happen to be the first woman he met.–

There should be some limit to pride as well as to everything else. And I, for my part, have never heard of anything more unreasonable.

MRS. RIIS. That's not the men's way.

RIIS. And how about the girls? What is their way? They don't care whether the man to whom they become engaged has been married before—ah, there I happened to use the word married. You may simply regard him as having been married before. And why not? That's what other girls do. Well, it's no use denying it! For I know that you know it! You have danced at more than one ball, haven't you? And what men are most sought after on such occasions? Exactly those—those whose names are smilingly connected with that of Don Juan. They take the wind out of the sails of everybody else. You have seen it yourself a hundred times.—And does it happen only at balls? Don't such men marry? As a rule *they* make the best marriages of all.

MRS. RIIS. That's true.

RIIS. Of course, it is true. And as a rule they become pretty good husbands at that.

MRS. RIIS. Hm-m?

RIIS. Oh, yes, indeed, they do!—Well, good gracious, there are exceptions! But the truth of the matter is, that marriage has an ennobling influence. And just here we meet with woman's highest mission. The very highest of all her missions!

SVAVA. [*Who has risen*] Oh, if need be, I can listen to that kind of thing from you. For I have expected nothing better.

RIIS. Thanks very much!

SVAVA. [*Coming down the stage*] One might think that marriage was a sort of higher ablutionary institution for men——

RIIS. Ha, ha!

SVAVA. And that men had a right to throw themselves into it just when they wanted—and in any manner suiting them.

RIIS. Oh, no——

SVAVA. Oh, yes—and it is flattering—so very flattering to me, your own daughter, that you hold me particularly fitted for that kind of higher laundry work. Nevertheless I shall have nothing to do with it.

RIIS. But this beats——

SVAVA. Now you listen to me a little! I don't think I have been talking too much these days.

RIIS. No, we haven't been able to get a word out of you.

SVAVA. You, papa—you carry around a lot of principles for exhibition purposes.

RIIS. For what?

SVAVA. By which I don't mean to say that they are not yours. But you are so good, so honest, so refined in everything you do, that I don't care a rap about your principles. But I do care about mother's. For she has formed my own. And when I want to apply them, she runs away.

MRS. RIIS *and* RIIS. But, Svava——!

SVAVA. It is mother I am angry with—it is her I cannot bear with.

RIIS. Really, Svava!

SVAVA. For if there be any one thing about which mother and I have been especially agreed, it is the unseemly way in which men prepare themselves for marriage—and about the marriages which are the outcome of it. We have been following up this matter for many years, mother and I. And both of us have become convinced that it is *before* marriage most marriages are spoiled.—And then, when mother began to change her tone a while ago——

MRS. RIIS. No, you can't say I have done that. For I believe Alf is honest——

SVAVA. When mother began to change her tone—well, I could not have been more surprised if somebody had come and told me that he had met mother on the street while she was sitting here talking with me.

MRS. RIIS. But all I ask is that you take time. I don't oppose you.

SVAVA. No, let me speak now.—Just one instance! Once, when I was about half-grown, I came running in here from the park. We had recently bought the place, and I was very happy about it. And then I found mother standing here, leaning up against the door and crying. It was a beautiful summer evening. "Why are you crying, mamma?" I asked. For a long while she pretended not to see me. Then I went closer to her and asked again: "Why are you crying, mamma?" But I never touched her. She turned away from me and walked back and forth several times. Then she came up to me. "Child," she said, and drew me close to herself. "Never give up anything of what you think good and right—not for any price! It's the most cowardly thing you can do, and you'll regret it terribly. For you will have to give up more and more and more." I don't know what she had in mind: I have never asked her. But the summer evening, and mother crying, and her words—the force of those words—it would be impossible to exaggerate what the memory of it all has been to me. *I* cannot give up anything. Don't ask it of me!—Everything that made marriage beautiful to me is gone. My faith, my trust—gone! No, no! This cannot be the way in which it should begin. And it is sinful of you to try to persuade me. To reach it through such disappointment—such humiliation? No, then I'll rather remain unmarried—even if it be in a strange country. I can find something to fill up my life with, I am sure. It is only for the moment I feel lost. And anything is better than to fill up

one's life with impurity. If you don't reject such things at
once, you become guilty of them yourself. Perhaps there
are those who can bear such things. Not I. No, I cannot!—
You think it is pride. Because I am angry. But if you
knew what he and I had agreed and planned—then you
might understand! And if you knew what I have thought
of him, how high up I had placed him—well, then you might
also understand how unhappy I am now! How boundless
my loss is!—Who's crying? Mother!— [SVAVA *runs across
the stage, kneels down beside her mother and puts her head in her
lap; long silence;* RIIS *goes out to the right*] Why cannot we
three stick together? If we do, what have we to fear? What
could happen? Papa, what could happen?—Where is papa?
[*Catches sight of* DR. NORDAN *outside*] Uncle Nordan! Well,
I never expected! [*She runs up the stage to meet him, throws
herself into his arms and bursts into tears*]

THIRD SCENE

SVAVA. MRS. RIIS. DR. NORDAN. *Later* RIIS.

NORDAN. Oh, you little goose! You dear, silly little
goose!

SVAVA. Oh, you've got to talk to me now!

NORDAN. Well, why do you think I am here?

SVAVA. And I who thought you were up in the mountains
and couldn't be reached!

NORDAN. Well, where do you think I was? But telegram
after telegram, as far as they could reach—and then messenger after messenger—and then, last of all—but I suppose, I
dare not even mention his name now?

RIIS. [*Who has reappeared from the right*] At last! The
way we have been waiting for you!

MRS. RIIS. [*Who finally has risen and come forward*] Thank you for coming, dear doctor!

NORDAN. [*Looking at* MRS. RIIS] There must be stormy days here.

MRS. RIIS. *You* don't need to be told anything.

NORDAN. Well, off with you now, both of you! Let Noodle-kin and me have it out between ourselves.

MRS. RIIS *goes out to the left, accompanied by* SVAVA.

RIIS. All I want to say is that in a little while——

NORDAN. ——comes the whole Christensen host. I know! Go now!

RIIS. [*Whispering*] Nordan!

NORDAN. Yes, yes—oh, yes—no, of course not! [*Drawing away from* RIIS] Don't you think I know all that? Get out of here!

As RIIS *goes out to the right,* SVAVA *returns from the left.*

SVAVA. Dear Uncle Nordan—at last I shall have some-body who agrees with me!

NORDAN. Oh, that's what you expect?

SVAVA. Oh, uncle, what days these have been!

NORDAN. And nights, I suppose?—Although you don't look so very bad after all.

SVAVA. I have slept the last couple of nights.

NORDAN. Oh, you have! Then I think I see how the matter stands.—You are a tough one, you are!

SVAVA. Don't begin now to say a lot of things you don't mean, uncle!

NORDAN. That I don't mean?

SVAVA. For that's what you always do. And we haven't time for it now. I am on burning coals.

NORDAN. Well, what haven't you gone and stirred up?

SVAVA. There you begin now!

NORDAN. Begin? Who the deuce has made you believe

that I say anything but what I mean? Come now and let's
sit down!   [*He places a chair in the middle of the floor.*

SVAVA. [*Putting her chair near his but at a right angle to it*]
All right!

NORDAN. I understand that since I saw you last, you have
issued a brand-new commandment in regard to love. My
congratulations!

SVAVA. Have I?

NORDAN. A supernatural, Svava-istic one. Probably de-
vised from the science of spherical harmonics. "There is but
one love, and it has but one object." *Dixi!*

SVAVA. Have *I* said that?

NORDAN. Are you not spurning a young man because he
has dared to love before he saw you?

SVAVA. So *you* are also regarding it in that manner?

NORDAN. In *that* manner? As if among rational people
there were any other? A splendid young fellow actually
worships you. One of our best families fling their double
doors wide open for you as if you were a princess. And then
you retort: "You haven't been waiting for me ever since you
were a little boy—*avaunt!*"

SVAVA. [*Rising abruptly*] Oh, you too, you too! And the
same text! The same stupid old text!

NORDAN. I may as well tell you this much at once: if you
don't take into consideration what can be said against you,
then you are a fool. It's no use whatever for you to rush
away from me and begin prancing up and down. For then
I'll begin to prance also. Come here and sit down. Or perhaps you don't *dare* to study the question more closely?

SVAVA. Oh, yes, I dare!   [*She sits down beside him again.*

NORDAN. For suppose now that the question happens to
be an extremely unsettled one, which is being discussed by
serious men and women all over the world?

SVAVA. But it concerns me alone. And to me it isn't unsettled at all.

NORDAN. You misunderstand me, child! In the last instance, you have to decide on your own case—you, and nobody
else. Of course! But when what you are to decide on is not
quite as clear as you may think; when, at this very moment,
it is occupying the minds of thousands and thousands—is it
not your duty then to show some regard for prevailing conditions, and for what is generally said and thought about
them? Is it not unconscionable, without some such regard,
to judge the individual case?

SVAVA. I see! And I think that what you demand of me
I have already done. Ask my mother.

NORDAN. Oh, yes, you and your mother have talked and
read a whole lot about marriage, and woman's emancipation,
and the abolition of special privileges for special classes—and
now all privileges of sex are also to be abolished. But what
about the particular question at issue?

SVAVA. What is it you think I have overlooked?

NORDAN. This! Have you the right to be as exacting
toward man as toward woman? What do you say?

SVAVA. Yes, of course!

NORDAN. Is it really so much a matter of course? Suppose
you were to make some inquiries. Of a hundred people you
asked, ninety would answer "no"—*even among the women
themselves!*

SVAVA. I don't know—it's beginning to change.

NORDAN. Very well. But knowledge is needed after all
to settle the question.

SVAVA. Do you really mean what you are saying?

NORDAN. Never mind! And for that matter, I always
mean what I say.—A woman can marry at sixteen. A man

has to wait until he is twenty-five or thirty.—That makes a difference!

SVAVA. There is a difference! For we have many, many, many more unmarried women than men. And these women are showing themselves capable of self-control—while the men find it easier to make a law out of their lack of self-control.

NORDAN. That kind of talk shows nothing but ignorance. The human creature is a polygamous animal, just like many other ones, and this theory is strongly supported by the fact that we have so many more women than men. This is something you have never heard before, I guess?

SVAVA. Yes, doctor, I have!

NORDAN. Don't laugh at science! What the deuce are we to believe in otherwise?

SVAVA. If you would only let the men have as much trouble with their children as the women? Why don't you let them, uncle? Then I think we would soon have a new set of principles. Oh, just let them, uncle!

NORDAN. They haven't the time. They must run the world.

SVAVA. Yes, they have chosen their own part!—But tell me, *Doctor* Nordan: is it not cowardly not to live in accordance with one's own teachings? [*She kneels down beside him.*

NORDAN. Yes, of course, it's cowardly!

SVAVA. Why, then, don't you live in accordance with yours?

NORDAN. I? Why, I have always been a monster! Don't you know that, dear?

SVAVA. Dearest Uncle Nordan—you have such long white locks—why do you let your hair grow that way?

NORDAN. Oh—there are reasons!

SVAVA. And what reasons?

NORDAN. Don't let us talk of that now.

SVAVA. But you have already told me.

NORDAN. Have *I?*

SVAVA. I wanted to touch your hair once, and you wouldn't let me. And then you said: "Do you know why I won't let you do it?"—"No," said I.—"Because nobody else has done so for thirty-four years."—"Who was the last one that touched it?" I asked.—"It was a little girl whom you resemble," you answered.

NORDAN. No, did I really tell you that?

SVAVA. "And she was a younger sister of your grandmother," you said to me.

NORDAN. So she was. Yes, yes, so she was. And you resemble her, child.

SVAVA. And then you told me that once—the year you entered the university—she was standing beside you and held as much as she could of your hair in one of her hands. And then she said: "You must never wear your hair shorter than it is now."—She went her way, and you went yours. And a little while afterward you wrote and asked her if you two hadn't better stick together for life. And she answered, yes. But a month later she died.

NORDAN. Did she die?

SVAVA. And ever since, this funny Uncle Nordan has considered himself married to her. [NORDAN *nods*] And the very night when you told me this—and when I lay awake so long, thinking it over and over—then I made up my mind that I should early choose one in whom I could place my whole trust— And I chose badly.

NORDAN. No, did you, Svava?

SVAVA. Don't ask me about it now!—But then I chose again, and felt secure. For never did a pair of eyes look more faithfully into another.—And the way we had everything in common! Day after day, each one bringing some

new discovery, each one seeming too short. Oh, I dare not
think of it now!—It is a sin to deceive in that way: not with
words, to be sure, but by permitting us to dream and to surrender ourselves. No, not with words. And yet with words,
too. For don't they listen to our words, and say nothing,
and so make them their own? They take pleasure in our
innocence as in a piece of unspoiled nature—and just by so
doing, they deceive us. For the result of it is a certain inti-
macy, a certain mutual banter, that can only have one basis—
that is, as we see it. And then it turns out to be ambiguous
after all.—I don't understand how anybody can act like that
toward one whom he loves? For he did love me!

NORDAN. And he does now!

SVAVA. [*Rising*] But not as I loved him! *I* had not been
giving myself away by piecemeal during the passing years.
My thoughts of love, and of being loved, were too high for
that. But for that very reason my desire was strong.—Oh,
to you I dare say so. And when it was free, it nearly swept
me off my feet. But I felt so absolutely safe with him, and
so I let him see it, and I took pleasure in his seeing it.—It is
this that hurts me now. For he was not worthy of it. He
said to me: I cannot bear that anybody else touches you.
He said to me: when I catch a glimpse of your arm, then I
remember that it has been lying around my neck, and that
nobody, nobody else can say the same.—And I felt happy
and proud at hearing him say it: for it was true. A hundred
times I had told myself that somebody would say just that
to me some time. But what I had not thought was that the
man speaking thus to me would himself—oh, abominable!
Then it gets a meaning that makes me hate him! Yes, the
mere thought that he has had his arms about me, that he
has touched me—it sets me trembling to my innermost soul!
—I lay down no rules for others. But the rule for myself

springs from my own self. My whole nature, from beginning
to end, determines it. Let *me* alone!

NORDAN. This is more serious and goes deeper than I had
any idea of. Nobody else looks at the matter in such a way,
and Alf least of all. He merely feels hurt—hurt and insulted
because you don't trust him.

SVAVA. I know it.

NORDAN. Well, don't be so brusque about it. For it is
just the way most people would feel about it.

SVAVA. Hm-m?

NORDAN. Most of them would think: other girls forgive
that sort of thing—just because they love.

SVAVA. And some would answer: had she *not* loved, she
might also have forgiven.

NORDAN. And yet, Svava? And yet——?

SVAVA. But, uncle, can't you understand! And I fear I
cannot explain it to you. For to do so, I should be able to
explain what it is we put into a man's appearance, nature,
walk, when we love him—into his voice, into his smile. And
it is just this that is gone. The meaning of it all is gone.

NORDAN. For a while, yes—until you have had time to
breathe——

SVAVA. No, no, no! Do you recall a song I have often
been singing to you—about the image of the loved one?
How it always appears with a burst of joy, as if bathed in joy?
Do you recall it?

NORDAN. Yes.

SVAVA. Well then—*that* is just what it doesn't do any longer!
It does appear, of course; but only pain comes with it.—
Always!—And a thing like that should be forgiven? Because
other girls have forgiven? But did they then never love,
those other girls? Can you tell me that? For what I have
loved is gone. And I don't intend to sit down and try to

dream it back again. I shall find something else to occupy myself with.

NORDAN. Well, you are in a bitter mood now. Your ideal has been thoroughly smashed. And, of course, it's of no use to talk as long as the pain of it lasts. And for that reason— only one thing—one single little thing—but that one thing you must promise me!

SVAVA. If I can.

NORDAN. You can. There are many things to be considered here. Ask for time to think it over.

SVAVA. Oh—mother has written to you.

NORDAN. Well, what of it? Your mother knows what is at stake here.

SVAVA. At stake? You talk so mysteriously as if we were not safe? Are we not? My father speaks of leaving the country. Why?

NORDAN. I suppose he thinks himself compelled to do so.

SVAVA. My father? For economical reasons?

NORDAN. Not at all! No, but you will have to face a lot of hostile gossip. For there is a challenge in what you do.

SVAVA. Oh, we are not afraid of criticism!—Of course, my father has very peculiar principles, as you know. But as far as his life is concerned—? I hope nobody has any doubt on that score?

NORDAN. Now listen, girl; nobody can prevent people from making up things. Be careful!

SVAVA. What *do* you mean?

NORDAN. I mean that you ought to take a walk in the park and pull yourself together a little before the Christensens are at the door. Try to calm yourself down, and then come in and ask for a little more time. That's all! They will grant what you ask—because they are forced to. Nothing has happened, and every road remains open. Do that now!

SVAVA. I *have* thought. And you will never bring me around.

NORDAN. All right—then what remains is nothing but a formality?

SVAVA. Hm-m? There is something else behind what you say.

NORDAN. My, but you are wilful! Can't you do this—for your mother's sake, let us say? Your *mother* is a very good woman.

SVAVA. What are they to think when I come in and say: "Please give me a little more time!"—Oh, no, I cannot!

NORDAN. Well, what would you say?

SVAVA. Nothing at all, if I could choose. But if I must——

NORDAN. Of course, you must!

SVAVA. Then I'll go out and think it over. [*As she goes toward the door*] But it won't be what you want.

NORDAN. [*Who remains standing on the same spot as before*] But it must be just that!

SVAVA. [*Stopping at the door*] You said: Your mother is a very good woman—that's what you said. It seemed as if you were putting stress on *mother*?

NORDAN. Well?

SVAVA. And my father?

NORDAN. A good woman—your father?

SVAVA. Why do you try to evade it with a jest?

NORDAN. Oh, hang it, because it is serious, of course!

SVAVA. Is my father not to be trusted——?

NORDAN. Sh!

SVAVA. My father?—Could it be possible that—? Is that what people are saying? [*When* DR. NORDAN *remains silent and motionless*] It's a shame! Impossible! Impossible, I say! [*She goes out quickly.*

FOURTH SCENE

NORDAN.   RIIS *comes from the right.*

RIIS. What is the matter with Svava?

NORDAN. [*Walking back and forth*] There was nothing else to do.

RIIS. [*Following him*] Nothing else to do?   But what?

NORDAN. No, I'll be darned if there was anything else to do!

RIIS. Is that so?   But what was it?

NORDAN. What did you say?

RIIS. No, *you* said——

NORDAN. What did *I* say?

RIIS. You said that there was nothing else to do— And you quite scared me.

NORDAN. Did I?   Well, you didn't hear right.

[*Goes away from him.*

RIIS. Didn't I?   Why, you even said you would be darned!

NORDAN. I didn't do anything of the kind.

RIIS. Well, then you didn't.—But what happened with Svava?   Can't you tell me?

NORDAN. What happened with Svava?

RIIS. Why are you so preoccupied?   Did things go wrong?

NORDAN. Preoccupied?   Why should I be?

RIIS. Well, you know best.   But I was asking about Svava. What happened with Svava?   It seems to me I have a right to know!

NORDAN. You, Riis?

RIIS. Yes. [*As* NORDAN *puts his arm through his*] What is it now?

NORDAN. Did you see Svava?

RIIS. As she rushed out into the park? Yes.—My dear fellow, what was it?

NORDAN. It was the Greek tragedy.

RIIS. The Gr——?

NORDAN. Just the name. Just the name. You know what it means, don't you?

RIIS. Something sad?

NORDAN. Not at all! Something very funny! It came to Greece with the cult of Dionysos. And in his train there was a goat——

RIIS. [*Pulling his arm away*] A—? But what——?

NORDAN. Yes, you may well be surprised. For the goat sang.

RIIS. He—sang?

NORDAN. Yes, and he is singing still, don't you know—and painting—oh! His pictures appear in every exhibition. And he works in bronze and marble. Splendidly! And what a courtier he is! He designs the costumes and decides what society——

RIIS. Have you gone clear out of your head?

NORDAN. Why so?

RIIS. I am merely waiting for all that damned nonsense to blow over. Of course, we are accustomed to almost anything when you are in this mood, but to-night I cannot understand a blessed word of what you are saying.

NORDAN. Oh, my dear fellow, is that so?

RIIS. Can't you tell me what my daughter said? It's perfectly ridiculous that I can't find out! Now, be brief and plain: what did she say?

NORDAN. You want to know that?

RIIS. And he asks me that!

NORDAN. She said· it is a pity about all the innocent little girls that, generation after generation, come tripping along. That's what she said.

RIIS. Tripping where?

NORDAN. That's just it: where? And she said: they are brought up in pious ignorance, and finally those trustful ones are swathed in a long, white veil, in order that they may not see where they are going.

RIIS. But this is mythology again. Why can't you——

NORDAN. Listen! It's your daughter speaking— *But I will not*, she said. I will walk securely into holy matrimony and sit beside the hearth of my native land and rear children before the sight of my husband. But he must be chaste as I am, or he will defile my child's head when he kisses it, and to me he will bring dishonour.—Now, that's what she said, and when she said it, she looked so beautiful!

[*A door-bell is heard ringing.*

RIIS. Now, there they are! There they are! How in the world is this going to end? We are immersed in the most unreasonable theories! We are buzzing about in the midst of a gigantic mythology! [*Rushes toward the door.*

FIFTH SCENE

DR. NORDAN. RIIS. MR. *and* MRS. CHRISTENSEN. MRS. RIIS. MARGIT. *Later* ALF.

RIIS. [*Meeting the new-comers and speaking while they are still outside*] Welcome! I wish you welcome of all my heart! —But where is your son?

CHRISTENSEN. [*Still outside*] We couldn't make him come.

RIIS. I am very sorry. Although, of course, I understand.

CHRISTENSEN. [*Appearing in the doorway*] Every time I

come here, I have to admire your splendid place over again, my dear Riis.

MRS. CHRISTENSEN. Oh, this old park! I wish that in due time— Ah, doctor—how is everything going?

NORDAN. So-o-o——

RIIS. [To MARGIT, who has followed the guests in] Please tell Mrs. Riis—will you? And—oh, there she is! [MRS. RIIS enters through the door on the left] And Miss Svava.

NORDAN. She is out in the park—over to the right!

[MARGIT leaves.

RIIS. No, the other way!—That's it!—Walk straight ahead till you find her!

MRS. CHRISTENSEN. [Simultaneously to MRS. RIIS as both come down the stage] Oh, my dear, I have thought of you so much these days! Such an annoying story!

MRS. RIIS. May I ask if you knew anything about it before?

MRS. CHRISTENSEN. What hasn't a mother—and a wife— to know these days, dear? As you may recall, she was in my house. Come here a moment!

She relates something in whispers, gradually raising her voice a little, so that toward the end such words can be heard as "discovery" and "turned out."

RIIS. [Offering chairs to the ladies] If you please!—Oh, beg your pardon, I didn't see— [Rushes over to CHRISTENSEN] Excuse me, but are you really comfortable there, tell me?

CHRISTENSEN. Thanks, it's as bad here as anywhere else. For it's mainly this sitting down and getting up again that gives me trouble. [After looking around] I have been to see him.

RIIS. Whom—Hoff?

CHRISTENSEN. Decent chap. Stupid.

RIIS. Well, if he only keeps his mouth shut——

CHRISTENSEN. He will.

RIIS. Thank heaven! Then it's all between ourselves.—I suppose it cost something?

CHRISTENSEN. Not a cent!

RIIS. Why, you got out of that cheap.

CHRISTENSEN. Yes, didn't I?—However, it has cost me plenty before—but *he* knows nothing of that.

RIIS. Oh? When he failed?

CHRISTENSEN. No, when he married.

RIIS. Oh, I see!

CHRISTENSEN. And I thought that ended the story. What kind of whispering game are the ladies playing?

MRS. CHRISTENSEN. [*Coming toward the centre of the stage;* RIIS *arranges chairs for her and for his wife*] I was telling about this matter with Miss Tang. One might almost say she had risen out of her grave.

CHRISTENSEN. Pardon me, but—isn't your daughter at home?

RIIS. We have sent for her.

MRS. CHRISTENSEN. I hope she, too, has learned a thing or two these days, poor thing! She has been suffering from a fault that often belongs to very clever people—I mean self-righteousness.

RIIS. Exactly! Quite right! Call it arrogance!

MRS. CHRISTENSEN. No, I wouldn't call it that. But pride, perhaps.

MRS. RIIS. What makes you think so?

MRS. CHRISTENSEN. Several talks I have had with her. Once I spoke of the husband as our lord and master. In these days of new-fangled ideas it is just as well to impress such things on our young girls.

CHRISTENSEN. Yes, the Lord knows!

Mrs. Christensen. And when I reminded her of what
Paul said, she replied: "Yes, those are the bars behind which
we women still are imprisoned." Then I knew that something was bound to happen sooner or later. Pride always
goes before a fall.

Christensen. No, dear—no. That line of reasoning don't
hold. No, really!

Mrs. Christensen. Oh, is that so?

Christensen. No! For first of all, it was not Miss Riis
that fell, but your own darling son. Secondly, he didn't fall
on account of Miss Riis's pride—in fact, I think he fell several
years before Miss Riis gave vent to her pride. So that when
you knew that his fall would result from Miss Riis's pride,
then you knew something that you didn't know at all.

Mrs. Christensen. Yes, you scoff!

Christensen. Oh, I have to attend a committee meeting
at one sharp. May I ask what has become of your daughter?

Riis. Yes, I am also beginning to——

Nordan. [*Who has kept in the background, sometimes in the
room and sometimes outside, says now to* Margit, *who is just
passing by the door from right to left*] Didn't you find her until
now?

Margit. Yes, I have been down once before with Miss
Svava's hat and parasol.

Nordan. Is she going out?

Margit. I don't know.   [*Goes.*

Christensen. Well, well!

Riis. What's the meaning of this?

                                    [*Is about to leave the room.*

Nordan. No, no! Not you!

Mrs. Riis. [*Has risen and goes toward the door*] I think I
had better——

Riis. Yes, you go!

NORDAN. No, *I* will go! For I fear I have been the cause— [*Going*] I promise to bring her back.

CHRISTENSEN. Well, well!

MRS. CHRISTENSEN. [*Rising*] I fear, my dear, that our visit is inconveniencing the young lady?

RIIS. You must have forbearance with her! It comes from all these romantic ideas, I tell you; from all this reading which her mother has not held properly in check.

MRS. RIIS. I? What is it you are saying?

RIIS. I am saying that this is an important moment. And such moments seem to bring clearness—just as if—yes, they do!

CHRISTENSEN. Your husband, Mrs. Riis, seems to have had the same revelation which came to our minister recently —that is, to my wife's minister. It was just after dinner—a very good dinner, too—and that's a time when brilliant ideas are likely to come. We were talking about how much more woman has to learn now than she had in the past. It didn't matter much, said somebody, for she forgot all about it as soon as she was married. And then the minister cried out joyfully: "Yes, my wife has already forgotten how to spell, and I am hoping she will soon forget how to write also."

MRS. CHRISTENSEN. The way you mimic people—I just have to laugh—although it's sinful.

[CHRISTENSEN *looks at his watch.*

RIIS. And they are not coming yet!—Will you go, or must I——?

MRS. RIIS. [*Rising*] I'll go. But they haven't had time yet——

RIIS. [*Close to his wife*] This is your fault! It's perfectly plain to me.

MRS. RIIS. I don't think you know what you are saying.

[*Goes out.*

Rīīs. [*Coming back to the middle of the room*] I have to apologise—very much! This was the very last thing I should have expected of Svava. For I dare say that the laws of common courtesy have never before been violated in this house.

MRS. CHRISTENSEN. Something may have happened.

RĪĪS. Why, I never thought— Good God!

MRS. CHRISTENSEN. Don't misunderstand me now. I mean that a young girl is so sensitive to emotion—and then she hesitates to show herself.

RĪĪS. All the same, Mrs. Christensen, all the same! In a moment like this— Well, you must pardon me, but I cannot bear this. I simply must see for myself what is the matter.

[*He hurries out.*

CHRISTENSEN. If Alf had been here, I suppose he would also be running around the park after the lady.

MRS. CHRISTENSEN. But, dear!

CHRISTENSEN. Are we not alone?

MRS. CHRISTENSEN. Yes, but nevertheless——

CHRISTENSEN. Well, then I can only say as a famous man said long before me: Why the devil did he venture on board that galley?

MRS. CHRISTENSEN. Now be patient for a few moments! It's absolutely necessary.

CHRISTENSEN. Necessary? Pooh! Riis is more afraid of a breach than any one of us. Didn't you notice him a moment ago?

MRS. CHRISTENSEN. I did, but——

CHRISTENSEN. She has already gone far beyond what she has a right to.

MRS. CHRISTENSEN. That's what Alf thinks also.

CHRISTENSEN. Then he should have been on hand to say so. It was what I wanted.

MRS. CHRISTENSEN. Alf is in love—and that makes a man timid.

CHRISTENSEN. Oh-h!

MRS. CHRISTENSEN. Yes, being in love as often as you are is a different thing. [*She gets up*] There they come— No— not Svava!

CHRISTENSEN. Isn't she coming?

MRS. CHRISTENSEN. [*Speaking at the same time as her husband*] I don't see her.

RIIS. [*Appearing outside*] Here they are!

MRS. CHRISTENSEN. And your daughter?

RIIS. Svava, too! She just asked us to walk ahead. She wanted a chance to pull herself together.

MRS. CHRISTENSEN. [*Sitting down again*] There you see! It was as I thought. Poor thing!

MRS. RIIS. Now she'll be here in a moment. [*Close to* MRS. CHRISTENSEN] You must forgive her—it has been a hard time for her.

MRS. CHRISTENSEN. Goodness gracious, I understand perfectly. The first time you experience a thing of that kind, it's something dreadful.

CHRISTENSEN. Really, this is becoming quite amusing!

NORDAN. Now then! She just asked me to walk a little ahead.

RIIS. I think we have waited long enough.

NORDAN. She's right behind me.

RIIS. There she is!

> *Goes over toward the right;* MRS. RIIS *and* NORDAN *meet* SVAVA, *who is coming from the left.*

CHRISTENSEN. One might think it was the Queen of Sheba!

SIXTH SCENE

The same as before. SVAVA. *Later* ALF.

SVAVA *has put on hat and gloves, and carries a parasol.*
MR. *and* MRS. CHRISTENSEN *have both stood up. She
greets them with a slight movement of her head and walks
over to the corner on the right in the foreground. Everybody sits down in silence;* NORDAN *furthest to the left;
then* MRS. RIIS, MRS. CHRISTENSEN, CHRISTENSEN;
and way over to the right, but in the background, RIIS,
who alternately sits down and gets up again.

MRS. CHRISTENSEN. My dear Svava, we have come here
to—well, you yourself know why. What has happened has
caused us a great deal of sorrow. But it's something that
cannot be undone. We don't want to justify Alf's conduct.
But it seems to us he might be forgiven, particularly by one
who feels that she is loved, genuinely loved. For that is
something entirely different!

CHRISTENSEN. Of course!

RIIS. Of course!

NORDAN. Of course!

CHRISTENSEN. And even if you don't agree to this, I hope
you can agree with regard to Alf himself. For we believe,
my dear Svava, that in his character you have a guarantee
of absolute faithfulness. I know that if it should be demanded
of him, he will give you his word of honour.

MRS. RIIS. [*Rising suddenly*] Oh, no, no!

MRS. CHRISTENSEN. What is it, my dear?

MRS. RIIS. Nothing of that kind! Why, the marriage
ceremony itself is the same as a vow.

NORDAN. But perhaps two might be more effective, Mrs. Riis?

MRS. RIIS. No, not that! No vows!   [*Sits down again.*

CHRISTENSEN. I have been noticing the remarks of our friend here, Dr. Nordan.—Tell me, my dear sir, do you also hold that my son's action must absolutely prevent his marriage with a respectable woman?

NORDAN. On the contrary! Such a thing never prevents a man from marrying—and marrying very well at that. So that in this case it is Svava alone who in every respect acts peculiarly.

MRS. CHRISTENSEN. I shouldn't say that. But there is something Svava has overlooked. She is acting as if she were free. But she is far from free. An engagement is a marriage. At least, I am old-fashioned enough to look at it that way. But then he to whom I have given my hand is also my lord, my master, and I owe it to him—as to everybody else in authority—to hold him in honour whether his actions be good or bad. I cannot cast him aside or run away from him myself.

RIIS. That's old-fashioned and solid! I thank you with all my heart, Mrs. Christensen!

NORDAN. I also——!

MRS. RIIS. But if it is too late *after* you are engaged——
[*Checks herself.*

MRS. CHRISTENSEN. What do you mean, my dear?

MRS. RIIS. Oh, no—it wasn't anything at all.

NORDAN. If it is too late after the engagement, Mrs. Riis means—why not then tell the truth before the engagement?

RIIS. Well, there came the only thing still wanting!

CHRISTENSEN. Ah, but there would be style to that! Suppose hereafter a proposal should come to be something like this: "My dear young lady, up to date I have had so and so many love affairs—to wit, so and so many serious ones, and so and so many lighter ones." That would be an excellent introduction, wouldn't it, to——

NORDAN. ——to a declaration that he has never loved anybody else.

CHRISTENSEN. Not exactly that, but——

RIIS. Why, there's Alf!

MRS. RIIS. Alf?

MRS. CHRISTENSEN. Yes, there he is!

RIIS. [*Going to meet him*] That's right! I am glad to see you!

CHRISTENSEN. We-ell?

ALF. In the end I couldn't help myself. I had to come.

CHRISTENSEN. And right you did.

RIIS. It was the only natural thing.

> ALF *steps forward and bows very deeply to* SVAVA. *She acknowledges his greeting, but without looking at him. He steps back.*

NORDAN. Hello, my boy!

ALF. Perhaps my presence is not convenient?

RIIS. Far from it—on the contrary!

ALF. It seems, however, as if Miss Riis didn't wish to have me here?   [*Silence.*

MRS. CHRISTENSEN. But in a family conference like ours just now? Don't you think so, my dear?

RIIS. I assure you that you *are* welcome. It is just what you have to say that we are all waiting for.

CHRISTENSEN. That's right.

ALF. I have not succeeded in getting a hearing before now. I have repeatedly been turned away. Both I and my letters. And so I thought—that if I came now, I might be heard.

RIIS. Of course! Nobody would think of anything else.

NORDAN. You will be heard.

ALF. Perhaps I may regard Miss Riis's silence as a permission? In that case—well, it isn't much I have to say either. All I want is to recall the fact that when I applied for the hand of Miss Riis, I did so because I loved her with all my heart—her, and no one else. The greatest happiness I could imagine, and also the greatest honour, was to be loved by her in return. And nothing has changed since then.

[*He makes a pause as if expecting an answer.
Everybody looks at* SVAVA.

ALF. If Miss Riis expects me to say more than that—if she expects me to make apologies—well, I can't see the matter in that light. I can't feel myself under such an obligation to anybody. [*Silence*] What I might offer voluntarily—what I might be anxious to tell under other circumstances—of that I cannot speak now. But I am under no such obligation to anybody. My honour demands that I insist on this. The only thing for which I am responsible is my future. And in respect to that I must admit it has offended me deeply that Miss Riis has for a moment been able to doubt me. It has offended me very deeply. Never in my life have I been doubted in the same way before.—I must ask, with all proper respect, that I be taken at my word. [*After another pause*] Well, that's all.

MRS. RIIS. [*Rising instinctively*] But if under similar circumstances, a woman should say the same thing—who would believe her?

Silence. SVAVA *bursts into tears.*

MRS. CHRISTENSEN. Poor child!

RIIS. Believe her?

MRS. RIIS. Yes, believe her.—Believe her if, with a past like that behind her, she dared to assert that she would always remain a faithful wife?

CHRISTENSEN. With such a past?

MRS. RIIS. Perhaps the expression is poor. But why demand that she trust the man more than he will trust her? For he wouldn't believe her at all.

RIIS. [*Coming up behind his wife*] Have you gone clear crazy?

CHRISTENSEN. [*Half rising*] If you pardon me, ladies and gentlemen, I think the two young people should be permitted to settle the matter.   [*Sits down again.*

ALF. I must confess that I have never given a thought to what Mrs. Riis is talking of, because it could never happen. No decent man would ever choose a woman of whose past he was not absolutely sure. Not one!

MRS. RIIS. But how about the decent woman, Alf?

ALF. That's a different thing.

NORDAN. To put it exactly: a woman owes the man both her past and her future, a man owes the woman only his future.

ALF. If you like—yes.

NORDAN. [*To* SVAVA, *as he gets up*] I did wish you to postpone your answer, Svava. But now I think you ought to answer at once.

> SVAVA *goes up to* ALF *and flings one of her gloves in his face. Then she disappears into her room.* ALF *makes a complete face-about to look after her.* RIIS *rushes into his room on the right. All are on their feet.* MRS. CHRISTENSEN *takes hold of* ALF's *arm and goes out with him.* CHRISTENSEN *follows them.* MRS. RIIS *runs across the stage to the left.*

NORDAN. That was the gauntlet, all right.

MRS. RIIS. [*In front of the locked door behind which* SVAVA *has disappeared*] Svava!

CHRISTENSEN. [*Returns and says to* NORDAN *before the latter*

has noticed him or had a chance to turn around] It is war, then?
—Well, I think I know something about war! [*Goes out again.*
    Nordan *turns around to look after him and remains
    standing that way.*
Mrs. Riis. [*At the door as before*] Svava!
    Riis *comes out of his room in great haste, with hat and
    gloves on and a walking-stick in his hand; runs after
    the* Christensens.
Mrs. Riis. Svava!

Curtain.

ACT III

A garden, at the end of which is seen the rear of a pretty one-story house.

FIRST SCENE

NORDAN. ALF. CHRISTENSEN.

Dr. NORDAN is sitting on a chair in the foreground, reading. An old man-servant opens the door of the house.

SERVANT. Doctor!

NORDAN. What is it? [ALF *appears in the door*] Oh, is it you? [*Rising*] Well, my boy?—But how you look!

ALF. Never mind that! Can you give me some breakfast?

NORDAN. Have you had no breakfast yet? Haven't you been home? Not home all night? Not since yesterday? [*Calling out*] Thomas!

ALF. And when I have eaten, I must have a talk with you.

NORDAN. Of course. My dear boy! [*To* THOMAS] Get ready some breakfast in there.

[*Pointing to a window on the left side of the house.*

ALF. And I suppose I'll have to straighten out my appearance a little too?

NORDAN. Go with Thomas! I'll be there in a moment. [THOMAS *and* ALF *go into the house; at that moment a carriage is heard stopping in front of the house*] There is a carriage now! See what it is, Thomas!—No practice! Going away to-morrow!

SERVANT. It's Mr. Christensen, sir! [*Goes out again.*

77

NORDAN. Ho-ho! [*Goes over to the window on the left*] Alf!

ALF. [*In the window*] Yes?

NORDAN. Your father! If you don't want to be seen, just pull down the shade.

The shade is drawn.

SERVANT. This way, please!

CHRISTENSEN. [*In evening dress; around his neck is seen the big cross worn by a Knight Commander of the Order of St. Olav; a light coat hangs across his shoulders*] I hope you will pardon me!

NORDAN. Certainly!—In all your glory?—Congratulations!

CHRISTENSEN. Oh, we freshly baked ones have to make our bow at court to-day. But on my way to the palace I thought I would stop for a moment with you, if you will let me.—Have you heard anything from that quarter? From the Riises?

NORDAN. No. I suppose they are waiting for the "war" to begin.

CHRISTENSEN. Well, it's coming! I intend to start it this very day. But I thought she might have become a little more reasonable? Women act ugly about that kind of thing as a rule. But afterward they become so much the meeker.

NORDAN. I don't think so. But I bow before your greater experience.

CHRISTENSEN. Thanks! But as a family buffer of long service, you must have a still greater.—Yesterday she was like an electric eel.—And she knew how to hit! I don't think the boy has been home ever since. I am almost glad of it. For it means there must be some shame in him. And I had almost begun to doubt it.

NORDAN. It is this matter about the "war" that interests *me*.

CHRISTENSEN. Oh, are you so keen on that? Well—I guess

that matter will take care of itself. The case of Mrs. North can be opened up again any day, my dear fellow. It rests with the bank, don't you know.

NORDAN. But what has it to do with your son's engagement?

CHRISTENSEN. What, you ask? My son is jilted by Miss Riis because she does not approve of his relations *before* the marriage. Her father maintains similar relations *in spite* of his marriage! *Tableau vivant très curieux*—to use the language of which Mr. Riis himself is so fond!

NORDAN. Oh, that's disgusting! For your son *alone* is to blame in this matter.

CHRISTENSEN. My son is not to blame at all. He has done nothing whatever that could bring harm or dishonour to the Riis family. Nothing whatsoever! He is an honest man who has given his promise to Miss Riis, and this promise he has kept. Who dares say anything else? Or that he does not *mean* to keep it? To doubt him is an insult, my dear doctor. There must be apologies—and peace—or war! For I am not going to stand this. And if my son intends to do so, I shall despise him.

NORDAN. *I* believe that your son's promise was honestly meant when he gave it. It is possible that he might have kept it also—but I don't know! I have learned to doubt. I am a physician. I have seen too much. And yesterday he did not appear to advantage.—Yes, you must pardon me. But on top of his lively bachelor life, and with the heritage that is back of him—if anybody doubted him—if his fiancée doubted him—do you really think that would be so very remarkable—my dear sir? Do you think he had a right to become offended? To demand apologies? Apologies for what? Because somebody dared to doubt his virtue?—Just think of it!

CHRISTENSEN. Oh, fiddlesti——

NORDAN. One moment! I am only half through. For you spoke also of peace—which means marriage. And if your son cares to marry a woman who does not feel sure of him, then *I* shall despise him.

CHRISTENSEN. Well——!

NORDAN. Well, I shall. That shows how opinions may differ. According to the way I feel about it, your son has simply to submit—and to wait. Wait and keep quiet. Always provided, of course, that he is still in love.—Now you know what I think of the matter.

CHRISTENSEN. First of all I presume that most suitors have erred in the same way as my son. At least, that is my own belief. Furthermore I presume that they have the same unfortunate "heritage"—a word on which you lay especial emphasis out of friendly consideration for me. But is that any reason for a majority of engaged young women to behave as Miss Riis does? To raise an outcry, to run away, to make a scandal? If it were, what a hubbub there would be! The result would be the most diverting anarchy ever heard of in this world— No, these doctrines now confronting us are against the nature and order of things. They are false. And when, in the bargain, they are hurled at our heads in the form of judgments by a Supreme Court of Morals, then I strike back! Good-bye! [*Starts to leave, but turns back*] Against *whom* would these Supreme Court decisions be directed, do you think? As a rule, against the best and ablest young men in the country. And *these* are the men that we should put in a class by themselves as special objects of derision!—And against *what* would those decisions turn? Against the better part of the world's literature and art; against a great deal of what is most beautiful, most entrancing in our own time—above all, against the great cities of the world. Against those world-miracles—the cities of vast millions. You cannot deny it!—Just that life which keeps apart from marriage, or breaks it up, or tries to change the whole institution—yes, you know very well what I mean— all that which we describe as "seductive" in fashions, in luxury, in sociability, in art, in literature—it is just this which contributes more than anything else to the richness of life in the big cities. It is one of their main sources of power. Nobody who has seen it, can doubt this. But everybody pretends not to understand. Is then all this to be destroyed? Are the best among our youths to be made outcasts? Are the great cities of the world to be ruined?—Yes, people de- mand so much in the name of morality, that at last they demand what is immoral.

NORDAN. Ah, you are, indeed, applying the superior ability of a statesman to your little war.

CHRISTENSEN. Nothing but common sense, my dear fellow. But that's all that's needed. And you may be sure that the whole city will be on my side.

SERVANT. Doctor!

NORDAN. Well, I declare!   [*He hurries toward the house.*

SECOND SCENE

The same as before. MRS. RIIS.

MRS. RIIS. May I come in?

NORDAN. Of course you may!

MRS. RIIS [*To* CHRISTENSEN, *who has saluted her*] My visit is really for you.

CHRISTENSEN. I am delighted!

MRS. RIIS. I happened to be at the window just as your carriage drove up and you stepped out. And so I thought I should seize the opportunity—for yesterday you uttered **a** threat against us. Am I right? You declared war against us?

CHRISTENSEN. It seems to me that it was declared, and that I merely accepted it?

MRS. RIIS. And what is the object of your war, if I may ask?

CHRISTENSEN. I have just explained my position to the doctor. But I doubt whether it would be chivalrous to do so to you.

NORDAN. Then I shall do it. The war is directed against your husband. Mr. Christensen means to take the offensive.

MRS. RIIS. Of course! For you know that you can reach him. But I have come to ask you to reconsider.

CHRISTENSEN. [*Smiling*] Is that so?

MRS. RIIS. Once—it is many years ago now—I picked up my child in my arms and meant to leave my husband. Then he mentioned a name. He used it as a shield. It was the name of a very powerful man. And he said: "Observe how forbearing that man's wife is. And because of her, the whole community is forbearing. And those who will benefit by it are their children."—Those were his exact words.

CHRISTENSEN. Well? In so far as advice was suggested, it was good advice. And you took it, didn't you?

MRS. RIIS. In our country it is a shame to be a divorced wife. And it brings no honour to be the daughter of such a woman. The wealthy, the powerful people, those that set the tone, have caused it to be so.

CHRISTENSEN. Oh, well——?

MRS. RIIS. This was my excuse when I stayed for the sake of my child's future. But it was also my husband's excuse —he being one who follows the example set by others.

CHRISTENSEN. We all do, madam.

MRS. RIIS. But the men of most power less than others.

And in this respect they are setting examples which are very
tempting to the rest.—I can hardly be mistaken in assuming
that, during these last days, I have heard *your* ideas from my
husband's lips. But if mistaken in this, I was surely right
in hearing *you* back of what your son said yesterday?

CHRISTENSEN. I stand by every word my son spoke.

MRS. RIIS. So I thought. Well, it will be a strange war,
this one of yours. For you are back of everything that has
happened from first to last. You are the whole war—on both
sides.

NORDAN. Before you answer!—May I submit to you, Mrs.
Riis, whether you want to make the breach incurable? Is a
conciliation between the two young people to be rendered
impossible?

MRS. RIIS. It *is* impossible.

NORDAN. Why?

MRS. RIIS. Because all confidence is gone.

NORDAN. Now any more than before?

MRS. RIIS. Yes, for I must confess that until yesterday,
when Alf's word of honour was offered—and until he himself
demanded that he be trusted on his word of honour—until
then I had not recognised my own story. And yet, that's
what it was—*word for word!* That's the way we began!
Who can guarantee that the sequel will not be the same?

CHRISTENSEN. My son's character is a guarantee of that,
madam.

MRS. RIIS. Character?—Yes, you think that a character
is developed by following secret, lawless ways from youth up!
But that is the way to develop faithlessness. And those who
complain that real characters are so rare, should seek the
cause right here, I think.

CHRISTENSEN. It is not one's youth that determines the
matter. What settles it is how one marries.

MRS. RIIS. Why should faithlessness cease with marriage? Can you tell me that?

CHRISTENSEN. Because then there is love.

MRS. RIIS. Then there is love?   As if there had been no love before!—It is just in this respect that the men have fostered a complete delusion.   No, love cannot bring lasting faith when the will itself is impaired.   And it is.   Impaired through the life the bachelor leads.

CHRISTENSEN. And yet I know very sensual men with strong wills.

MRS. RIIS. I am not talking of strong wills, but of clean ones.   Of loyal and noble wills.

CHRISTENSEN. If my son is to be condemned by that kind of nonsense, then I praise the Lord that he got away before it was too late.   Yes, I do!—And this will be enough!

[*Starts to go.*

MRS. RIIS. As to your son—?   Doctor, tell me—and so that his father may hear it before he leaves—that time when you refused to come to the engagement party, had you already heard something about Alf Christensen?   And was what you had heard of such a nature that you couldn't trust him?

NORDAN. [*After a moment's hesitation*] No, not exactly!

MRS. RIIS. Do you hear that?—But then I must ask you, doctor: why didn't you say anything?   Why, in the name of God, did you keep silent?

NORDAN. Listen, Mrs. Riis; when two young people, who at bottom suit each other—for they do, don't they?

CHRISTENSEN. Yes, they do—I admit that.

NORDAN. When they all at once fall insanely in love with each other—what can a man do?

CHRISTENSEN. Oh, he can manufacture stories, exaggerations, scandals!

NORDAN. And then I must confess—as I think I have said before—that I have grown accustomed to the fact that things in this respect are not as they should be—I looked upon this engagement as upon others—as upon most of them—as a lottery. It might come out well; it might turn out badly.

MRS. RIIS. And my daughter, of whom you are fond—for I know you are—her you would stake in a lottery! Could anything give a better idea of how matters stand?

NORDAN. Yes, there is something—for you yourself, Mrs. Riis—what did you do?

MRS. RIIS. I?

CHRISTENSEN. Good!

NORDAN. *You* learned also what Hoff had told—and more besides.

CHRISTENSEN *laughs in a subdued way.*

NORDAN. And yet you helped your husband—if not to make Svava overlook the whole thing, at least in trying to smooth it over.

CHRISTENSEN. Bravo!

NORDAN. And you called me in to assist you in getting more time.

CHRISTENSEN. In matters like these, you know, the mothers distinguish to some extent between theory and practice.

NORDAN. It was only when I saw Svava—how deeply she took it, and how she had come to fear it—that my own eyes were opened. And I listened to her until my sympathy became aroused. I, too, was young once, and believed—and loved. But all that happened so long ago. And I have grown so tired——

MRS. RIIS. [*Who in the meantime has seated herself at* DR. NORDAN's *small reading table*] Oh, God!

NORDAN. Yes, Mrs. Riis, let me be quite frank about it: it is just the mothers who have gradually blunted my feelings. Because they themselves don't seem to care.—And as a rule they are perfectly aware of what they are dealing with.

CHRISTENSEN. They are, my dear fellow, they are! And Mrs. Riis is no exception. For you must admit, madam, that you, in your time, did your best to hang on to a young man with a pretty lively past!—And for that matter, he held a fine position socially, that young man—something I mention quite incidentally.

NORDAN. Oh, well, well!—But no sooner have the daughters a chance to make what their mothers call a "good marriage," than the old ones forget their own sufferings.

MRS. RIIS. But we don't know that it is the same thing over again.

NORDAN. You don't know?

MRS. RIIS. I tell you that I didn't realise it. We always believe that the men chosen by our daughters are so much better. We believe the guarantees to be better, the conditions to be changed. And it *is* so! It is a sort of mirage that deludes us.

CHRISTENSEN. Through the expectation of a good marriage —yes! I quite agree with you, madam, for the first time. Otherwise I have an idea that all this proves something else, too. Perhaps, after all, the women don't suffer so much by the fact that men are men? How is that? Perhaps the trouble is more violent than deep-going—something like sea-sickness? When it's over—well, then it is over. And when the time comes for the daughters to board the ship, their dear mammas think: oh, well, they'll bear it as we did. Only get them started! For they want so badly to see them started—that's the whole trouble!

MRS. RIIS. [*As she gets up and moves toward the foreground*] Well, if it be so, then it is nothing to laugh at! For then it

proves to what depth a woman may sink through her life
in common with a man.

CHRISTENSEN. Well, I'll——!

MRS. RIIS. Yes, for every new generation of women comes
with a stronger and stronger demand for a decent life. The
mere sense of motherhood is enough to develop that demand.
It is meant for a protection to those that cannot protect
themselves. Even bad mothers have the feeling of it. And
if, nevertheless, they surrender, and if each new generation
of women sinks as deeply in marriage as you say, then this
must be caused by the special privilege which man asserts.
For it is this privilege which has developed him.

CHRISTENSEN. Which special privilege?

MRS. RIIS. That of living as he pleases while still unmarried, and of being taken on his word of honour when he chooses
to enter marriage. As long as woman cannot stop this dreadful privilege, or make herself independent of it—so long will
one half of mankind remain a victim of the other half—of that
other half's lack of self-control. This one privilege has proved
itself stronger than all the work ever done for freedom on
this earth. And that is nothing to laugh at.

CHRISTENSEN. You are dreaming of another world than
ours, madam, and of natures different from ours. And, of
course—if you pardon me!—therein lies the only answer
needed.

MRS. RIIS. Why don't you then give the same answer in
public? Why don't you step forth into full daylight and
acknowledge your views?

CHRISTENSEN. Are we not doing so?

MRS. RIIS. No—not in this country. On the contrary!
For publicly you place yourself under *our* flag, while secretly
you desert it. Why have you not the courage to unfold a
flag of your own? Let those bachelor habits be established

as quite proper! Then the fight will begin at last. And then each innocent bride may at last know where she is going—and in what capacity.

NORDAN. That means the abolition of marriage—nothing more or less.

MRS. RIIS. Well, wouldn't that be better? For now it's being destroyed—long before it is begun!

CHRISTENSEN. Yes, and the man is at fault, of course. That's the fashion nowadays. It's part of the "work of emancipation." His authority must go!

MRS. RIIS. The one he has gained during his life as bachelor.

NORDAN. Ha, ha!

MRS. RIIS. Don't let us cover up the thing with phrases. Let us rather speak of what the poet has called "the blighting of the hearth." For what it means is just blighted marriages. And whence does it spring—this chilling, gruesome materialism, this pleasure-craving brutality? Where does it come from?—I might describe something that lies still nearer at hand. But I won't. I shall not even mention the prevalent family diseases.—But drag it out into the open! Perhaps then it will break into flames, too. And our consciences will be smitten by it! And it will become the most important matter of all in every home! *This* is what is wanted!

CHRISTENSEN. Now we have worked ourselves up to such an elevation that it doesn't sound impressive at all when I say that I am expected in certain "very exalted" quarters. But nevertheless you'll have to excuse me.

MRS. RIIS. I hope I haven't delayed you.

CHRISTENSEN. No, there is plenty of time. I am only longing—please, don't take it badly—to get away from here.

MRS. RIIS. To your—equals?

CHRISTENSEN. I am glad you remind me of them. It

makes me realise that I shall probably not have to meet you
or yours any more?

MRS. RIIS. No, you have received your dismissal from us.

CHRISTENSEN. Well, thank heaven! Now I only hope to
be able to distribute the ridicule in accordance with justice.

MRS. RIIS. To do so, you need only publish your auto-
biography.

CHRISTENSEN. No, rather your family principles, madam!
For they are really too funny for anything. And when I describe the way they are put into practice within the family
itself, I have reason to think that people will laugh rather
heartily. Or to speak seriously: I'll get after your husband
in his reputation and in his business, until he has to leave the
city. I am not going to accept a humiliation like this without paying back in equal coin.   [Starts to leave.

NORDAN. But this is revolting!

ALF. [Appears in the doorway of the house] Father!

CHRISTENSEN. You here?—And how badly you look!
Where have you been, my boy?

ALF. I got here just ahead of you, and I have heard everything. I may as well tell you at once, that if you begin that
kind of warfare, then I'll go around everywhere telling why
Miss Riis broke her engagement with me.—I'll tell it just as
it is.—Yes, you can sneer at me as much as you please. But
I'll do it. And I shall begin at once.

CHRISTENSEN. I think you can save yourself the trouble.
After the breach your reputation will probably travel a great
deal more quickly than yourself.

NORDAN. [Goes over to ALF] To be plain, Alf: do you still
love her?

ALF. You ask because you think she has wronged me?
But now I understand why she did it—and why she had to
do it. Now I understand!

CHRISTENSEN. And forgive her?   Without further ado?

ALF. I love her more than ever—and no matter what she thinks of me.

CHRISTENSEN. Well, well, well!—Then there is nothing more to say about it.   You insist on your right to play the part of lover—and to us self-respecting people you leave nothing but to grin and bear your bad acting as we may best. —I suppose you'll go right over and pay your duty call on account of yesterday's festivities?   And ask for a respite till to-morrow?   While, with as much haste as propriety will permit, you hurry through some kind of purgatory?   May I ask the location of that institution and its methods?—No, my boy, don't get melodramatic!   When you can stand what you got from that little Riis girl yesterday and from her mother to-day, then you can also stand a few gibes and prods from your own father.   I have had to stand the whole engagement, and the breach, too!   And being sprinkled with moral waters on top of it!   Oh, damn it all!   I hope I don't stink of the thing when I get up to the palace! [*He goes toward the house.   In the doorway he turns about for a moment*] Your travelling money will be waiting for you at the office. [*Goes out.*

NORDAN. Does that mean another exile?

ALF. Of course!   [*He shows great excitement.*

MRS. RIIS. Now you'll have to come over with me, doctor, and that at once!

NORDAN. How is she taking it?

MRS. RIIS. I don't know.

NORDAN. You don't know?

MRS. RIIS. Yesterday she wanted to be alone.   This morning she left the house very early.

NORDAN. Then something must have happened?

MRS. RIIS. Yes.   You said yesterday that you had given her a hint about—about her father.

NORDAN. And then?

MRS. RIIS. Then I felt that the time to keep silent was over.

NORDAN. And you——?

MRS. RIIS. I have written to her.

NORDAN. Written?

MRS. RIIS. It came more naturally.   Then we didn't have to talk it over.   I wrote, and tore up—and wrote again. The whole afternoon yesterday and all night.   Wrote! There wasn't much of it.   But it came hard.

NORDAN. And now she has got it?

MRS. RIIS. This morning, when she had eaten and was starting out, I sent it after her.—And now, dearest friend, I want *you* to come and talk to her.   And then you tell me when I can come.   For I am afraid!   [*She covers up her face.*

NORDAN. I saw, the moment you came in, that something important had happened.   And you were so hot-headed!— Good God, how this thing has spread and grown!

MRS. RIIS. You shouldn't go away, doctor!   Don't go away from her now!

NORDAN. Oh, that's what it was!—Thomas!

SERVANT. Yes, sir!

NORDAN. You don't have to pack.

SERVANT. Not pack!—Your stick, sir!

[*Handing* NORDAN *his walking-stick.*

NORDAN. Will you take my arm, madam?

The SERVANT *opens the door for them.*

ALF. [*Stepping forward*] Mrs. Riis!—Will you let me speak to her?

MRS. RIIS. Speak to her?—Oh, that's out of the question!

NORDAN. Why, you heard yourself what she has to think of to-day.

MRS. RIIS. And if she didn't want to speak to you before, she certainly will not do so now.

ALF. When she asks for permission to see me, will you then tell her that I am here? And I'll stay here till she asks!

MRS. RIIS. But what's the use of it?

ALF. Well, that's our concern. I know that she wants to speak to me.—Just tell her that I am here! That's all that's needed! [*He walks away and disappears in the garden.*

NORDAN. He doesn't know what he is saying.

MRS. RIIS. Let us be going, doctor—I am afraid!

NORDAN. And so am I!—Hm—so now she knows *that!*

[*They go out.*

ACT IV

Same room as in the first two acts.

FIRST SCENE

SVAVA. DR. NORDAN.

SVAVA *comes in, walking very slowly; looks around the room; goes up to the door and steps outside for a moment; comes back into the room; when she turns around again,* DR. NORDAN *is standing in the doorway.*

SVAVA. Is that *you*—? Oh, Uncle Nordan! [*She sobs.*
NORDAN. My dear—dear little girl! Now be brave!
SVAVA. But haven't you seen mother? They said she had gone over to you?
NORDAN. She will be here in a moment.—But, do you know—we two ought to take a long walk instead of talking with your mother or anybody else. A long, quiet walk? What do you say?
SVAVA. No, I cannot do that.
NORDAN. Why?
SVAVA. Because I must get through with it.
NORDAN. What do you mean?
SVAVA. [*Paying no attention to his question*] Uncle——
NORDAN. Yes.
SVAVA. Does Alf know this? Did he, too, know it?
NORDAN. Yes.
SVAVA. Of course, everybody but me. Oh, I have such a longing to hide myself—hide myself! And that's what I am going to do.—Now I can see things as they are. There is a

93

big mountain against which I have put my hands to push it away. And the others have stood around laughing at me. —But I want to speak with Alf.

Nordan. With Alf?

Svava. I behaved very unwisely yesterday. I should never have gone in. But you just carried me along. I hardly knew that I went with you.

Nordan. Then it was that about your father—what I said about your father—that——

Svava. I didn't understand at once. But when I was alone —mother's peculiar anxiety, my father's threat to leave the country, all sorts of remarks and symptoms—so many, many things that I had not understood, or hardly even noticed— and all at once—they were there!—I pushed the thing away from me, and it came back.—It came back, and it came back! —And then it was as if every limb of mine had been lamed. —When you took hold of my arm and said, now you *must* come in—at that moment I could hardly think at all. Everything was in a whirl!

Nordan. Well, I acted like a big fool—and twice in succession at that!

Svava. No, it was better. Much better. Of course, it didn't come about in the right way. I must speak to Alf. For it mustn't remain that way.—But otherwise it was better. And now I must get through with it.

Nordan. What do you mean by that?

Svava. Where is mother?

Nordan. My dear girl, you shouldn't do anything to-day. Better not speak to anybody at all. If you do—well, I don't know what may happen.

Svava. But I know.—Yes, it's of no use!—You think I am all nerves to-day? Well, so I am. But if you oppose me, it will only get worse.

NORDAN. I don't oppose you either. All I want——

SVAVA. Yes, yes, yes!—But where *is* mother?—And *you* have to get hold of Alf! I couldn't go to him—could I? Or do you think he is too proud to come here after what happened yesterday? Oh, no, that isn't like Alf! And tell him that he must not be too proud toward one who has been so humiliated.

[*She cries.*

NORDAN. But do you really think you can——?

SVAVA. Oh, you don't know what I can do. Only I must get through with this. For it has lasted long enough now.

NORDAN. I have to ask your mother, then——?

SVAVA. Yes—and Alf?

NORDAN. Yes, after a while. But if you——

SVAVA. No—no "but!"

NORDAN. And if you need me, I shall not go away until you are "through," as you call it.

SVAVA *runs up to him and puts her arms around him.*
DR. NORDAN *goes out.*

SECOND SCENE

SVAVA. *A little later* MRS. RIIS.

MRS. RIIS. [*Approaching* SVAVA] My child!   [*Stops still.*

SVAVA. Yes, mother, I cannot meet you—my whole body is shaking. And don't you know what it is? Has it not occurred to you that you cannot treat me like that?

MRS. RIIS. Treat you, Svava?

SVAVA. Heavens, mother! That you let me live day after day, year after year—without letting me know what kind of thing I was living with? To let me preach the most extreme principles in a house like ours?

MRS. RIIS. But you didn't want me to tell my own child that——?

SVAVA. Not while I was still a child! But when I grew up? Yes, by all means! Hadn't I a right to choose whether or no I wanted to stay in such a home? Hadn't I a right to know what is known to everybody else—or what they might learn at any minute?

MRS. RIIS. I have never thought of it in that way.

SVAVA. Never thought of it in that way? Mother!

MRS. RIIS. Never! To spare you; to keep peace in our home—while you were a child; and later, to let nothing interfere with your studies, your interests, your pleasures—for you are not like others, Svava!—to do that I have watched with the utmost care lest any such knowledge reach you. I thought it my duty! You have no idea of how far I have stooped in order to—for your sake, child!

SVAVA. But you had no right to do so, mother!

MRS. RIIS. No right——?

SVAVA. No! For when you lowered yourself for my sake, you lowered me, too!

MRS. RIIS. [Deeply moved] Good God, Svava——!

SVAVA. Why, I am not reproaching you, mother!—Dear mother, I wouldn't do that for anything in the world!—It only makes me so inexpressibly sad, so shocked—for your sake—that you could be carrying within you such a secret! Never for a moment dare to be yourself with me! Always something to hide! And that you could hear me praise what was not worthy of praise—that you could see me trust— could see me give my love to—oh, mother, mother, mother!

MRS. RIIS. Yes, I have felt it that way myself. Oh, yes! A thousand times! But I didn't think I could dare! Oh, it was wrong—wrong! Now I see! But would you have had me go my own way the moment I myself found out?

SVAVA. That's more than I dare to answer. You have settled that yourself. Every one must settle that—in accordance with her own strength and the strength of her love. But when it kept on until I was grown up—! And that's the reason, of course, why I made a second mistake! I was brought up to be mistaken.

> RIIS *is heard humming a song as he approaches from the left.*

MRS. RIIS. Merciful heavens, there he is!

RIIS. [*Is seen passing the left-hand window in the background, but at the door he stops and exclaims*] Oh, that's right!

> [*Then he turns and walks away hurriedly.*

MRS. RIIS. But, child, what a changed look came over you! Svava, you frighten me! You cannot mean to——

SVAVA. But what have you been thinking, mother?

MRS. RIIS. That I have stood so much for your sake, that you, perhaps, might stand a little for my sake.

SVAVA. Of this? Not in the least!

MRS. RIIS. But what do you want to do?

SVAVA. Go away from here, of course!

MRS. RIIS. [*Utters a cry*] —Then I go with you!

SVAVA. You? Go away from father?

MRS. RIIS. It is for your sake I have stayed with him. Without you, not a single day— Oh, *you don't want me!*

SVAVA. Mother, dear!—I must get accustomed to all that's new to me. Even you seem new to me. And, of course, I have been mistaken about you also.—I must be by myself.— Oh, now, don't get so miserable!

MRS. RIIS. This on top of all! O God, this on top of the rest!

SVAVA. Mother dear—I cannot do otherwise. Now I shall give myself wholly to my kindergartens. I must, I must!

And if I am not permitted to be alone, I shall go still farther away.

Mrs. Riis. This is the worst of all! This is the worst!—There I hear—yes, it's him! Don't say anything now! More than this I cannot endure! Not all at once!—Try to be kind, Svava! Do you hear?

> *Humming as before,* Riis *comes again, but now with an overcoat carried over his arm.* Svava *rushes toward the foreground; after a moment's wavering, she sits down far over to the left, with her back turned toward the centre of the room so that she appears in half profile to the audience; she looks nervously for something with which she can seem occupied.*

THIRD SCENE

Svava. Mrs. Riis. Riis. *Later* Alf.

Riis. [*Puts the overcoat on a chair; he is in full dress and wears the badge of St. Olav*] Good morning, ladies, good morning!

Mrs. Riis. Good morning.

Riis. First big news item: with whom did I drive from the palace?—Christensen!

Mrs. Riis. Really?

Riis. The thundering Jove of yesterday—exactly! With him and my brother the Director-General. And I was the first one he shook hands with when he arrived at the palace. He made conversation with me, he introduced me to people —a regular exhibition it was!

Mrs. Riis. Well!

Riis. Of course, nothing happened yesterday. Nowhere in the world was any gauntlet thrown—least of all in the face of his first-born! Christensen, the worshipful Knight Commander of to-day's make, has a longing for peace. In the end we had a glass of champagne together at my brother's.

MRS. RIIS. That was very nice.

RIIS. Therefore: be in good spirits, ladies! Nothing has happened. Absolutely nothing. We'll begin the feast all over again, with a fresh, clean table-cloth, on which not a single drop has been spilled.

MRS. RIIS. That's very fortunate.

RIIS. Yes, isn't it? Our dear daughter's rather violent discharge of electricity has relieved her own mind and cleared up the ideas of other people—the air is now agreeably refreshing, not to say fecund.

MRS. RIIS. And at the palace? How was it?

RIIS. Well, my dear—looking around at our little group of fresh-baked worthies, I dared not persuade myself that virtue is the thing rewarded in this world. However, some sort of solemn proclamation was spread before us. There was something we should save—it must have been the State, now I think of it—or perhaps it was the Church? Well, I don't know, for I didn't read it. But everybody signed.

MRS. RIIS. You also?

RIIS. I also! Why not keep in good company? Up there, on life's mountain tops, one gets a more pleasing, a more untrammelled view of life. Up there, all are friends. They came and congratulated me—and in the end I couldn't make out whether it was on my own behalf or that of my daughter. Nor did I know that I had so many friends here in the city, not to say at Court. But in such glorious company, and in an atmosphere laden with praise and flattery and pleasantries, what's the use of examining things too closely? And then, nothing but men, just men! There is after all—if the ladies will pardon me—something charming at times to be sur-

rounded only by men, by men in a festive mood. The conversation becomes a little more highly spiced, more to the
point, more full-blooded, and the laughter much more hearty.
One understands one another almost before the word is
spoken.

MRS. RIIS. You seem very happy to-day?

RIIS. Yes, so I am, and no mistake! And I should like
everybody else to be happy also. Of course, life could be a
great deal better; but when you see it from those heights,
you know also that it might be much worse. And as far as
we men are concerned—well, we have our faults. But at
bottom we are awfully amusing. And I bet you, life would
be pretty tedious without us.—Let us then take life as it is,
my dear, darling Svava! [*As he goes toward her, she rises*]
What is this? Are you still in a bad humour? After having
slapped him in the face with your own glove, and in full
family council at that? Can you reasonably ask more of life?
I think you ought to be laughing aloud— Or is something
the matter? What? Oh, what is it now again?

MRS. RIIS. It is——

RIIS. It is——?

MRS. RIIS. Oh, it is— Alf will be here in a moment!

RIIS. Here? Alf? In a moment? Hooray! Then I understand! But why didn't you tell me at once?

MRS. RIIS. You have been talking ever since you came in.

RIIS. Yes, I think I have! Well, even if *you* take it seriously, my dear Svava, I hope you won't object to your
"noble" papa taking it humorously? For it does amuse
me extremely. My spirits went up the moment I guessed
from Christensen's manner that everything was all right.
And now Alf will be here in a moment? Then I understand
everything. Once more: hooray! Why, this is after all the
finest thing that has happened so far to-day! I feel as if I

simply *had* to accompany his entrance with a triumphal overture.   [*He goes humming toward the piano.*

MRS. RIIS. Oh, no, dear! Please, don't!

> RIIS *begins to play as if he didn't hear her;* MRS. RIIS
> *goes over to him and stops him, pointing at the same
> time to* SVAVA.

SVAVA. Let him play! Just let him play, dear! This inno-
cent gaiety which has amused me ever since I was a child—
[*She breaks into tears, but checks herself quickly*] Disgusting!
Horrible!

RIIS. You look as if you wanted to throw more gloves
to-day. So it isn't over yet?

SVAVA. No, it isn't.

RIIS. Perhaps you want to borrow mine, if your own
shouldn't——

MRS. RIIS. No—not that way!

SVAVA. Yes, that way, too. Let him mock at us! One
possessing his moral resolution ought to mock at us.

RIIS. What do you mean by that? Do you call it lack of
moral resolution that I don't care for old maids or sour-faced
virtue?

SVAVA. Father—you are——!

MRS. RIIS. Oh, Svava!

RIIS. No, let her finish! It is quite a novel sensation to
see a well-bred girl throw gloves in the face of her fiancé and
innuendoes in the face of her father!—Especially when it is
done for morality's sake!

SVAVA. Don't mention morality! Or do so to Mrs. North!

RIIS. Mrs.—Mrs.— What has she got——?

SVAVA. Oh, be quiet! I know everything you have——

MRS. RIIS. Svava!

SVAVA. That's right!—For mother's sake we'll go no further!—But when, yesterday, I threw that glove of which you

have so much to say, I knew this. And that's why I did it!
It was meant for everything of this kind, for the beginning
and the continuation, for him and for you! Then I understood your righteous zeal in this matter—as well as the moral
indignation which you showed and voiced to mother.

MRS. RIIS. Svava!

SVAVA. Oh, that politeness of yours, that concern for
mother which I have so often admired—and your jests, your
good-humour, your elegance—I have just learned what it all
means!—No, no, I can no longer believe in anything! Oh,
it's horrible, horrible!

MRS. RIIS. But, Svava!

SVAVA. All life has become unclean to me. The nearest
and dearest has been blackened. And for that reason I feel
it since yesterday as if I had been made an outcast. And
what else am I? Cast out from all that I loved and treasured,
and this without any fault of my own! And yet, what I feel
most, is not pain. No, it is humiliation, shame. All that I
have dared to say is now turned into words merely—and all
that I have dared to do on my own behalf is nothing but big
words—and this without any fault of my own! For it is
your fault!—I thought I knew something about life. But I
was to learn a lot more. I suppose the meaning of it was to
make me stoop so low that at last I should fit into it.—Now,
and now only, has it become clear to me what you were
teaching me all the time—while you appealed to God and to
my mother for support. But it was all of no use!—It is a
great deal, I should say, to live through the thoughts I have
had to face, yesterday, last night, to-day. But once done, it
is done for ever. Afterward there is nothing that can surprise!—Oh, that a man has the heart to let his own child live
through such a thing!

MRS. RIIS. Look at your father!

SVAVA. Yes—if you find what I say to you very hard— then remember what I used to say to you. Not longer ago than yesterday morning, on this very spot. Then you have a measure of what I have thought of you, father—and of what, because of it, I now feel in *here!*—Oh——!

RIIS. Svava!

SVAVA. You have ruined my home for me. The very memory of the time spent in it is spoiled. And I cannot think of it as a home for the future either.

RIIS *and* MRS. RIIS. But, Svava!

SVAVA. No, I cannot! All sense of security is gone! And then it is no longer a home. Since yesterday I am a tenant only.

RIIS. My child—don't say that!

SVAVA. Yes, I am your child. You have only to say it as you did now, and I feel it deeply. And all we have lived together, we two! All the fun we have had on our travels; all that we have read together, played together—now it cannot even be remembered—I cannot go back to it in my mind! And that is why I cannot stay here!

RIIS. You cannot stay here?

SVAVA. No, it would remind me of too many things—all of which are now spoiled.

MRS. RIIS. And you'll see that it is just as hard to leave.

RIIS. But—*I* can go!

MRS. RIIS. You?

RIIS. And you can stay here with your mother. But— Svava——?

SVAVA. No, I cannot accept that—no matter what happens——

RIIS. Don't say anything more! I beg you, Svava! Don't make me too, too miserable! Remember that not until to-day— Never have I dreamt of making you— If you cannot endure me any longer—if you cannot—then let me go away. It is I—who am the guilty one. Svava, don't you hear? I, not you! You must stay here!

MRS. RIIS. Mercy, there is Alf!

RIIS. Alf!   [*Silence.*

ALF. [*Stops in the doorway; pause*] Perhaps I had better leave again——?

RIIS. Leave again?—Leave again, you say?—By no means! Oh, no!—You couldn't come more conveniently! Really, you couldn't! Dear fellow—my dear fellow, let me thank you!

MRS. RIIS. [*To* SVAVA] Do you want to be left alone?

SVAVA. No, no, no!

RIIS. You want to speak to Svava, do you?—I think the most proper thing I can do is to retire. You two ought to have a chance to talk it out. Be by yourselves. Yes, of course! And with your permission, I'll disappear. You don't mind? I have really some very important business in the city. You must pardon me! I am only going to make a quick change. Pardon!   [*Goes into his room.*

ALF. Of course, I can come some other time.

MRS. RIIS. But you want badly to have a talk with her at once?

ALF. There can be no question here of what I want. I can see—and Dr. Nordan told me—that Miss Riis has been under a great strain. But I thought it my duty to come just the same.

SVAVA. And I thank you for it. It is more—much more than I have deserved. But I want to tell you at once that what happened yesterday—I mean, the way it happened— the reason of it was that I had just learned something I had never known before. And all was mixed in my mind.

[*She can no longer hide her emotion.*

ALF. I knew that what happened yesterday—you would regret to-day. I know how kind you are. And in that lay my one hope of seeing you again.

Riis. [*Comes from his room, having partly changed his dress*] If anybody wants anything done in the city—I'll attend to it—no? I have thought that the ladies might like a trip abroad. How does it strike you? When one's thoughts are about to become—what shall I say?—too severe, or rather, too heavy—it offers a remarkable diversion. I have often noticed it myself. Oh, quite often!—Think it over, will you?—I might as well make arrangements at once, if perchance—how about it? Well: good-bye for a while! And think it over! I myself think it would be fine.

> *Goes out through the door in the background and turns to the left.*

> SVAVA *looks smilingly at her mother for a moment; then she hides her face in her hands.*

Mrs. Riis. If you don't mind for a moment, I must——

Svava. Mother!

Mrs. Riis. I cannot help it, child. I must try to calm down a little. And I shall only be in there. [*Pointing toward the room on the left*] And soon I shall be here again.   [*Goes out.*

> SVAVA *sinks down on a chair by the table, wholly overcome by her emotion.*

FOURTH SCENE

Svava. Alf.

ALF. Now I have a feeling that the whole matter has come back to us two.

Svava. Yes——

ALF. I suppose you know that since yesterday I have done

nothing but make up speeches to you?—But now that doesn't help me a bit.

SVAVA. But it was kind of you to come.

ALF. Let me then ask just one thing of you—but that one I ask with my whole heart: *wait for me!*—For now I know what road leads up to you. We had laid out a plan of life, we two, and although I shall be alone about it now—I want to carry that plan through! And I shall! And then, perhaps, some day, when you see how faithful I have been—? I have been ordered not to bother you, and least of all to-day. But let me have an answer—quietly, very quietly. Won't you?

SVAVA. But why?

ALF. I need it to live on. For I am one of those men to whom life means the more the higher hangs the prize.—An answer!

SVAVA. [*Tries to speak, but bursts into tears*] You see, everything upsets me to-day. I cannot.—And what do you want? That I shall wait? What does it mean? To be through— and yet not through; try to forget—and yet build up new hope. [*Again overcome by her feelings*] No!

ALF. I can see that you ought to be left alone. And yet it is impossible for me to leave.

> SVAVA *rises in order to hide her emotion;* ALF *follows her and kneels beside her.*

ALF. Only a word for me!

SVAVA. But don't you understand, then, that if you could once more give me the joy that springs from nothing but complete trust—do you think I should be waiting for you then? No, I would come and thank you on my knees! Can you for a moment doubt that?

ALF. No, no!

SVAVA. But now I don't have it.

ALF. Svava!

SVAVA. Oh, please!

ALF. Good-bye!—Oh, good-bye!—But to meet again!—To meet again! [*He starts to leave but turns back at the door*] I *must* have a sign. A sure sign! Hold out a hand to me!

> SVAVA *turns toward him and holds out both her hands.*
>> ALF *goes out.*

MRS. RIIS. [*Comes through the door on the left*] Did you give him any promise?

SVAVA. I think I did!

> [*She hides her face against her mother's shoulder.*

Curtain.

BEYOND OUR POWER

(OVER EVNE)

THE FIRST OF THE TWO PLAYS OF THIS NAME

1883

PERSONS IN THE PLAY

PASTOR ADOLPH SANG

CLARA SANG, *his wife*

ELIAS
RACHEL } *their twin children*

MRS. HANNA ROBERTS, *sister of Mrs. Sang*

{ THE STRANGER
{ BRATT, *a minister*

KRÖYER, *a minister*

THE BISHOP

BLANK
BREY
FALK
JENSEN } *ministers*

THE OLD WIDOW

ÅGOT FLORVÅGEN

SEVERAL MINISTERS

BEYOND OUR POWER
(OVER EVNE)

ACT I

A poorly furnished room with walls of crudely dressed logs. In the right wall is a window in two parts that open separately outward. There is a door in the left wall. A bed stands near the middle of the room, a little to the right, and so placed that the head is in a line with the doorway, facing it. By the bed stands a small table covered with bottles, saucers, and such things. A wash-stand and a few chairs make up the rest of the furniture.

FIRST SCENE

CLARA SANG *is lying in the bed. Her clothing is white, and the bed has a white cover. Her sister,* MRS. HANNA ROBERTS, *is standing at one of the windows.*

HANNA. How the sun is shining on the leaves of the birches! And how tender the leaves are up here!

CLARA. But now I smell the bird-cherry blossoms.

HANNA. I am looking and looking, but I cannot see a single bird-cherry tree.

CLARA. You cannot see it, but it's there. The smell of it is carried down here by the morning breeze.

HANNA. But I smell nothing.

CLARA. Oh, after such a rain the slightest current from the outside carries its own scent.

111

HANNA. And you smell bird-cherry blossoms?

CLARA. Most distinctly!—And I think you had better close the lower window.

HANNA. All right. [*She closes the window.*

CLARA. Who was it that said there was danger of a land-slide?

HANNA. That old fellow—the strokesman of the boat that brought us in. It rained and rained, and then he said: "This is dangerous weather—after a rain like this, things get loosened up in the mountains!"

CLARA. I thought of nothing else last night. We have had slide after slide here, you know. Once—well, that was before our time—the church was carried away.

HANNA. The church?

CLARA. Not from where it is now. It stood farther away then.

HANNA. Is that why it has been placed right up against the garden wall?

CLARA. Yes. And when they open up the church windows in the summer, as they have done now, I can lie here and hear Adolph singing at the altar. That is, if our door here is open, and also the door to the living-room—and, of course, the window in the living-room must be open. He sings so beautifully. And when both doors stand open, I can see the church from this place. Come over here! That's why the bed is placed just here, you know.

HANNA. [*Going over to the bed*] Oh, dearest, that I should come back to find you in such a condition!

CLARA. Hanna!

HANNA. Why didn't you write?

CLARA. First of all, America is so far away. And then—but we'll leave that to some other time.

HANNA. I didn't understand your answer yesterday, when I asked about a doctor?

CLARA. Adolph was here, so I didn't want to answer. We have no doctor.

HANNA. You have no doctor?

CLARA. Well, he came and came—and he's a good way off at that—but nothing happened. And when I had been lying a whole month here without sleep——

HANNA. A whole month without sleep? But that is impossible!

CLARA. It's close to six weeks now!—Well, then it didn't seem to matter much whether the doctor came or not, don't you see? My husband asked him what my trouble was, and he gave it an ugly-sounding name. Adolph hasn't told me what it was, so I don't know. And since then we have not sent for him again.

HANNA. Are you not talking too much?

CLARA. Whole days go by without my saying a word. At other times I talk continuously. I have to.—I suppose Adolph will soon be back from his morning walk now, and then he will bring me flowers.

HANNA. Couldn't I pick some for you, as you long so much for them?

CLARA. No, thank you, for there are some that I cannot endure. But he knows them.—But, Hanna, you haven't told me yet about your meeting with the children on board the steamer. And I want so badly to hear about it.

HANNA. Everything was so upset here yesterday.

CLARA. And then you were all tired. Think of it—the children are still asleep. From seven to seven! That's youth, sure enough!

HANNA. Well, they needed it. But I can only sleep a few hours at a time. And yet I don't feel tired.

CLARA. That's what happens to everybody who comes up here where the midnight sun is shining. They seem to be startled out of their usual sleepiness.—But the children—are they not sweet?

HANNA. And such innocents! But in features they don't resemble you, nor Sang either—that is, except their eyes. That came home to me later.

CLARA. Tell me, tell me!

HANNA. For if they had resembled you, I should have recognised them at once. You must remember, of course, that I had seen neither one of you since you were young. Well, I saw them as they were coming aboard, and later also, although they were travelling second-class——

CLARA. Yes, poor things, they couldn't afford better.

HANNA. And yet I didn't recognise them. Then I happened one morning to be standing on the upper deck, and they were walking rapidly back and forth right below where I stood —to keep themselves warm. And each time they turned their backs to me to walk forward, I kept on seeing those eyes of theirs just the same. For those eyes were familiar to me. And then some gulls passed us so close that they made Rachel reach out both arms. She was scared, you know, for they seemed to be coming right at her. But that movement of her arms—it was exactly yours. And then I knew the eyes also. They were Sang's.

CLARA. And then you went down to them at once?

HANNA. Do you need to ask? And the first thing I said was: "Is your name Sang?" And they didn't have to answer. I knew it perfectly. And then I said: "I am Aunt Hanna from America." And, of course, all three of us were very deeply moved.   [*Both sisters weep quietly.*

CLARA. Rachel had written to you that you should come over and see me! How was that?

HANNA. That's right. And it's something for which I shall always be thankful to Rachel. And how sweet she was! I had them moved over to the first cabin at once, and got her tucked up in a big shawl. She was just freezing. And I got him a plaid.

CLARA. Dear!

HANNA. But, do you know—yes, it's part of the story— just then a squall seemed to turn the whole fiord black. We were at the foot of a towering mountain wall, naked and grey. A flock of gulls came out. Some of them flew right over our heads, screaming. Everything seemed so cold. A few poor huts along the shore were the only houses in sight, and we had travelled miles and miles without seeing any others. Nothing but peaks and rocks. This is the Northland, I thought. Here these poor frozen children have been brought up. Yes, I'll never forget it! It was horrible!

CLARA. But it isn't horrible.

HANNA. Oh, Clara!—Now, lying there, as you are—can you remember what a fine, high-spirited thing you used to be?

CLARA. Oh, yes! And I don't know how I am going to begin to explain everything to you. Good gracious!

HANNA. Why didn't you cry out across the sea to me? To me who had plenty and who could in so many ways have saved you from being worn out? Why didn't you write the truth? You have kept it hidden from me all these years. —Rachel was the first one who wrote and told me the truth.

CLARA. Yes, yes—that's the way it was—and the way it had to be!

HANNA. But why?

CLARA. If I had written as it was, and all of you had come rushing—I didn't want to be helped. Because I couldn't be helped.

HANNA. But then you actually lied——?

CLARA. Of course, I did. I have been telling lies all the time—and to everybody. What else could I do?

HANNA. There are things here that pass all understanding. I come across one after the other.

CLARA. Listen, Hanna. You used the words "worn out." You said that you could have saved me in many ways from becoming worn out. Have you ever known a worn-out person capable of asking for help? Or one who knew how to resist?

HANNA. But before you *had* become worn out?

CLARA. You don't know what you are talking of.

HANNA. Well, explain—if you can?

CLARA. No, I cannot—not all at once—but by and by, perhaps.

HANNA. You didn't share his faith to begin with, did you? How strange that was! And was *that* one of the reasons?

CLARA. No.—Well, it's a long story!—But it wasn't that. Our natures are so different—and yet it isn't that either. If Adolph had been like other men, ramping and raging—oh, then it would have been easy—I think! But long before he knew me, all his strength—and he has strength, I tell you!—had become absorbed by his work. It had turned into love and self-sacrifice. It had been made wholly and completely beautiful. What do you say to the fact that in our house a harsh word has never yet been heard? Nothing like a "scene" has ever occurred. And we shall soon have been married twenty-five years. He is constantly radiant as with the joy of the Sabbath. For to him the whole year is made up of Sundays.

HANNA. Heavens, how you love him!

CLARA. It is not enough to say that I love him. I don't *exist* without him. And then you talk of resistance?—That is, at times I have had to, when matters have been going too far beyond our power.

HANNA. What do you mean by that?

CLARA. I'll explain it to you later. But who can resist what is all goodness, all sacrifice for others, all joy and happiness? And who can resist when his childlike faith and supernatural powers sweep everybody else along?

HANNA. Supernatural, you say?

CLARA. Haven't you heard of it? Haven't the children told you?

HANNA. What?

CLARA. That Adolph, when he prays intently, gets what he prays for?

HANNA. Do you mean that he works miracles?

CLARA. Yes!

HANNA. Sang?

CLARA. Haven't the children told you?

HANNA. No.

CLARA. But that's remarkable.

HANNA. Not a word has been said of anything like that.

CLARA. But then they have not at all— Oh, they thought you knew of it! For Adolph—well, to the whole country he is "the wonder-worker." Of course, they thought you knew of it. And they are so diffident.

HANNA. But does he work miracles? *Miracles?*

CLARA. Didn't you get an impression of something supernatural the moment you saw him?

HANNA. It would never have occurred to me to use that word—but now, when you speak of it— He gives you, in the very highest degree—what shall I call it?—an impression of spirituality?—a most wonderful impression. As if he didn't belong here!

CLARA. Yes, don't you think so?

HANNA. I do.

CLARA. Do you know, that sometimes I lie here completely tied up in a knot, with my legs drawn up to the chin almost— well, I don't dare to show you, for that might bring it on. And like that I sometimes lie whole days together when he is away, utterly unable to stretch out my limbs. Oh, it's dreadful, I tell you! Once, when he was up in the mountains—oh, those journeys into the mountains!—I was lying here for eight— think of it, eight!—days in that state. And no sooner did he appear in the doorway, so that *I* saw him and *he* saw me, than my arms and legs began to yield. And then he came up to me, and passed his hands over me, and in a moment I was lying as straight as I am now! And it is always like that—up they will come, up they will come! And the moment he enters the room, it passes!

HANNA. How very strange!

CLARA. And what do you say of this? Sick people—that is, sick people who really believe—it has happened, not once, but a hundred times—when he came and prayed with them, they got well.

HANNA. Actually well?

CLARA. Absolutely well! And more than that. There were sick people he couldn't reach—oh, you know the distances we have here—and to those he would write that, on such and such a day, at such and such an hour, he would pray for them, and that they must pray themselves at the same time. And from that hour their sickness would take a turn for the better. This is true! I know of many such cases.

HANNA. Wonderful!—But you have never written me a word of all this.

CLARA. Didn't I know you? Do you think I cared to ex- pose him to your scepticism?—We have an old minister's widow here—you must see her! She lives only a little ways

from here. She is the most venerable old lady I have ever
seen.—Well, she had been paralysed for fifteen years when
Adolph first came here—that's twenty-five years ago. *Now
she goes to church every Sunday!* And she is close to a hundred.

HANNA. And he cured her?

CLARA. Just by praying for her and by getting *her* to pray!
Oh, how he can pray! And then there was the case of Ågot
Florvågen. It's the most remarkable of all. For she was
dead as far as we could see. Then he took one of her hands
in one of his, and he put his other hand on her heart to warm
it, and she began to breathe again. Now she is living with
the old widow—right by here!—I might keep on like this till
to-morrow morning, just telling and telling. Oh, here and
elsewhere, among thousands and thousands of believing ones
all over the country, his name has a glamour attached to it
such as was never heard of. And now it is getting to a point
where it doesn't leave us in peace a single day.

HANNA. Then I may also see this—what you speak of—
while I am here?

CLARA. As surely as I am lying here unable to raise myself
an inch from the bed!

HANNA. But why shouldn't the miracle come to you also,
Clara? Why hasn't he cured you long ago?

CLARA. [*After a pause*] There is a special reason.

HANNA. But can't you tell me?

CLARA. No.—Yes, I mean. But later.—You'll have to
open a window again. It's getting close in here. More air,
please!

HANNA. Yes, yes, dear!   [*She opens the upper window.*

CLARA. He ought soon to be here now. This morning he
is staying away very long. If I could only smell the flowers.
Now, after the rain, there must be masses of them. And it's
seven o'clock—almost seven!

HANNA. [*Looking at her watch*] Yes, so it is!

CLARA. Ever since I have been lying here like this, I have been able to tell the time exactly.—Am I not going to get a breath of fresh air?—I think the wind must have gone down—Why don't you answer?

HANNA. I didn't hear what you said.—I simply cannot get over my surprise.

CLARA. Well, I suppose there is nothing more remarkable in this country. Perhaps not in our entire age.

HANNA. What do people say about it? How do the peasants regard him?

CLARA. I believe that anywhere but here it would have attracted twenty times—nay, a hundred times—as much attention. Here it is only as it should be.

HANNA. But, Clara—a miracle is a miracle.

CLARA. Yes, to you and me. But there is something in nature up here that demands the unusual even of us. Nature itself seems to have passed the limits of reason up here. Almost the entire winter is one long night. And the summer is one long day, when the sun remains above the horizon all the time. You have seen it at night, haven't you? But do you know that the mists from the ocean at times make it appear three and four times larger than it is? And then the colour effects produced at sea, on the mountains, and in the sky—running all the way from a fiercely glowing red to the gentlest, most delicate whitish-yellow! And then the colours painted by the Northern Lights on the wintry sky! More subdued, of course; but still there is in them such a wildness of pattern, such a restlessness, such change without end— And then all the other monstrosities of nature! Flocks of birds that run into the millions; schools of fish that would reach "from London to Liverpool," as one man wrote. Do you see these mountains rising straight out of the sea? They are not like other mountains.—And the ideas of the people are proportionate. They are simply boundless. Their legends and their fairy tales give you a sense of somebody piling continent on continent and then hurling the icy peaks of the North Pole on top of everything else. Yes, you may smile! But listen to their tales. Talk to the people. Then you will soon see that Pastor Adolph Sang is a man to suit their own hearts. His faith fits the place. He brought with him a fortune when he came here, and he has given away almost everything. That's the way it had to be! That's Christianity! And now, when he travels miles and miles to visit some poor, sick creature, and when he prays so that their innermost souls are laid open, and the light seems to get right into them, unreflected—! At times they catch sight of him far out at sea in impossible weather—he alone in a tiny, little boat—or perhaps one of the children, or both, may be with him—for he has been taking them along since they were six years old. Perhaps he works a miracle before he is off to another fisher village—and there again the same! It is as if they just expected it of him. And even more than that! If I hadn't held back—well, then we shouldn't have enough to live on to-day, and probably he would not be living. Not even the children would be spared, perhaps— Of myself it is no use talking. For I have reached the end.

HANNA. But then you haven't held back——?

CLARA. So it may seem. But I have. Not by remonstrances. That would have done no good. No, I am forced to invent something—something new every time—or he'll see through it. And it brings me to despair!

HANNA. Invent something, you say?

CLARA. There is one sense he lacks entirely: the sense of reality. He never sees anything but what he wants to see.

Thus, for instance, he cannot see anything evil in anybody. That is, he sees it, but he doesn't care. "I hold on to what is good in men," he says. And when he is talking to them, they become good—absolutely every one! When he looks at them with those childlike eyes of his—what else could they do? But then, of course, it turns out badly afterward. For he ruins us for the sake of such people.—But that's the way he lives, without the least regard for actual conditions of any kind, small or great. If permitted, he would take our last cent—what we were to live on to-morrow! "God will surely give it back to us, for it is what he has told us to do."—When the weather is such that the hardiest sailors won't venture out in a ship, not to speak of the pastor's sail-boat, then he wants to start out in a mere skiff—and perhaps with his own little child in the stern at that!—He has ventured across the mountains in a fog and wandered around up there for three days and nights without a vestige to eat or drink. They went in search for him and brought him back. And a week later, with the fog still lasting, he wanted to try the same trip again. Somebody was ill and wanting him!

HANNA. But can he stand it?

CLARA. He can stand everything. He goes to sleep like a tired child, and sleeps, sleeps, sleeps. Then he wakes up, eats, and begins it all over again. He lives in some region apart from the rest of us: for he is innocent through and through.

HANNA. How you do love him!

CLARA. Yes, it is the only thing that is left of me. This difficulty about the children finished me.

HANNA. The children?

CLARA. They took harm from staying here. No regulation or discipline: it turned them topsy-turvy. Never any check on whatever was held right! Never any reasoning—only inspiration! They were already grown up and had learned nothing but to read and write.—And how I fought to get them away from here! And then, for five years, to keep them over there, and to get them some education! It took the last remnant of my strength. Now it is all over with me.

HANNA. Dearest, dearest!

CLARA. You don't mean to—you are not pitying me, are you? Me, who have had for companion on my journey the best man on earth, the noblest will in all mankind!—In that way one does not live so long as otherwise—true! But one cannot have everything. And to choose something else— oh, dear!

HANNA. But he has destroyed the rest of you.

CLARA. He has! Exactly! That is, he has not destroyed *all*—for he was not permitted to do so. And he would have destroyed himself, too, had he been given a chance. He is always going beyond his power.

HANNA. Beyond his power? When he really works miracles? And comes out of everything unharmed?

CLARA. Don't you think the miracles also depend on the fact that he is going beyond his power?

HANNA. Now you scare me. What do you mean?

CLARA. I mean that the prophets must have been like that. Those of the Jews as well as of the Pagans. In certain directions they were capable of more than we because they lacked so much in other directions. Yes, that's the way it has seemed to me.

HANNA. But don't you *believe?*

CLARA. Believe? What do you mean by that? We sisters come from a more or less neurotic old family of sceptics—an intellectual family, I dare say. I admired Adolph. He was unlike all others, better than all others. I admired him until I fell in love with him. It wasn't his faith that did it: to me

that was only one of his peculiarities.   How far I now share
that faith with him—I don't know.

HANNA. Don't you know?

CLARA. I have been so harassed, I tell you, that I have had
no chance to make up my mind about it.   Such a thing takes
time.   I have had my hands full trying to steer us straight
from one wave crest to another.   The effort of it has wasted
me prematurely.   Long ago I lost the power of dealing with
large problems.—It's barely possible for me to tell what's
right and wrong.   Oh, in a crude way, of course—but not in
a finer sense!   I must do what I can.   And so with my faith,
too!   More than that is beyond my power.

HANNA. And he knows it?

CLARA. He knows all.   Do you think I could hide anything from him?

HANNA. But does he not want you to believe what he believes himself?

CLARA. Not in the least.   This matter of faith, if we are
not to be lost—it is God's own concern, he says.   Ours is to
be true.   If we are, the faith will come—here or elsewhere.
Oh, there is nothing inconsistent about him!

HANNA. But isn't he working for the spread of his faith?

CLARA. In his own way.   Never, *never*, by pressure.   He
shows absolutely the same consideration for everybody.   For
everybody—do you understand?   Oh, there is no one like
him!

HANNA. You still see him as you did in those first days of
rapture!   And this although your eyes have grown old!

CLARA. Yes, though my eyes have grown old.

HANNA. But now as to your faith in his miracles—at
bottom you don't believe in them at all?

CLARA. What are you saying?   There is nothing else in
the world in which I believe so completely!

HANNA. When you don't dare let him go out in a storm —when you don't dare feel sure of getting back what he gives away, even if it be all you have left—then you don't believe in them.

CLARA. Rather than permitting such a thing— Oh, this is where my strength lies, I tell you!

HANNA. All right. But it is not the strength that springs from faith.

CLARA. No, you mustn't— If there should be some contradiction here—what of it? All of us are full of contradictions —all but he! And then, you know, to throw oneself and one's children into the sea—that's not faith: it is to tempt God.

HANNA. But it seems to me that a miracle may be wrought then as at any other time—whether our own lives are at stake, or those of other people.

CLARA. But to *put* one's own life in danger?

HANNA. When it is done to save others? That cannot be called to tempt God.

CLARA. Listen—no, let's drop it. I am too tired. All I know is that if he wants to take the children's livelihood and give it to people that are bad and useless, or if he wants to start across the mountains in a fog, or put to sea in a storm —then—then I just throw myself across his path. I'll do anything I can think of, absolutely *anything*, to stop him!— Suppose he should try to do something of that kind just now —I have not been able to stand on my feet in many a month —but then I could do it! Then I could! I am sure of it! At such moments *I* can also work miracles. For I love him and the children.   [*Long pause.*

HANNA. Can I help you in any way?

CLARA. Let me have some eau de Cologne. Put some on my temples. And let me smell it too, of that you brought me yesterday. Hurry up, please! Can't you get the cork out?—The corkscrew is over there—no, no, over there! And open the lower window—the lower one also!

HANNA. Yes, yes!

CLARA. Thank you!—If the ground were not so damp after these horrible rains, I should go outside a while—can't you get the cork out?

HANNA. In a moment!

CLARA. Push in the screw a little further—but not too far —that's it—that's it—now—no—*jasmin!*

HANNA. Jasmin?—There is no jasmin!

CLARA. Jasmin, jasmin—! It is he! I hear him! It is he! The Lord be thanked! Now I'll be quiet—quiet! Oh, the blessing of it! There—he is!   [SANG *enters.*

SECOND SCENE

SANG. Good morning again!—Good morning, dear Hanna! Oh, that we have you here—that we have you here!—Such a morning as this, so full of song and fragrance, you don't have in America—or anywhere else in the world!

CLARA. And my flowers?

SANG. Do you know what happened, Clara?

CLARA. You gave them away?

SANG. No! Ha-ha! Not this time, as Tordenskjold[1] said. —Oh, but you are a bad one!—Here we have ranted and raged at this endless, horrible raining, and been afraid of landslides and falling rocks—and all sorts of disasters. And the rain has done nothing but bring us a great blessing!—When at last I saw the sun again this morning, and went out—what a

---

[1] A famous Danish admiral of Norwegian birth, who had many hair-breadth escapes in his numerous encounters with the Swedes.

flowery host there was to meet me! I have never before seen
anything like this year! Oh, the richness of colour and odour
all around me—and all of a sudden it filled me with such a
sense of joy that I couldn't but think it a shame to step on
the things that brought me such happiness. And so I turned
aside, and found a path, and this I followed, looking down into
all those dewy eyes at my feet. What a crowding there was
among them! What a will to live in that crowd! What
passion! Even the smallest among them craned their necks
to reach the sun. How eager, how greedy, they were! Really,
I think some of them must have rushed ahead at such a rate
that they will send their pollen dust courting before the day is
over! And I have already seen several bumble-bees. They
didn't know where to turn in the midst of all that fragrance.
For there were thousands and thousands of blossoms, and each
thousand tried to surpass all the rest in passionately tempting odours. Oh, such doings! And you may be sure there is
individuality, too, in all this millionfold multiplicity. Yes,
there is! And so I couldn't pick a single one of them.—But
I have something else for you to-day!

CLARA. [*Who has been signalling to her sister while* SANG
was speaking] Have you?

SANG. I, too, will try to raise on high a flowery cup

CLARA. Dear, what is it?

SANG. Well, I suppose you never thought me mean enough
to keep anything to myself? But I can!

CLARA. I have noticed for a long time that there was
something——

SANG. Have you really? And I who haven't said a word
this time!—But when your illness didn't frighten me as much
as the rest, there was good reason for it.

  CLARA. But what is it?

HANNA. Yes, what is it? She is getting excited!

SANG. Now I'll tell at once. I have helped so many and cannot help her—because she is self-willed, and I cannot pray with her as I should. And I have no power over those that don't pray themselves—that is, when they can pray at all. And so I wrote to our children to come home. And last night, when I sent them to bed so early, I told them why I did so—that I wanted them to have a good night's sleep, and then be ready at seven in the morning to help me pray at their mother's bedside.

CLARA. Oh, dearest, dearest!

SANG. We'll weave a prayer chain around you! One of us at your feet, one at your head, and I right in front of you! And we won't cease until you fall asleep. Not until then— not until you sleep! And then we'll repeat it until you get up and walk with the rest of us. That's what we are going to do!

CLARA. Oh, you dear soul! ·

HANNA. What did the children say?

SANG. You should have seen them! How it stirred them! I tell you, their faces were as white as sheets. And then they looked at each other.—But I guessed that they wanted to be left alone.—I can see that you are stirred by it, too. Your eyes close. Perhaps you also want to be left alone?—For we are going to have a visitor—a wonderful visitor—and it is necessary to be prepared!—What time is it?

HANNA. After seven.

SANG. Not yet, for then they would be here. You have forgotten to set your watch according to our local time.

HANNA. Oh, no, I haven't.

SANG. Then you haven't set it right, my dear. How can you imagine that grown-up children would oversleep when called to pray at their mother's bedside?

HANNA. I'll go up to them.

SANG. No, no, no! They must not be disturbed these last few moments. I know what it means.

HANNA. They won't hear me. I'll just take a peep at them.   [*Goes out.*

SANG. Now be careful, please!

THIRD SCENE

SANG. It's fine of her to be so eager about it.

CLARA. Dearest!

SANG. Your voice is troubled—? Oh, do be hopeful now! I have never felt more certain of myself. And you know from whom that feeling flows.—Clara!—My beloved! [*He kneels beside her bed*] Before we join in the great prayer, let me thank you! I have been thanking the Lord for you to-day. In the midst of all this spring-time glory I have been thanking Him. So boundless was the joy within me and without me. And in my mind I have gone over what we have principally lived together. Do you know, I think I love you the more for not wholly sharing my faith? It keeps you still more in my thoughts. Your devotion to me comes wholly from yourself, from your will—and from nothing else. And I am proud of the fact that, by my side, you have remained true to yourself. But when I realise that you—without believing as I do—have sacrificed your life for my sake——

CLARA. Adolph!

SANG. I'll put my hand over your mouth if you speak. Now it's my turn!—Oh, it's a great thing you have done. We other ones, we are giving our faith; but you are giving your life. What confidence you must have in me! And how I love you!—When the fervour of my faith frightened you, and you trembled for me, or for the future of the children, and when, perhaps, you didn't quite consider what you were

doing—*I* know that you didn't have strength enough left to
do otherwise.

CLARA. No, I hadn't!

SANG. It is my fault. I have not known how to spare you.

CLARA. Adolph!

SANG. I know it's so! You have sacrificed yourself little by
little. And not for the sake of your faith, not for the hope of
some reward here or there—but out of love alone. How I
love you!—All this I wanted to tell you to-day. If Hanna
hadn't gone out, I should have asked her to leave me alone
with you a little while.—I thank you! This is your great
day! And now the children will soon be here.—Let me kiss
you again as I kissed you that first day!

FOURTH SCENE

SANG. Well?

HANNA. It's *past* seven.

CLARA. I knew it.

SANG. Is it past seven? And the children?

HANNA. They were asleep.

SANG. Asleep?

CLARA. I knew it.

HANNA. Elias was dressed. He had thrown himself on the
bed as if he didn't want to sleep, but just rest a little, and
sleep had overtaken him in spite of himself. Rachel was
sleeping with her hands folded on the cover. She didn't hear
me.

SANG. I have asked too much of the children. That's
what I always do.

HANNA. They had hardly slept for two days and nights—
or since we met.

SANG. But what did the Lord mean then, by giving me such strength to-day? And by making me feel so certain of myself?—I must try to discover it! [*Going out*] Pardon me a moment, dear friends!—Why exactly this day——?

[HANNA *enters.*

FIFTH SCENE

CLARA. Did you wake them?

HANNA. Of course.—Do you know what I think is the matter?

CLARA. Good Lord, yes!—Oh, I am trembling already!

HANNA. Can anything be done about it?

CLARA. No—nothing except what I can do myself to soften it.—Oh!—There was a something in their eyes yesterday—now I understand what it was.

HANNA. They have lost their father's faith.

CLARA. They have lost their father's faith.—The poor things, how they must have been struggling and suffering! Loving and respecting him more than anything else on this earth, as they do!

HANNA. That's why they were so quiet yesterday.

CLARA. That's why the slightest thing moved them so easily.—Oh, and that's why Rachel wrote for you. Somebody had to be here—and she herself didn't dare.

HANNA. I think you are right.—How they must have been wrestling with this!

CLARA. Oh, the poor things, the poor things!

HANNA. Here comes Elias.

CLARA. Is he coming?

ELIAS. [*Throwing himself on his knees beside his mother's bed and burying his face in his hands*] Oh, mother!

CLARA. Yes, yes—I know everything.

ELIAS. You know?   Oh, it couldn't be worse!

CLARA. No, it couldn't.

ELIAS. When he said last night, that at seven o'clock this morning——

CLARA. Don't now!   I cannot bear it!

HANNA. Your mother cannot bear it.

ELIAS. I won't—I knew it had to come.   In one way or another.   It had to come in the end.

HANNA. Can you bear to hear it?

CLARA. I must hear.—Tell me——

HANNA. What is it?

CLARA. Elias—are you not there?

ELIAS. Here I am, mother.

CLARA. And Rachel?

ELIAS. What do you mean, mother?

CLARA. Where is Rachel?

ELIAS. She's getting up.   She was awake with me till midnight.   But then she couldn't any longer.

CLARA. Children, how—oh, how—how did it happen?

ELIAS. That we lost father's faith?

CLARA. That you lost your father's faith, children?

[SANG *enters.*

SIXTH SCENE

SANG. Have you lost your faith?—My boy—   Have you lost your faith?

HANNA. Look at Clara—look at her!

SANG. [*Hurries over to the bed and puts his hands on* CLARA] It'll stop!   It won't come!—Thank God!

CLARA. It's—passing—but you must hold me.

SANG. I will hold you!

CLARA. And don't let me cry—oh!

SANG. No, no! No crying! [*He bends down over her and kisses her*] Now you must be strong!—Clara!—There now! Don't be sorry now! You must remember how sorry *they* have been. In their suffering and pain, they have wanted to spare us. Shouldn't we, then, spare them now?

CLARA. Yes.

SANG. That's why this attack came. So that we might have time to think. Or we might have showed bitterness toward them. Especially I, in my eagerness. Where is Rachel?

HANNA. She's coming. She was awake with Elias till midnight.

SANG. Those children, those children!—How could you—? No, no! I don't want to know it. You have always been honest. What you have done—you had to do.

ELIAS. I had to. But it was dreadful.

SANG. Your faith came too easily, here with me. I am all emotion. And perhaps this is the beginning of a faith that cannot be lost.

ELIAS. I feel like a criminal—but I am no such thing.

SANG. Do you think I could doubt you for a moment, my boy? You mustn't misunderstand because I cannot quite control myself. It is because I have counted so much on your faith. So it will take some time before I— No, no, no! Forgive me, Elias! How could you help it? [RACHEL *comes into the room but withdraws shyly to the background;* SANG *catches sight of her*] Rachel!—Oh, Rachel! [*She comes forward and kneels beside him*] Ever since you were a little child, *you* have given me more faith than any book— How can this be possible?—No, if they have been able to win her over, then I must know the way of it— For that anybody could take *you* from me——

RACHEL. Not from *you*, father!

SANG. Pardon me! Oh, I didn't mean to hurt you—
Come to me! [*She throws herself into his arms*] I promise you,
children, that from now on, I shall not mention this matter
again.—But first I must know—you cannot wonder at that
—how it could happen.

ELIAS. If you were to talk with me for days, father—I
don't think I could get to the bottom of it!

SANG. No, that's beyond me.   I cannot argue about faith.
That's something I don't understand at all.

ELIAS. But you have to hear me——

SANG. If it can be of help to you, that's another matter.
And then you know that I want to hear.—But can't you tell
me briefly—just in a few words?   What was it that made you
—that—well—that decided you, children?

ELIAS. I think I can tell in a few words.   Rachel and I
—we discovered that the Christians were not as you had told
us they should be.

SANG. But, children——

ELIAS. You sent us to the best ones you knew.   And I do
think them better than all the rest.   But soon Rachel and I
agreed on something, and she was the first to say it: there is
only one real Christian, and that's father!

SANG. Oh, but, children!

ELIAS. If they had proved a little more or a little less
what you are—then we wouldn't have been so disappointed.
But they are something else—something entirely different.

SANG. What do you mean?

ELIAS. Their Christianity is merely a convention.   In their
life and in their teachings, they bow down to the established
order—to the order established in their own time and place.
To institutions, customs, prejudices, economical conditions,
and all sorts of things.—They have picked out every loophole

in the faith, so that they can make it fit in with whatever happens to be.

SANG. Are you not too severe?

ELIAS. *You* seek out what is most ideal in it, and strive for that—and *this* makes the difference!

SANG. But, dear children, what have *you* to do with this difference?

ELIAS. It has set us thinking, father— You cannot won-. der at that?

SANG. Think as much as you please. As long as you don't judge.

RACHEL. I don't think we have been judging. And do you know why? Because we saw that their teachings were as natural to them as yours is to you.

SANG. Well——?

ELIAS. But what is then Christianity? It cannot be what they teach?

SANG. Suppose it isn't? What does it matter? When they act according to their understanding?

RACHEL. But, dear father, is Christianity then something which only one in a million can reach?

ELIAS. Must all the rest be mere bunglers at it?

SANG. Whom do you call a Christian?

ELIAS. Him alone who, from Jesus, has learned the secret of perfection, and who is striving after it in *everything*.

SANG. I think that a charming definition! You have some of your mother's delicate discernment!—Oh, it was always‘ my cherished dream that you some time— No, no, no— I have given you my promise, children—and I *shall* keep it. You were saying—? Yes, that's good: it's splendid!—But listen, my son: may not everybody *try* to become a Christian without being called a bungler on that account? What do

you say? Is it not here that faith helps out—that the merits
of one make up for the shortcomings of millions?

ELIAS. Now you have said it! When we strive with our
whole heart—*then* faith does the rest.

SANG. Well, then?

ELIAS. But there is only one human being who puts this
into practice—and that one is you. The rest—oh, don't be
afraid! I am not saying this to accuse anybody. What
right have I to do so?   The rest—either they ask for so little
that their peace need not be disturbed—they do just what
suits them; or they try really—and overreach themselves.
Yes, that's just the word!

RACHEL. Yes, that's the word. And it was this thing,
father dear, that made me say to Elias: if those ideals are so
little suited to man's powers and conditions even at the present time, how can they have come from Him who is om-
niscient?

SANG. And it was you who said that?

ELIAS. We could not dispose of Rachel's doubts. And so
we began to study.   We traced those ideals backward through
history—and we were carried *beyond* the beginning of the
Christian era.

RACHEL. They are—all of them—much older than Christianity.

SANG. I know it, children.

ELIAS. Dreamers proclaimed them long before——

SANG. Oriental and Greek dreamers proclaimed them in a
time of despair; a time when the best ones longed for nothing
but to flee to some land of new birth—just to get away! I
know it, children.—So this was what made you fall? Merciful heavens!—As if that land of new birth, the millennium,
were less true for being an old, an immensely ancient, Oriental
dream?—And if it has kept us waiting so long for its coming

that weak souls are beginning to call it an impossible dream—
and the demands that lead to it, impossible ideals—what does
it prove?—Nothing about the faith, but much about those
that preach it. Oh, yes—much about those that preach it.—
I won't speak of them, but will only tell what happened to
myself. I saw that Christianity was crawling on its belly—
and carefully dodging every little hillock at that. Why can
it be doing so, I asked myself. Can it be because—if it stood
straight up—it would pull everything off its hinges? Is
Christianity impossible? Or don't men dare?—If only one
dared—would not thousands dare with him? And so I felt
that I must try to be that one man. And I think everybody
should make the same attempt. Otherwise he is not a true
believer. For to believe is to know that nothing is impossible
to faith—and then to show this faith.—Do you think I say
this as a boast? No, as an accusation against myself! For
although so much grace has been granted me, and I have
built so high, I, too, every so often, fall away from the Lord.
—Have I not been going around here and thought it impossible that she could be saved by me alone? Have I not been
distrustful and looking to others for help?—That's why God
took all help away from me. For this reason he permitted
that you also should stumble over "the impossible," and come
and tell me about it. For in such manner his hour had to be
prepared. Now he wants to show us all what *is* possible!—
Oh—how I have misunderstood! But now I do understand.
I must do it *alone!* Now the command has come. Now I
can do it.—That's why the great grace of preparedness descended upon me just this morning! Everything fits together
now. Do you hear, Clara? It is no longer I speaking, but
the great certainty that's within me—and you know from
whom it always springs! [*Kneeling beside her*] Clara, my
precious friend, why shouldn't *you* be as dear to the Lord as

anybody that believes wholly? As if the Lord were not the
father of everybody.—The Lord's love is no privilege of those
that believe. The privilege of those that believe is to *feel*
His love and rejoice in it—and, in His name, to make the impossible possible.—You patient, you faithful one! Now I
leave you in order to try it. [*He rises to his feet*] Yes, to try
it! I am going over to the church, children, because I want
to be alone. I will not leave it again until, from the hands
of the Lord, I have received sleep for your mother; and after
the sleep, health, so that she may rise up and walk among
us.—Be not afraid! I feel within me that he will grant it!
He will not give it to me at once, for this time I have doubted.
But I shall not give up— I shall wait for my Lord, who is
stern and kind.—Good-bye! [*He kneels over his wife in brief
prayer*] Good-bye! [*He kisses her; she does not move; he gets
up*] Thank you, children! Now you *have* helped me nevertheless. More than anybody could guess. Now I shall
myself ring out the call to prayer. At the first sound of the
bell you know that I have begun to pray for your mother.
Peace be with you!   [SANG *goes out.*

HANNA. [*Who instinctively has opened the door for him*] This
is—this is——   [*She bursts into tears.*

ELIAS. I must see—I must see him go into the church.
                                            [*Goes out.*

RACHEL. [*Coming forward*] Mother!—Oh, mother!

HANNA. Don't talk to her! She sees you—but don't talk
to her!

RACHEL. I am afraid!

HANNA. From here, where I am standing, I can see your
father. Now he will soon be at the church— Come!

RACHEL. No!—I can stand it no longer! I am afraid!—
Mother!—She is looking at me, but she doesn't answer me.—
Mother!

HANNA. Be quiet, Rachel!   [*The bell is heard.*

RACHEL. [*Sinks down on her knees; a little later she cries out, but in a subdued tone*] My God—Hanna!

HANNA. What is it?

RACHEL. Mother is asleep!

HANNA. She's asleep?

RACHEL. Mother is asleep!

HANNA. Really——?

RACHEL. I must find Elias. I must tell him about it!
                    [*She goes out.*

HANNA. She is sleeping like a child. O God!

> She kneels down; then a rumbling as of thunder is heard
> —prolonged, deepening, constantly deepening, growing
> more and more awesome; cries are heard outside; the
> house is trembling; and still the roar is increasing.

RACHEL. [*Outside*] The mountain is falling! [*Shrieks; comes running in*] The mountain is falling right on the church! On us—on father—on us! It's rolling, it's roaring—it's like night—oh!   [*She cowers down and hides her face.*

ELIAS. [*Outside*] Father!—Father!—Oh!

HANNA. [*Beside the bed*] Now it's coming! Now it's coming!

> The roar is at its loudest; then it decreases little by little;
> then the bell is heard again.

HANNA. [*Leaping to her feet*] It's still ringing! He's alive!

RACHEL. He's alive!

ELIAS. [*Outside*] Father is alive! [*Coming nearer*] The church is still there! [*Comes in*] The church is still there. Father is alive. Right in front of the church, the slide turned aside—turned to the left. He's alive, he's ringing the bell— O God!   [*He throws himself down beside the bed.*

RACHEL. [*Drawing nearer*] Elias! Mother——?

HANNA. She's sleeping!

ELIAS. [*Jumps up*] Is she sleeping?

RACHEL. Yes, she's sleeping—   [*The bell continues to ring.*

HANNA. She is sleeping just as quietly!

Curtain.

ACT II

*A small room, with walls made of logs. In the rear, a door
opening on a porch. This door stands wide open, disclosing
a view of a narrow landscape abruptly shut off by a bare
mountain-side. There is a door in the right wall, and a big
window in the left. Above the door leading to the porch
hangs a cross, into which, under a glass cover, is fitted a
gilded crucifix. In the foreground, to the left, stands a sofa,
and in front of this a table with some books on it. Chairs
are placed along the walls.*

FIRST SCENE

*Elias enters from the porch, moving quickly and restlessly.
He wears leather breeches and low shoes, and above the
breeches nothing but a shirt. His head is uncovered.
He stops for a moment. Then he goes over to the window and listens. A hymn sung by a male voice is
plainly heard, though coming from a distance. Elias
is deeply moved. Rachel enters softly through the
closed door on the right, which she closes again behind
her. Her brother makes a sign to her to stop and
listen.*

Rachel. [*Also moved, says in a low voice*] Let me open the
door to mother's room.
Elias. [*In the same voice*] Is mother awake?
Rachel. No, but she'll hear father. [*She goes out to the*
141

right, but returns soon and leaves the door open behind her; speaks in a very low tone] She smiled.

ELIAS. [*As before*] Oh, Rachel!

RACHEL. [*Showing emotion*] Elias—don't say a word—I cannot bear it!

ELIAS. Look at that, Rachel! Could you imagine anything more beautiful? Hundreds of people around the church, and all of them still as still can be. And in there he is praying and singing without being aware of the people outside. The windows are open, but they are set too high for him to look out. And those without are scared almost to death lest he hear them and be disturbed by it.—Look! He was speaking of a prayer chain. All those people around the church—there is a prayer chain for you!

RACHEL. Yes. [*They listen to the song, which ceases after a while*] He is singing a great deal to-day.

ELIAS. Close the doors now. I have so much to tell you. I have been here twice to look for you.

RACHEL. [*Goes softly out to the right; on her return, she closes the door behind her; then she says in somewhat louder voice*] A whole lot more people have arrived this afternoon.

ELIAS. And they are constantly coming—from miles off! You cannot see them all, for many of them are in the groves, listening to the lay preachers. They don't disturb father over there. And then the people go back and forth between the groves and the church.—And now, look over there, toward the shore.

RACHEL. What is it? The ground is black with people. What can it be?

ELIAS. It is the mission ship that has just come in.

RACHEL. The mission ship?

ELIAS. Don't you know that a lot of people from the East have rented a steamer to take them to the big mission conference in the city?   Now that steamer is at anchor in the fiord.

RACHEL. Here?

ELIAS. Here!

RACHEL. But why do they come here?

ELIAS. For the sake of the miracle.   When our delegates—Pastor Kröyer and another man—boarded the ship down at the pilot station——

RACHEL. —then——?

ELIAS. —and told what happened here yesterday, and how father was still in the church, all by himself, praying——

RACHEL. Now I see!

ELIAS. Then not a soul among them would go on, but all wanted to come here instead.   The bishop and the ministers begged them to keep their words and promises.   But they insisted on staying here.   And so the others had to give in. And now they are here.

RACHEL. The ministers also?

ELIAS. The bishop and the ministers—of course!

RACHEL. But they'll not come in to us?—Elias, you shouldn't be dressed like that.

ELIAS. I can't stand clothes.

RACHEL. You can't stand——?

ELIAS. They scorch me.   And then I have a craving—well, as if I wanted to walk through the air.   I can't describe it, but sometimes it seems as if I could do it!

RACHEL. But, Elias!

ELIAS. There he is!   There he goes now!

RACHEL. Who?   That man over there?

ELIAS. It must be he!   Yes, it is!   They carried him over here this morning, sick as sick can be—and now he is walking about—there you can see him!—It happened this morning, just as father sang for the first time.   Nobody had expected him to sing. It made all of us burst into tears. And then the sick man got up without any help. We didn't notice it until he was walking around among us.—Mother will also get up, Rachel! I can see it as if it were already happening.

RACHEL. Yes, she will get up. I have expected it any moment. But I tremble when I think of it.—Why are you looking at me like that, Elias?

ELIAS. Because—at times, when you speak, it seems almost as if it were verse. And it's the same when the others talk.

RACHEL. But, Elias——

ELIAS. And then again—as just now—I hear nothing but the sound of what you say—not the meaning. For at the same time I hear something—something that is *not* spoken.

RACHEL. That is not spoken?

ELIAS. Most often it seems to be father calling—calling me by name—as he did yesterday morning. [*With emotion*] He had something in his mind when he gave me that name. It sings and it accuses—and with his voice. Incessantly, at times. It haunts me. And in the midst of it I feel a longing to plunge into some great danger. For I am certain that I should come out of it unharmed. No, don't be scared! Why, there is nobody here.

RACHEL. Come, Elias, and sit with me beside mother. There is peace in her presence.

ELIAS. I cannot.—Rachel, answer me before God—search your final, your subtlest doubt, and answer me: is this a miracle that we have experienced here?

RACHEL. Merciful heavens, Elias!—Why do you always come back to this?

ELIAS. But is it not dreadful that perhaps the only two people still doubting are his own children?—Just now I would give my life to feel certain.

RACHEL. Don't, Elias! I beg you!

ELIAS. Tell me only what you do believe. This thing with the landslide? It's too big a thing to be merely accident. Don't you think so? And mother's sleep? The moment he began to ring the bell—sleep! And she slept in spite of the landslide. She sleeps as long as *he* is praying.—Is not this a miracle? And why shouldn't that other thing have been a miracle also—a great miracle?

RACHEL. I almost think it was, Elias.

ELIAS. You do?

RACHEL. But I am none the less afraid of it.

ELIAS. Afraid of it, if it be a miracle? But then you don't believe it was a miracle?

RACHEL. Yes.

ELIAS. For this cannot merely depend on some magnetic power of healing? Or on the power of his personality? No, it must be something more! Is it a miracle? Do you feel sure?

RACHEL. I cannot go into this now. It was to escape it that I sought refuge beside mother. Her honesty seems to fill up the whole room and put an end to all such questions.— Now, there is something else that is of more importance, Elias!

ELIAS. Something else?

RACHEL. After all this! What will come next—when she has got up? For that is not the end of it. In the last instance——

ELIAS. In the last instance?

RACHEL. In the last instance it is a question of her life!

[*She begins to cry.*

ELIAS. Rachel—? My God!

RACHEL. Mother has no power of resistance left. And he will go right on—right now!

ELIAS. With what?

RACHEL. With this—whatever it be!

ELIAS. But suppose it be a miracle, Rachel? Why need we then be afraid?

RACHEL. I cannot overlook the consequences—to mother and father—to all of us.—You don't understand me at all?

ELIAS. No.

RACHEL. No! But to me it does not matter what it is. It will destroy us. It will kill us in the end!

ELIAS. The miracle?

RACHEL. Yes, yes! There is no blessing in it! A horror, that's what it is!—Elias!

> [*She drags him into the middle of the room.*

ELIAS. What is it?

RACHEL. There is a man out there who is staring right at this window—a peculiar man—so very pale——   ·

ELIAS. In a coat that is buttoned all the way up?

RACHEL. Yes.—[*With a subdued cry*] There he is in the room, too!

> *She falls back as if she were facing a ghost, and finally she takes flight into her mother's room.*

ELIAS. In the room?—Here?

> *At that moment a* STRANGER *walks up to the porch from the left, crosses the threshold, and stands still just inside the door while he searches the room with his eyes.*

SECOND SCENE

ELIAS. [*As the* STRANGER *appears*] Yes, there he is!

STRANGER. Will you permit——?

ELIAS. Who are you?

STRANGER. Does it matter?

ELIAS. I have seen you here since yesterday.

STRANGER. Yes, I came here across the mountains.

ELIAS. Across the mountains?

STRANGER. I saw the landslide from above.

ELIAS. Really?

STRANGER. And I heard the bell. And this morning I saw the sick man who got up and walked when your father sang— And now I want to ask: is your mother sleeping in there?

ELIAS. Yes. But not in the next room. In the one beyond.

STRANGER. But if she should get up—then she would come in here? She would turn toward the church, where he is— don't you think? And so she'll come—here?

ELIAS. Yes, now when you speak of it——

STRANGER. And so I ask of you—beg of you—may I be here? Wait here? See it? I have been filled with a burning desire—and now I cannot resist any longer. I'll not come in again until driven to do so. I'll not stay around here—and be in the way. But if the impulse should become irresistible, to come in here, and wait, and see—will you let me?

ELIAS. Yes.

STRANGER. Thank you!—And I want to tell you: this day will decide my whole life!

[*He goes out through the porch to the right.*

THIRD SCENE

ELIAS. This day will decide my whole life! [KRÖYER *enters the porch from the left*] Kröyer, did you see him? The man to the right, there?

KRÖYER. Yes, who was he?

ELIAS. You don't know him?

KRÖYER. No.

ELIAS. Certainly a remarkable man!—This day will decide my whole life! O Lord! That's the word for me, too!

KRÖYER. That's what I expected, Elias—that this day must be a great one for you. Who could resist what is happening here? If it were nothing but these hundreds of people praying around the church; and he within, unconscious of the rest. I cannot think of anything more beautiful!

ELIAS. Yes, don't you think so?—Oh, I'll throw aside all fear and doubt—this day will decide! What a word that was!—I have struggled and suffered without getting anywhere. And then it is *given* to me! And at once I feel more at peace.—I want to talk to you!

KRÖYER. No—not now. I have a message for you.

ELIAS. For me? From whom?

KRÖYER. I have just returned with the mission ship.

ELIAS. I know.

KRÖYER. And now the bishop and the ministers are asking if they can have the use of this room for an hour or so?

ELIAS. For what purpose?

KRÖYER. They feel it necessary to discuss what attitude they are to take toward what's happening here. And we know of no other place where we can be by ourselves.—Yes, it's no use getting surprised. We professionals, we members of the preachers' union, must try to look more rationally at such things than the rest, don't you know?

ELIAS. It will fill the room with a lot of loathsome discord.

KRÖYER. Which may turn into harmony. For who can resist the miracle?

ELIAS. You are right! And yet—in here? As if they were putting a wedge between my father and my mother? And if father should begin to sing again? Then we couldn't open the door to let mother hear?

KRÖYER. What do you think your mother or your father would have answered?

ELIAS. Yes—beyond all doubt. You are right. They can have the room. But let *me* get out of this.

KRÖYER. I'll arrange it. Are both doors closed between this and your mother's room?

ELIAS. Yes.

KRÖYER. Then I'll close the window, and also that door, as soon as they are here.

ELIAS. Let *them* lock themselves in! I'll go out to the people where there is more sympathy. They are trustfully expecting that something great will happen to-day—and perhaps they will not have to wait much longer.

KRÖYER. [*Following*] Shall we pray for that, Elias?

ELIAS. Yes. Now, I will try! [*Both go out to the left.*

FOURTH SCENE[1]

KRÖYER. [*Comes in from the left*] Will you please step in?
He goes over to the window and closes it; in the meantime the BISHOP *and the* MINISTERS *enter; then* KRÖYER *goes back to the door and closes it.*

BLANK. You, Kröyer, who are acquainted in this house, can't you get us something to eat?

BISHOP. I know that we are making ourselves ridiculous. But the truth of it is that we were dreadfully seasick.

BREY. We couldn't keep anything down.

BISHOP. And when we got into smooth water at last, and they had just begun to cook something for us——

BREY. Then came the miracle!

FALK. I am so *frightfully* hungry.

KRÖYER. I fear nobody in this place has given any thought to food to-day, but I'll see. [*Goes out.*

---

[1] All the ministers, and especially the elderly one named Blank, speak with artificial precision, very broad vowel sounds, and a preaching drawl, as if they were always in the pulpit.

JENSEN. I have regular food hallucinations. I have read about that kind of thing—but then you read so much you cannot believe. It's especially partridges I see.

FALK. Partridges!

JENSEN. And I smell them, too: broiled partridges!

BLANK. Partridges?

SEVERAL. Are we going to have partridges?

KRÖYER. [*Returning, speaks while still in the doorway*] Sorry. I looked in the kitchen and in the dining-room also. Not a thing. And no people around.

BREY. Not a single soul?

FALK. I am so *frightfully* hungry.

BISHOP. Well, my dear friends, don't let us become altogether too ridiculous. We have to submit to the inevitable. Let us get on. Will you please be seated. [*He seats himself on the sofa; the others take chairs*] Very briefly and very quietly —for we know that this is the habitation of a very sick person—we must try to agree how to behave in this matter. I have always held the opinion that the minister—as a rule— should remain neutral toward any excitement of this kind. Neither affirm nor deny until the excitement has subsided sufficiently to permit of a judgment. For this reason I wish with all my heart that we might have gone on. But we were not permitted to go on.

MINISTERS. [*In murmurs to each other*] We were not permitted to go on! No, we were not permitted to go on.

BISHOP. Everybody wanted to make for this spot, where the miracle was supposed to be at home, so to speak. And I don't reproach them on that account. But being with them, on board the same ship, our opinion will be demanded. And when we reach the conference, our opinion will again be asked for.—What is it, then?

KRÖYER. If you permit me—with all due respect: either we believe in the miracle, and act accordingly; or we don't believe in it, and act accordingly.

BISHOP. Hm?—There is a third way, my young friend.

MINISTERS. [*Murmuring among themselves*] There is a third way! Indeed, there is a third way!

BISHOP. The older one grows, and the more experienced, the more difficult it becomes to form a conviction—and especially in regard to supernatural things.—In the present case, time and conditions will hardly permit an investigation. And suppose we were to arrive at conflicting opinions? What impression do you think a clerical fight about miracles would make in these days of scepticism? A fight to decide whether or no miracles are worked at the present hour somewhere in the Northland?—I see my old friend Blank asking for the floor.

BLANK. If I have understood Your Grace right, we have no need of first deciding whether a miracle has occurred or not. That is for God, our father!

BISHOP. That is for him! That's the word! I thank you, old friend.

BLANK. I maintain that miracles are as much regulated by natural law as anything else, although we cannot see the law. I maintain exactly the same thing as has been maintained by Professor Petersen.[1]

FALK. In that book he never gets published.

BLANK. But which he will get published some time.—But if it be as I said—what importance can then be attached to any single miracle—whether near-sighted creatures like ourselves can see it or not? If the congregation believes it sees

[1] Professor Fr. Petersen, of the University of Christiania, a liberal theologian who, about the time this play was written, tried to "reconcile the scientific insistence on universal conformity to law with the Christian faith in miracles" (Just Bing: Norsk Litteraturhistorie).

a miracle, then we'll praise the Lord together with the congregation.

BISHOP. Then you want to acknowledge the miracle after all?

BLANK. Neither acknowledge nor refuse to do so. We merely praise the Lord together with the congregation.

BISHOP. No, my old friend, we cannot get out of this by singing hymns.

MINISTERS. [*Murmuring to each other*] We can't get out of this by singing hymns. No, this we can't get out of by singing hymns.

BISHOP. Mr. Brey has the floor.

BREY. Really, I cannot understand what should prevent us from acknowledging the miracle at once. Is it, then, so rare? I am seeing miracles all the time. In our congregation we are so accustomed to them that the strange thing would be *not* to see them.

FALK. I wish Brey would be kind enough to tell us something about the miracles that happen in his congregation.

BISHOP. No, that would lead us too far afield.—You got up—do you wish to speak?

JENSEN. Yes. In this case everything depends on the fact confronting us. Is it a miracle—several, perhaps—or is it no miracle at all?

KRÖYER. Precisely.

JENSEN. Every separate miracle must be investigated. But to do so, we must have some technical evidence, some evidence of a medical character, or perhaps the testimony of witnesses taken down by a reliable lawyer. With *this* at hand—then only can we ministers safely submit our spiritual evidence. And with "spiritual" I don't mean the kind of thing we hear from lay preachers and a lot of other people supposed to be inspired or supplied with divine grace. As usual, I have in mind plain, solid, sober truth—and the more plain, solid, and sober it be, the more "spiritual" it will prove.

FALK. Hear!

JENSEN. Perhaps it will be found, then, that a miracle never occurs in this way. Never! It does not occur when it is expected and hailed by hundreds—nay, thousands perhaps—in a state of excitement and curiosity. Yes, curiosity! The miracle comes in an honest, plain, quiet, sober way to those who themselves are honest, plain, quiet, sober.

FALK. This is as if it were spoken out of my own heart!

KRÖYER. With Falk's permission, I should like to point out something. Since I settled here as minister, I have repeatedly seen that none become more easily the prey of superstition than the very people that are most sober-minded.

BLANK. That's just my experience! Verily!

KRÖYER. Their suspiciousness makes them often deny what is clearly seen by everybody else. Instead they are attacked from behind, so to speak, by mysterious fears, and thus they are moved by things wholly invisible to the rest of us. I have grown to think that the craving for the supernatural has to such an extent become a heritage of man that if we resist it in one way——

BLANK. —it gets hold of us in another. That's just what I have come to think.

FALK. Well, whether it start with the sober or the sottish, I want to ask once for all, if this means that we are now to surrender what the Church has gained of clearness and order, that we are to begin once more to flutter about like ordained *night owls?*

BREY. Are you looking at me?

[*All the ministers laugh aloud.*

BISHOP. Ssssshhh! Let us remember the invalid!

FALK. The craving for miracles is to the exercise of the faith what this activity by laymen is to the preaching of it—an excrescence, a disorder—or, if we go to the bottom of it, an atavism, a *regurgitation!*

> *The other ministers laugh in a suppressed way until several of them begin to cough.*

BISHOP. Sssssshhhh!

FALK. A miracle not acknowledged by the clergy—not appointed and confirmed, so to speak, by the highest church authorities, with His Majesty the King at their head—is to me nothing but a vagabond, a tramp, a *sneak-thief.*

> *The* BISHOP *laughs softly, and the ministers follow his example, while watching him closely.*

FALK. It is all right to have a simple mind. I had it once myself. But when, as in my case, the minister in a big city has to be sad with the bereaved ones around the grave at one o'clock, and merry with the joyful wedding guests at three; when he has to sit beside a poverty-stricken deathbed at four, and dine in the Royal Palace at five; then he becomes familiar with the infirmities of man. And what he learns by it is this: to rely very little on persons, and very much on institutions.— Where the miracle appears, there all institutions perish in the revolt of the feelings. For this reason the Catholic Church has tried to make an institution of the miracle itself. But thereby it has forfeited the respect of all intelligent people, so that only the stupid and the selfish ones remain within it.—Once I was in a company of ladies—only myself and about twenty ladies. [*Subdued merriment*] One of these ladies became hysterical, than another, then a third—six in all. [*Increasing merriment*] Then I poured water on them—first on those six—one by one [*he makes a motion with his hand as if pouring out water several times*]; but afterward on several of the rest, too—for that kind of thing is contagious.   .[*Loud laughter follows.*

BISHOP. [*Who is the first to recover himself*] Sssshhhh!
[*Then he bursts into open laughter again, and the rest with him;
finally he recovers his composure once more*] Sssshhhh!

FALK. I think that is the most wholesome way. Pour
water on it!

> *There is still a great deal of laughter and discreet coughing
> behind handkerchiefs; several of the ministers express
> eagerly their gratitude to* FALK.

KRÖYER. Of course, we know Falk, and we know that he
means what is right, in spite of his peculiar way of expressing
himself. I am inclined to think that if he should see—
well, that old lady, say—the minister's widow who is now
close to one hundred years old—*he* would be the last one to
pour water on her—although her presence among us is like
a living miracle, and her faith is infecting everybody. The
same thing holds true of the young girl Ågot Florvågen,
who is looking after the old lady. To *our* eyes, to *our* hands,
she seemed dead and cold. And *he* prayed over her and made
her rise up. If one man testify, you must believe! [*General
astonishment*] Both of them are here now.

SEVERAL. They are here?

KRÖYER. Perhaps they will come into this very room.
They are on their way to this house, although it takes them a
long time. The old lady wants to see for herself—she wants
to see her who was not awakened by the landslide.—Now, you
look at the old lady. Talk with her. Talk with the girl who
attends her. The replies you get will be plain and honest as
her own face. That would be of more help than all our doc-
trinal discussions. I do not say this in a spirit of reproach.
I used to think as you do now—up to the time I became a
minister in these parts. Nobody can be more painfully conscious than I am of what the Church has had to relinquish, of
what meagre doctrines and false constructions are left to us

—we are poor, with nothing left of the miracle—without courage to ask for a miracle—and we have to pretend either that we don't care for it, or that we have it and are rich in the possession of it!—I know every one of you well enough to know that if you only *dared*—if you could feel sure of witnessing a miracle so great that it met the test once for all prescribed by the Bible: "*All who saw it believed*"—oh, no matter how far you may have fallen short at other times, then you would become as children, you would surrender yourselves completely, you would sacrifice the days still left to you—only to proclaim it! [*Considerable emotion is shown, especially by the older men*] I dare to make these confessions on your behalf, my brethren, because my place is within the circle of the spirit —that circle of which it has been said: either within, or without! Once within, and all the tricks prompted by our poverty will collapse on their own accord, and we shall dare to admit the truth!—What will be left of Christianity, if we declare the miracle lost to the church?

ELIAS. [*Entering from the outside*] Pardon me—there is somebody here who wants to look at my mother. It's the old widow of the minister.

> *All rise. In the doorway appear the* MINISTER'S
> WIDOW *and* ÅGOT. ELIAS *opens the door on the*
> *right and disappears through it. The* MINISTERS
> *push back their chairs and make way reverently for the*
> *old lady.*

WIDOW. [*After having crossed the threshold*] Let me go, Ågot.—Now I want to be alone.—Quite alone.—For this place has been visited by the Lord—it is holy.—This place is holy —here you stand face to face—and then it is better to be alone. [*She stands now so that she can look through the doorway on the right into the room where* MRS. SANG *is lying; she drops a curtsey; then she raises both her arms in an outburst of exaltation;*

having had another long look, she curtseys again, turns around,
and walks toward the door leading to the porch] She was white—
radiantly white—and she was sleeping like a child. Now, I
have seen—such things shed light—oh, how they shed light on
everything!—Thank you for letting me be alone!

ÅGOT. But were you alone?

WIDOW. Quite alone. Nobody but myself. And she was
radiantly white.   [*They go out together.*

ELIAS. [*Coming in again from the right*] Both doors are
closed again. And now I'll close this one, too.

> *He goes out; the* MINISTERS *remain standing, without*
> *moving.*

KRÖYER. You didn't speak to her?

BISHOP. No.

KRÖYER. There is a light on every face as of sunshine.—
I can tell you why: people on whom the miracle has shed
its glamour, reflect the light of it.—Let us talk this over.

> [*They move together and sit down again.*

JENSEN. May I ask a question?—Don't you look upon
conversion as a miracle?

KRÖYER. What we call the miracle of conversion can be
traced psychologically, step by step, and for that reason it is
no miracle. It exists in other great religions, as well as in
the form of purely moral conversion, although the latter is a
silent one. But a Christianity which is founded on a wonder
and yet, in the course of the ages, has lost its power of working miracles—what is it? Nothing but moral precepts.

FALK. The characteristic feature of Christianity is not the
miracle, but the belief in resurrection.

KRÖYER. Which *all* the great religions have; which is common to all people with religious feeling.

BISHOP. What is your idea of Christianity, then?

KRÖYER. To me Christianity is infinitely more than a moral

code. More complete and more refined codes of this kind may be found outside of the New Testament. To me it is also infinitely more than the power of consecration: if it were not, then much else would equal it in rank.—Either Christianity is a life in the Lord that takes us beyond this world and all its precepts, or it is nothing at all. Either it is something more than mere consecration to an idea of any kind—that is, it must be a new world, a miracle—or it is nothing at all. [*He sits down, trembling and exhausted*] There was so much—I wanted to say—but—I cannot.

BISHOP. My dear Kröyer, the moment you came aboard this morning, I saw that you were overworked and ill. But that's what happens to every follower of Pastor Sang.

THE STRANGER. [*Has in the meantime opened the door in the rear and entered without closing the door again; he has drawn nearer step by step*] May I say a word?

All turn toward him, and some rise.

BISHOP. Is that you, Bratt?

SEVERAL. Pastor Bratt?

OTHERS. Is *that* Bratt?

BISHOP. You didn't come with us—how did you get here?

BRATT. Across the mountains.

BISHOP. Across the mountains? You are not going to the mission conference then?

BRATT. No, I wanted to come here.

BISHOP. I understand.

BRATT. It is the miracle that I am seeking.—And so I got here yesterday just as the landslide occurred. I was up there, only a little way off, and saw everything. And I heard the ringing of the bell.—And I have been here ever since.—And this morning I saw a sick man carried over to the church, and as the pastor began to sing within, the man rose, thanked God, and went his way. May I speak?

BISHOP. Of course!

BRATT. For I am a man in distress, and I am coming here to ask your help, brethren!

BISHOP. Speak, dear friend!

BRATT. I have said to myself: here I have met with the miracle at last. And the next moment: but was that a miracle after all?—For this is not the first place I have visited in order to find it. With blighted hopes I have turned back from every spot in Europe where the miracle was thought to dwell. Here, of course, the faith is bigger and simpler; and the *man* is great. What I have seen here has taken hold of me with supernatural power. But the next moment doubt has returned. This is the curse that rests on me, you see. I have incurred it by the seven years during which, as minister, I promised the miracle to those who would believe. I promised, because thus it was written—although I myself doubted —for I had never seen it come to anybody that believed. For seven years I preached that in which I did not have faith myself—and each time the dark days returned during those seven years—and they would come, just as did the wakeful nights—each time, because of my promise, I prayed with burning fervour: Where is that miraculous power which Thou hast promised Thy believers?   [*He bursts into tears.*

BISHOP. Oh, you lay bare everything. And that's what you have always done.

BRATT. In binding words, each one stronger than the other, He has declared that whosoever will believe shall possess this power. Yes, the power of deeds greater even than those done by the Son of Man.—What has then become of that power?— After eighteen hundred years of passionate labouring for the faith, is there not one who believes in such measure that he can produce a miracle among us? Is the Lord's own promise not yet redeemed? It cannot be that the power of belief has

been weakened.   For this faculty cannot have developed contrary to all other racial faculties—so that it became lessened
by constant practice.   No: after more than eighteen hundred
years of Christian preaching, it must in many, many families
have become a millennially increased heritage, and it is still
further multiplied by education.   And yet this power is not
strong enough to bring us the miracle?   All the merged long-
ings of the believing ones have not been able to produce one
individual with a miracle-working power strong enough to
make a believer of every one beholding it.   For this is necessary; it is the test provided by the Bible.   Time and again it
says: "All that saw it, believed."—A miracle it must be then,
that turns all who see it into believers.   But instead of it,
thousands upon thousands are falling away.   For in spite of
the promise, the miracle is not forthcoming.—A man possessing the knowledge of our own time, an educated woman of the
present day—these will not be satisfied with what was un-
questioningly believed by men and women of the past.   Not
because their faculty of believing has grown less, but because
it is better guarded.   Their devotion is so much deeper and
more intimate in character that, naturally, properly, it is
more difficult to win.   He who does win it will have the best
that exists so far on this earth!—Therefore you must give as
much, or it will never be yours! [*The ministers exchange remarks in whispers*]—Religion does no longer constitute man's
only ideal.   If, at least, it is to be the highest one, you must
prove it such.   Man can live and die for what he loves—for
his country, his family, his convictions.   And as these things
are the highest of all that exist within the limits of the natural, and as you want to show him something still higher
—well then, you must *pass* those limits!   Show him the
miracle!

    All appear strongly moved.

FALK. [*Rising*] Somewhere a scornful word is to be read about the race that will not believe without signs and wonders.

BRATT. And do you know the answer of the race?—"We ask only for the signs promised by the Lord Himself—promised to whosoever will believe. Or is there not yet a single one among you that really believes? What, then, do you want of us?"—Yes, that's what the race answers.—But offer a miracle to that same race—one that cannot be picked to pieces by the sharpest tools ever shaped by doubt—one of which it can be said: "all that saw it, believed"—and then you may yet be witnesses of the fact that not the faculty of belief is lacking, but the miracle. [*Stir among the ministers*] Our preaching need not put a premium on credulity. Faith has more roots, and stronger ones, even in the keenest sceptic. Can anybody familiar with civilised man be ignorant of this? Is there any minister whose experience has not told him that, as a rule, the danger lies in the opposite direction: for lack of what is genuine, men put their faith in what is false.

SEVERAL. [*In subdued voices*] That is true.

BRATT. If a miracle appeared among us—one so great that "all who saw it, believed"—? First of all, the vast millions would come running—those who live in need and are full of longing—those who are dissatisfied, and oppressed, and suffering, and hungering for justice.—If they were to hear that the Kingdom of God, in the ancient sense, had once more descended upon the earth—no matter where it be—then, weeping and rejoicing—yes, even if the greater number of them should know themselves in danger of dying on the way—why, they would rather die on that way than go on living on any other! Then they would crawl forth, each one out of his own town, his own hut, his own bed—the sick ones in the lead—to see the Lord revealed. But they would not be the only ones. All seekers after truth on this earth would follow them. First of all,

those whose craving for truth is greatest—all profound, serious thinkers, all noble minds. *Their* eagerness would be the
most beautiful to behold; their faith, of most importance.   It
is neither the craving for truth nor the faculty of believing
that is lacking in them: it is the miracle!—All demand certainty and peace in regard to life's greatest problems.   Even
the thoughtless, and those who have put such problems aside
as useless or futile.   All of them, without exception, have been
brought up to long for more than knowledge—that is, for
something in which to believe.   But first of all you must fur-
nish them with a guarantee!—a guarantee that what you
preach is true!   If they see *this*, then they will also believe
in what they do *not* see.—That's the way it has been from the
beginning.   Those who now will be satisfied with less—with
personal experience alone—they are like Mohammedans and
Jews and Buddhists.   These, too—all of them—appeal to
their own personal experience.   But what is lacking is the
guarantee that such experiences are universally valid.   And
it is *this* that I am seeking!   For it has been promised us!—
O God, my God, now comes the final test!

BISHOP. Bratt, Bratt!

BRATT. The *final* test.   For further struggle is beyond my
strength.   I shall resign from the ministry—resign from the
Church and from the faith—if, if, if——!

[*He bursts into tears again.*

BISHOP. My dear son!   You mustn't——

BRATT. No, don't speak to me—I beg you!   Help me to
pray instead!   For if the miracle be not here, it cannot be
anywhere!   This man is more than other men; he is the
noblest one the earth has borne.   A faith like his nobody has
ever seen.   Nor was there ever seen a faith like that aroused
by his faith.

ALL. It is true!

BRATT. And it is easy to understand. He was wealthy
when he came here. He has given all away. The number of
times he has risked his life to bring help to others cannot be
counted. The miracles which he is believed to have worked
are equally numberless. But just because they were so many,
I could not believe in them.

SEVERAL. [*In low voices*] That's just what happened to me!

BRATT. Perhaps the right thing would have been to think
the very opposite? That here exists what really is meant by
"faith"? That the essence of faith *is* the miracle? That it
must work miracles? Perhaps that is how we should have
thought of it?—And whatsoever our thoughts should have
been—we should not have regarded him with that professional
scepticism which, I am sorry to say, was shown by myself.
His love and his faith should have made me humble. I have
to accuse myself, and in my heart I am sincerely asking his
pardon.

ALL THE MINISTERS. [*Without exception*] I also! I also!

BRATT. We know no better man; there is no stronger faith
than his: suppose the miracle were found here?

General emotion.

JENSEN. [*In a whisper*] Look at the cross above the door!
Is it the evening sun—or what is it?

BRATT. I don't know. But you may be sure that if we
meet the miracle, then the meeting will be attended by thousands unseen by us. If only it be granted *us* to be there!—
If only it be granted us to be there! Think of it: to witness
something so great that "all who see it, believe!" And *we*
were to witness such a thing—you, and you, and I? It is too
much! It cannot be possible!—But if it prove possible—
then there can be no one else in our day, brethren—oh, full of
shortcomings, and lacking in faith, lacking in love, as we
are——

ALL. Yes, yes——!

BRATT. Then, in spite of all, there can be none on whom grace has been more richly bestowed; then we, unworthy ones, must be especially chosen! [*Deep general emotion*]—And as I look out upon this hemmed-in, barren land of the fiords, with the screaming gulls overhead, and as the thought comes to me, that the Kingdom of God began in the luxuriant regions of countries steeped in sun, through which ran the highroads of the world: what a proof it would be to see it resumed, in all its grandeur, in a poverty-stricken, outlying corner like this, on the edge of the everlasting ice——

FALK. [*Gets up, pale as death, and whispers*] Yes, yes!

SEVERAL. Yes, yes!

BRATT. Then it seems to me that everything fits together, and that the miracle *must* come.

All are now on their feet.

BISHOP. [*In a low voice*] Oh, that it would come, so that I might see it in my old age!

BLANK. Yes, if only the great faith would seize us! Not because we have deserved to see; but because we need it!

[*He falls on his knees; others follow his example.*

BRATT. Because the whole race needs it! More than at any other time. Because it has been promised. Because here it must be, if it be anywhere. [*He kneels*] His faith must be able to reach it! There is no greater faith than his on earth! And faith can do it! Oh, it can!

ALL. It can, it can!

BRATT. If it couldn't—then the whole thing would be impossible. Then there would be no truth in the rest either. Then there would be something excessive in all of it—something beyond our power——

FIFTH SCENE

RACHEL. [*Is heard calling in a scared voice from the room on the right*] Elias! [*Immediately afterward she enters in great haste through the door on the right and runs across the room to the window, which she flings open, as she cries out with all her might*] Elias! [*Thereupon she throws herself backward so that she would fall if she were not caught by* KRÖYER; *she bursts into violent weeping, but struggles to her feet again and points toward the other room in evident terror*] There! In there! She is no longer alone!—See—don't you see! [*All have risen; at that moment* ELIAS *appears on the porch; as she catches sight of him,* RACHEL *tears herself loose from* KRÖYER *and runs to meet her brother, crying*] Mother! Mother!

ELIAS. Has she risen?

RACHEL. Yes, yes.

ELIAS. And she walks?

RACHEL. Yes! But she is not alone!

ELIAS. This must be told!

RACHEL. But not to father!

ELIAS. No—from the roof, from the belfry—it must be rung out to the whole world!   [*He runs out.*

RACHEL. But you have no ladder! [*As he fails to reply, she repeats in alarm*] You have no ladder, don't you hear?

KRÖYER. [*Makes a silencing gesture and says in a low voice*] Hush!

BISHOP. [*Whispering*] Oh, listen!

SANG. [*Is heard singing in the church:*
            Alleluia, alleluia!
            Alleluia, alleluia!

ALL. [*Kneel down, whispering*] He knows it! He knows it!
      At that moment CLARA *appears in a white night-dress; her*

eyes are turned toward the church; she stops and reaches out her arms as if to meet the song.

ALL THE MINISTERS. [*Singing very softly:*
>Alleluia, alleluia!
>Alleluia, alleluia!

RACHEL. [*In the porch*] Now father is at the church door.

SANG. [*His voice is now heard strong and clear:*
>Alleluia, alleluia!
>Alleluia, alleluia!

The church bell begins to ring, and all the people outside join in the singing. There is a triumphant force in their song as if it sprang from a thousand throats. It is increasing in strength, for the people who were in the groves come running to join those at the church. For a while it seems as if the "alleluias" would lift the house off its foundations.

SANG appears in the doorway. His face is lighted up by the rays of the evening sun. All rise and fall back. He holds out both arms toward CLARA, who is standing in the middle of the room. Her arms are stretched out in response. Then he goes to her and takes her in his arms.

All around them the song is pouring forth. The room is full of people, and so is the porch; some have climbed up on the shoulders of those in front of them, and others are standing on the window-sill.

Then CLARA collapses in her husband's arms. The song dies out. Only the bell is still heard.

CLARA makes an effort to rise up again, but succeeds only in raising her head so that her eyes can meet his.

CLARA. Light flowed from you—when you came—oh, my beloved!

Her head sinks back, her arms lose their hold, her entire body collapses.

SANG. [*Still holding her, puts a hand over her heart; then he bends over her body in surprise; finally he looks up toward the sky, saying with childlike innocence*] But this was not the meaning of it—? [*He sinks down on one knee and puts* CLARA's *head on the other; once more he searches for signs of life; then he lets the body gently sink to the floor; and rising to his feet, he looks up again as he says*] But this was not the meaning of it—? Or—? Or——?

> *He puts his hand to his heart and sinks down on the floor.*
>
> RACHEL *has been standing as if turned into stone; now a wild cry breaks over her lips as she sinks on her knees beside the bodies of her parents.*

KRÖYER. What did he mean—by that word—"or——"?

BRATT. I don't know with certainty. But it killed him.

RACHEL. Dead?—It is impossible!

> *The bell continues to ring.*

Curtain.

THE NEW SYSTEM

(DET NY SYSTEM)

1879

CHARACTERS

Riis, *Director-General of Railroads*
Kamma Riis, *born* Ravn,[1] *his wife*
Frederick, *their son*
Karen, *their daughter*
Kampe, *engineer*
Hans, *his son, engineer*
Frederick Ravn, *canal inspector*
Larssen, *chief clerk*
Karl Ravn, *engineer*
Anna, *his wife*
Mrs. Ole Ravn, *mother of* Anna, *known as "Aunt Ole"*
Preuss, *engineer*
Mrs. Preuss, *born* Ravn
Mrs. Thomas, *born* Ravn
Mrs. Stange, *born* Ravn
Kahrs, *engineer*
Lange, *engineer*
Kraft, *engineer.*
Chairman of the Committee on Railroads
Miss Nora Holm
Miss Lise Gran
A Man-Servant *of the* Riises
A Maid *of the* Riises
Marie, *maid at* Kampe's
Several dinner guests

[1] *The name* Ravn *means* Raven.

THE NEW SYSTEM
(DET NY SYSTEM)

ACT I

A large room open to the rear and adjoining a veranda that looks out over the sea. The background shows a number of small islands and the outlines of the shore.

FIRST SCENE

KAMPE, *his son* HANS, *and* FREDERICK RAVN *are seated around a table.*

RAVN. Now let me tell you this. When you attack the Director-General (for an attack on his "new system" is an attack on himself—although the system is neither his nor new)—when you attack the Director-General——

KAMPE. Say, let's have a glass of something—Marie!

HANS. Not now, dad. It's too warm. [*As* MARIE *enters*] Please get us a couple of bottles of seltzer.

RAVN. No, listen to me now. When you attack my esteemed brother-in-law's "new system" (which is neither his nor new), then you forget what a Director-General means in our small circumstances.

KAMPE. Quite right!

RAVN. You act like a man who has been away from home seven years.

KAMPE. That's it!

RAVN. You act like one who has been in America.

171

KAMPE. All right!

RAVN. You think you can bring home with you the frankness which they use out there, and also the results which such frankness produces in big countries. It means that you are acting like a fool.

KAMPE. I am not so sure of the conclusion——

HANS. I have talked with engineers who differed from you.

RAVN. It must have been some credulous scatter-brains like my nephew Karl. No, the engineers in this country are like all the rest. Either they *have* public employment or they are *looking* for it. And if they are doing private work, then they either *have* made a success of it or they *want* to do so—and in neither case do they care to quarrel with those in power.

HANS. When I think of all those I met while studying abroad——

RAVN. Most of whom are married by this time. And the women know even better than the men on which side their bread is buttered.—Please remember that you have come home. Here you meet with the small souls of small circumstances. And they grow scantily and uniformly as turnips in a field.

KAMPE. Oh, I think we should have something strong on top of this.—Marie!

HANS. No, dad. It's too early in the day. [*To* MARIE, *who enters*] Bring us some cigars. Of course, I have to admit that it is harder to tell the truth in small circumstances.

RAVN. Harder? It's impossible!

KAMPE. Hm——?

RAVN. Well, you are thinking of truths that measure twenty to an inch. But the big truths that might lead to an explosion—they are not told.

KAMPE. Oh, they are told——

RAVN. Yes, told, but they fizzle out like powder set off in the open. I assure you that a small state couldn't stand the chemical process started by a powerful truth. It would go to pieces, darn it! No, stronger retorts are needed for that kind of thing.

HANS. The world's greatest truth came out of a small people.

RAVN. Which also dutifully went to pieces.

HANS. Not for that reason.

KAMPE. But this is getting awfully dry. Hadn't we better——?

HANS. Dad is right——

KAMPE. Well, at last!

HANS. We are getting away from the subject.

KAMPE. Ugh!

HANS. I know we are going to meet with difficulties; that they will evade the subject and resort to personalities. But if I can stand it——?

RAVN. Oh, you have got it all wrong! Well, I said to your father: don't let the boy stay away so long, I said; and don't let him get so far away. He will have to pay for it when he comes home.—Isn't that so?

KAMPE. Yes.

> *Rises and walks back and forth a couple of times; then he saunters out of the room, trying to appear as if he had no special purpose in mind.*

RAVN. Now, it is enough in itself that you have made this attack on a man of authority quite openly and with his name used——

HANS. But such things have happened before.

RAVN. Of course, they have. But when you, a young man without reputation—Oh, pish, the whole thing will just peter out.

HANS. Not while I am alive.

RAVN. Yes, be the whole show!

HANS. I shall keep on until parties are formed for and against—or perhaps no parties are ever formed in "our small circumstances," as you call them?

RAVN. Oh, yes, and with all the rottenness that goes with them—yes, indeed!

HANS. Just as in the big countries.

RAVN. Not in the same way. There is real conflict out there, often on a tremendous scale, and with it goes always a sense of spiritual uplift. You don't mind a little dirt spattered over you, when all your faculties are strained to the utmost. Yes, then you don't even mind wounds and prison walls. You go to defeat or victory in company with thousands. The flag is always held on high, and it draws new hosts from every new generation. In that way characters are formed, and firm wills. In that way you get statesmen, artists, writers, who have insight and purpose. But here? Just look at the same kind of men here—a small group of broken, sick, embittered fellows, with whom it is almost impossible to co-operate—and then, here and there, a man standing wholly alone.

HANS. But when they conquer at last——?

RAVN. Conquer? Oh, mercy! Where there is no fight there can be no victory. A lot of abuse and misrepresentation, of falsehood and hypocrisy; some stir and noise; but no fighting! It is as I told you; a small country couldn't even stand it. The slender threads out of which it is cautiously crocheted together would be torn to pieces—ugh!

[*Rises to his feet.*

HANS. Well, doubt and discouragement have certainly done their worst with you!

RAVN. You think so?

HANS. I do. For I can still recall how confident you used to be—as confident as your nephew Karl is now.

RAVN. Oh, his turn will come, too.

HANS. In those days you used to sparkle—sparkle like a diamond.   [*Smiles.*

RAVN. But it has been badly handled in the setting, boy. If you knock it and hammer it too carelessly, it breaks into fragments. A simile, by the by, that fits the case pretty well. It is particularly fitted to a family of enthusiasts in small circumstances.

HANS. But this "family of enthusiasts," as you call it, has nevertheless reached both fame and wealth.

RAVN. That happened in the old stirring days—long ago. And our fate has been that of other great men—who also had enthusiasm. Perhaps you haven't noticed it? But if it be true that great nations cannot exist without sacrificing thousands and thousands of their humblest members—then it is just as true that small nations cannot exist without sacrificing a certain number of their great and greatest!

HANS. Hm!

RAVN. See for yourself! To achieve success here you must have a will that is thoroughly tamed or very crafty. No man can reach the heights here unless he has the insinuating smile of a woman.

HANS. Are you thinking of your brother-in-law?

RAVN. No. As far as I can see, he smiles no more than anybody else. But have you noticed his son—my namesake —Frederick? Why, that rascal is really named after me— Oh, well, that was long ago!

HANS. Well, what of him?

RAVN. Oh—what a tone! So, you *have* heard?

HANS. You mean this thing with——?

RAVN. Speak up!

HANS. Speak up yourself!

RAVN. So I can: you mean Anna, my landlady's daughter —who has to go to America now.

HANS. Yes, I have heard of it.

RAVN. But *he* has already learned how to smile.

HANS. I am sure Frederick will make a success of it. Yesterday I heard that his father and Holste—the cabinet minister, you know—had come to an understanding.

RAVN. Quite likely. That's what the father did himself.

HANS. What do you mean? Did he also——?

RAVN. Desert a poor girl for the sake of his career—exactly! And do you know who it was? Anna's aunt.

HANS. Our old Marie?

RAVN. Sh! I think somebody is coming.

HANS. Karen!

SECOND SCENE

KAREN RIIS *enters.* KAMPE *follows a little later.*

KAREN. Pardon me!

HANS. Miss Ri—you here?

RAVN. Well, well!

KAREN. The road runs right by here.

HANS. Of course! But we have never before been honoured—at least not since my return.

KAREN. A couple of my friends and I were going to— How d'you do, uncle?

RAVN. Hello, my dear.

KAREN. We were passing by, and we thought it would be such fun to go out rowing—please, can we have the boat?

HANS. With the greatest pleasure! That is, I think my father has the key. But I'll——

RAVN. There's the old man now.

KAREN. Good evening!

KAMPE. [*Entering*] Good evening, Miss Riis. Why——?

KAREN. Can Nora Holm and Lise Gran and I have the boat for a little while?

KAMPE. If you can have the boat—? To lie out there reading novels?

HANS. Of course, you can have the boat! Let me have the key, and I'll——

KAMPE. Oh, I'll see to that! [*As he goes out*] Hm, hm, they are going to lie out there reading——

KAREN. Everything is as it used to be here.

HANS. Do you think so?

KAREN. Good-bye!

HANS. Good-bye! It was pleasant to have a look at you at least.

KAREN. One wouldn't think so, seeing that you never visit us any more.—Good-bye, uncle!

RAVN. Good-bye—and be careful, now!

KAREN. [*To* HANS] And Frederick likes you so much, you know.

KAMPE. [*Outside*] So it was a novel, after all? That's what I thought.

KAREN. [*Running to the door*] You are not reading while I am away, are you, girls?

HANS. [*Going after her*] Is it as interesting as all that?

KAMPE. [*Outside*] A story of life-saving!

HANS. Oh, a life-saving story?

KAREN. [*With a laugh*] Yes, and a woman who saves a man at that—just for a change. Good-bye!   [*Goes out.*

HANS. Good-bye!   [*Stands looking after her.*

THIRD SCENE

HANS. RAVN. *Later* KAMPE.

RAVN. [*Goes over to* HANS *and slaps him on the shoulder*] And with such a pretty view before your eyes, you intend to attack her father?

HANS. Not him! Only his system. I shall be very careful, you know.

RAVN. Ho, ho—ye-es! No, you had better let Karen be the woman who "saves a man," and for heaven's sake let that man be yourself, Hans!

HANS. But that's worse than a joke! I can prove that this so-called "new system" is costing the country millions. I am the only one who has gone to the bottom of the matter. Or at least, I am the only one who is willing to *tell the truth*. And then you advise me to keep silent—and to marry his daughter. And you say that's better!

RAVN. Well, hang it, I wouldn't advise you that way if I didn't think it better for the cause itself, too. An attack at this early moment, and without any authority to back it, will spoil everything. Wait!

HANS. For what?

RAVN. For the rest of the world, my boy! When the big countries have tried it out, then—say, in ten or twenty years —it will be almost ready for our acceptance also. Wait until the time when the judgment of the world at large is quietly being unloaded at our docks together with bales of cotton and silk and feathers and other noiseless goods. On its own in- itiative a small nation dares nothing!

HANS. And yet the system was adopted.

RAVN. And why? Because the engineers of other countries actually recommended it to begin with—fooled into doing so by one of our own men—the idiot!

KAMPE. [*Entering*] Why, are you still at it? The deuce take it, then you've got to have something to refresh yourself with. I have just discovered a bottle. [*Going to the door.*

HANS. Dad!

KAMPE. Keep quiet, boy! [*Out.*

RAVN. I have tried it, I can tell you. And it's of no use!

HANS. Hm!

RAVN. And now you are going to try *that*, too! Well, well! You have come home with your head full of illusions. So did I also once upon a time. But that was long ago—And look at your father. In railroad matters he is beyond a doubt our cleverest man—the man who has done most.

HANS. That's what I think. He actually astonishes me!

RAVN. Yes, but he wasn't "presentable," as they put it. And why not? Because, like you, he began by telling the truth—that's why! And it made a drunkard out of him. It was all *he* gained by it.

HANS. Hush!

KAMPE. [*Enters*] Here's the bottle! Come on! Don't be pig-headed now! A bottle like this can put some colour into small conditions. It can even make them look big. Here's to you! [*Drinks.*

RAVN *follows his example.* HANS *looks out over the sea.*

KAMPE. He's got his eye on those novel-reading little girls out there.

RAVN. You didn't treat them very well, did you?

KAMPE. Oh, I happened to think of how they are reading novels all the time, and always about courage, and enthusiasm, and that kind of thing—and for all that they are nothing but a lot of mincing good-for-nothings.

Ravn. It's hardly to be wondered at. They live in conditions where nobody ever dares anything, not as much as a contradiction even.

Hans. [*Interrupting*] I vouch for Karen. I can remember how she ran away from home as a child because her father wanted her to do something she didn't think right. Then she came to me, and I had to row her far, far away.

Kampe. I remember it also.

Ravn. [*Who has picked up his stick*] Karen has more of our blood. But upbringing, conditions—oh, you'll learn all about it now. You just publish that book of yours! Good-bye!   [*Holds out his hands to* Hans.

Hans. [*Without taking it*] There is one factor you constantly overlook when you speak of my book: the Diet.

Ravn. The Diet? No, I don't overlook it at all. Why, I am a member of it myself.

Hans. I am going to present my case in such clear light——

Ravn. Good-bye, Hans. It was nice of you to ask for my advice.

Hans. And it will be what you have said?

Ravn. Absolutely.

Kampe. Don't you want——?

Ravn. No, thank you. Good-bye!

Kampe. Good-bye!

Ravn. [*To* Hans, *who is seeing him out*] And what about your father? When your book appears, every engineer will understand that he has made the calculations. He will be discharged.

Hans. That's just what I am going to have a talk with him about.

Ravn. All right. Good-night!   [*He goes out.

FOURTH SCENE

KAMPE. HANS.

KAMPE. Well? What do you think of him?

HANS. What bitterness!

KAMPE. There's a lot of the same kind around here.

HANS. And he used to be such an enthusiast—like all the rest of the family.

KAMPE. Heaven only knows what happens to the enthusiasts in this country. That's the way they all end.—Well, well! God help the whole lot of us!   [*Takes a drink.*

HANS. Dad!

KAMPE. Yes.

HANS. Don't do it!

KAMPE. What?

HANS. That!

KAMPE [*Taking another drink*] Stuff and nonsense, boy! It's all over with me. And I cannot stand any kind of solemnity.

HANS. But if I don't want it——

KAMPE. Not another word! Let us talk of you. You'll have to face everything I've told you. But that's no reason why you should turn back. If we don't start some time to speak up in this country, each one in his corner, we'll never get anywhere. Now that's *my* new system.

HANS. It's old as the hills——

KAMPE. But remains always new. *Tell the truth!* And let come what must.—Do you know after whom you were named?

HANS. No.

KAMPE. I'll tell you. I broke into your mother's fine

family.   There I didn't feel very much at home.   And it was
the family that influenced your mother so that I didn't have
a chance to push ahead the way I wanted.   Well—I used to
go hunting when it became too much for me.   And for companion I took along old Hans, the cottager, and a more honest
man I never met.   It's after him you were named.   I invited
him to the party we gave when you were baptised, and I even
proposed a toast for him—great scandal—but lots of fun!—He
used to say when we were crawling along after reindeer out
on the bare rocks, and the fall winds were like razors, and we
got near enough to shoot: 'Give it to 'em, boy!'—And that's
what I say to you!

HANS. I am not going to give it to them, as you call it.

KAMPE. Call it anything you please!   But stick to it!
That's what I didn't do.—And now enough of that!

[Takes a drink.

HANS. But I won't stick to it.   For I'll never start.

KAMPE. You won't start?   What's that?   You don't mean
to say that his cawing really scared you?

HANS. No, but you scare me, dad.

KAMPE. I?—Oh—my example, you mean?   Never mind
that, Hans!   You won't fall down where I fell.   And I don't
want any kind of solemnity!—What have you got to do
with me?

HANS. Dad!

KAMPE. Twaddle!   I have helped you along.   And nobody has had more pleasure in it than I.   You 'tend to yours,
and I'll 'tend to mine—[preparing another glass]—and at
night I get myself a little 'night-cap' before I go to bed.
What's that to you?

HANS. All right—then I'll get myself a 'night-cap' also.

[Picks up a glass and reaches out for the bottle.

KAMPE. You, Hans?

HANS. Yes, I have come home to share your life in every respect.

KAMPE. You mean to do like me——? *[Stops short.*

HANS. Like you, I'll go to bed drunk every night and sleep it off beside you.

KAMPE. I forbid you to do so, Hans—! Oh, you ought not to joke like that, Hans,—you quite frightened me.

HANS. But if I start with anything while you are keeping up this kind of thing—where will it end for me?

KAMPE. What the devil have you got to do with me?

HANS. And *you* ask that, who have encouraged me into attempting something of a reformation. What would people say? " Why should *he* do any reforming? Let him at least begin with it in his own home!"

KAMPE. You think they'll say——

HANS. Don't you know the conditions we are living in? They'll lose no time in finding out who I am, that I am not a reliable person, that I am the son of a—— *[Stops.*

KAMPE. Drunkard. Speak out!—Well, as far as that is concerned, there is nothing to do about it. You have to bear it.

HANS. Bear it? Oh, no! To bring my own father into bad repute—that's something I cannot strive for.

KAMPE. It can't become worse than it is. Listen, Hans: when your mother couldn't—Oh, quit all this!—Don't you think I have tried?—Lord Jesus!

HANS. As long as you have not tried to place yourself in a new, independent position, which would occupy you fully, you have not tried at all.

KAMPE. What have you in mind?

HANS. You know I have accepted the agency for one of the biggest machinery concerns in America and England.

KAMPE. Yes, and I don't like it.   You are built for bigger things.

HANS. But I have done this for you.

KAMPE. For me?

HANS. *You* are to run the business.   We two will go into partnership.   The firm will be Kampe & Son.   I am never again going to leave you, dad, not for a single day, and this I say right to your face in remembrance of mother.

KAMPE. Hans, my boy—!   But it won't go.   And you are not to throw yourself away for my sake.

HANS. Throw myself away?   No, if there be *any* way for me to do something real big, it lies here.   You can be sure I see that clearly.

KAMPE. Hans, my boy!—Oh, that you are home again— No, this is madness, solemnity.   I should be fooling you.   I know myself.

HANS. But I won't let go on that account.   I have a better chance than mother had to be with you all the time.

KAMPE. I should only become a burden to you, Hans—and to myself also.—Yes, indeed, I could tell you a thing or two— but that will have to be some other time.   Ugh!   This sort of thing takes it out of you—I think I'll have to——

[Goes toward the table.

HANS. Dad!

KAMPE. Well, there you see.   It has gone so far with me that I don't know myself when I am doing it.   And it's for me you would sacrifice your future?   Stuff, rot—leave me alone!   *[Goes toward the table again.*

HANS. And if mother was still alive, dad?

KAMPE. Do you want to hurt me?   Do you think I haven't thought of it——   *[Covers his face with his hands.*

HANS. I cannot see how you could go on after mother was dead——

KAMPE. Will you keep quiet? You don't understand at all. It was then it became worse than ever—But I don't want to go on talking of this. I won't have any interference.

HANS. Dad!

KAMPE. You have no right. Don't I attend to my work? The rest is my own concern. I owe nobody an account. Nobody!

HANS. What is the matter with you now?

KAMPE. Well, I can't stand this kind of thing. Who but myself can understand why I do it? I need it. That's all there is to it. And I don't ask anybody's permission.

[*Takes a drink.*

HANS. No, this is more than *I* can stand!

KAMPE. If you only knew what I have stood for your sake!

HANS. You—for my sake?

KAMPE. A while ago you said I stood in the way of your future.

HANS. Oh, no——

KAMPE. Well, that's what it came to. You had made up your mind not to bear with me any longer.

HANS. But, dad——!

KAMPE. Now I am going to balance the account. I had a son somewhere out in the big world, and for *his* sake I had to work. But this work had become a hell on earth. I, who had done what placed the bigwigs where they now are, I was to be disposed of. I, who had once been held indispensable, was given all kinds of odd jobs to do, and was finally shunted into a sort of double-faced position as inspector and cashier for new constructions. I *had* to stick it out, for my son was constantly asking for still another trip, still another year.—Much that looks nasty can be drowned in a full glass, you know. That's just what happened. And you are the last one, you know, who has a right to say anything about it.

—What I have stood for your sake, you will never have to stand for mine. So you had better keep quiet.

        Goes over to the table and begins again to prepare a glass for himself.

HANS. Well, if you drink any more, dad, I'll go.

KAMPE. Now you are on the wrong tack. I won't submit to any commands.

HANS. I am not trying to command you. But I'll go.

KAMPE. Go? Where?

HANS. Away, and for ever.

KAMPE. Have you no heart?—All right, go on!

HANS. Merciful heavens! Do you dare to call me heartless because I cannot bear to see you like that?—Here I come home without an idea of the way things have gone. Then I offer you my future—not as a duty, or a sacrifice, or what you call it. Never was a thought more dear to me than that of doing so. Never have I been so proud of anything as of the hope that I might help you into your own once more.

KAMPE. Hans!

HANS. And then you won't listen to me even. You won't give me time to finish what I have to say. Yes, you don't even hesitate to put the fault on me. Under such circumstances there is nothing for me to do here. And it is dangerous to stay here—I have felt it already. So I guess I'll be going again, dad.

KAMPE. You don't understand me. When I belittle myself, it is in order not to make myself out better than I am. Rather worse, so that I don't deceive you.

HANS. But are you not willing to try?

KAMPE. O Lord, when I know it is impossible!   O-oh!

HANS. Will you listen to me?

KAMPE. Yes.

HANS. We are at the end of the quarter. You have just settled your accounts. Write out your letter of resignation this minute, right here. If they want to kick up a rumpus about it, don't mind them. They are only getting what they deserve. We pack this very evening, and leave to-morrow—then a month or two abroad!

KAMPE. Hans!

HANS. In the meantime my book is printed. We come back, publish it—and start business. Your name will make the firm respected. We shall be our own masters. We'll fight for what both of us believe in—and we'll work. What do you say of it, dad?

KAMPE. Oh, what a dream! If it could only be done, Hans—oh!

HANS. But you *want* to see it done?

KAMPE. What a question! But I have sunk too deep already.

HANS. That remains to be seen. There is still such a lot of power in you, dad.

KAMPE. Do you think so?

HANS. Now, let us get out of this—quick!

KAMPE. If I only dared to trust myself——!

HANS. It should help you to think that I am merely yourself as you were when you were young. Will you do it?

KAMPE. If I will——? But I don't dare. I'll sneak out of it—I know it!

HANS. But we shall always be together.

KAMPE. Oh, it would be——

VOICE. [*Heard from the outside*] Help! Bring the boat this way!

BOTH. It comes from the shore?

HANS. Somebody bathing!

VOICE. Help!

KAMPE. He is caught in the sea-weed! He is drowning!

HANS. But there is a boat coming. No, it's going away again! What do they mean by it? *[Runs out.*

KAMPE. [*Running*] The young ladies! They're rowing ashore! What was it I said? [*Outside*] Come here with the boat! This way!—Now, row! Keep together!

VOICE. Help! Help!

KAMPE. [*Outside*] We're coming now!

FIFTH SCENE

> KAREN RIIS. NORA HOLM. LISE GRAN. *They en-*
> *ter from the left, all badly frightened.* KAREN *runs*
> *back and forth.*

NORA. Do you see him?—I don't dare to look out!

LISE. No, he has gone down!

BOTH THE OTHERS. Gone down!

KAREN. We should have saved him.

NORA. [*Weeping*] But, Karen, we couldn't!

KAREN. It wasn't right, it wasn't right, it wasn't right! I'll never have peace again in all my life.—Can you see him?

LISE. No.

NORA. They generally come up again twice.

LISE. But he is caught in the weed.

KAREN. That's so. Oh, that's so.—Isn't the boat getting there?

LISE. There it is!

NORA. There it is!

KAREN. God be thanked!

LISE. Just where he went down!

NORA. The old man jumps in!

KAREN. O-oh!—   [*Silence.*

NORA. [*In a whisper*] How long he is gone!

LISE. There he comes!

KAREN. [*Joining* LISE] Has he got him?—Yes!

LISE. Now he has hold of the boat!

ALL.   [*Cry out, taking hold of each other.*

NORA. It's upsetting!

LISE. No, the old man let go!

KAREN. Hans is holding on to the man.

NORA. There is the old man on the other side of the boat.

LISE. He's holding it down.

KAREN. Now Hans got him into the boat. [*Coming down to the foreground*] God be thanked and praised!

[*She bursts into violent weeping.*

LISE. More boats are coming.

NORA. And what a lot of people! What are we to do? We can't go down there! Where are we now?

LISE. But, Karen! Don't!

KAREN. O-o-oh!

NORA. Let us get away from here! But which way?

LISE. Karen—dear Karen! [*They hasten out to the right.*

SIXTH SCENE

The stage is empty for a time. Then KAMPE *enters without shoes, his clothes dark and drooping, his hair clinging to his head. He comes in from the right and walks quickly across the stage toward a door on the left.*

HANS. [*Outside*] Wait, dad!

KAMPE. I am just going to change.

HANS. Oh, wait. [*Enters on the run*] What we were talking of before this happened—promise me now!

[*Embraces his father.*

KAMPE. You'll get wet, boy.

HANS. But you promise, daddie!

KAMPE. I'll do my best!

Curtain.

ACT II

The private office in the Director-General's home by the sea.

FIRST SCENE

RIIS. MRS. RIIS. FREDERICK.

RIIS. [*Sitting by the big desk that stands in the middle of the room; he is arranging documents and maps, part of which he puts into a travelling-bag; now and then he looks for something in a big cabinet with shelves which stands to the left of him*] Things don't happen in life as they do in books, or in the imagination of young people. For instance, it is very rare that anybody marries for love.

MRS. RIIS. [*Employed with some needlework*] But, dear, we married for love, didn't we?

RIIS. We two, my dear, are now too old to talk of love.

MRS. RIIS. Too old? Can you ever become too old to talk of love? To feel it—that's another thing.

[*She wipes her eyes.*

RIIS. [*To* FREDERICK] And now, when the girl gets out of here anyhow, I should think there might be an end to the whole story.—The whole thing was an irregularity.

FREDERICK. [*Standing in front of his father and partly turned away from the latter; his hands rest on a big T-square from the office*] I really didn't know how much I had come to love her. Now, when she is going, I feel as if I couldn't stand it.

RIIS. Why, that kind of thing has happened to all of us.

MRS. RIIS. But, dear, you don't mean to say that.

RIIS. I am not speaking of ourselves now, my dear—There

191

is a regulating principle in life that pulls us into line again, if we have gone a little astray.   Our acquaintances, the mutual relations between us and—   Do you think I should be sitting here now if I had let my passions run away with me?

MRS. RIIS. But there has to be passion, dear—a passion for what is good.

RIIS. Quite right, my dear—and the principal good for Frederick is his future.   He must passionately—the word fits excellently—devote himself to his future.   My social position will help to start him.   But he must do the rest himself.

MRS. RIIS. Happiness, dear, does not merely consist in that kind of thing.

RIIS. Of course not.   But if you neglect it, you'll see!   It means, in the highest sense, to miss your destiny.

MRS. RIIS. Our destiny, dear, is to enter into eternal bliss.

RIIS. Certainly.   But that doesn't make it wrong to become as happy as possible in this life, my dear.

MRS. RIIS. No, but to be happy we should follow the best impulses of our own hearts.

RIIS. Your mother is quite right. [*He rises and walks past* FREDERICK] This is dragging you down, my boy.

MRS. RIIS. But she is a very nice girl, and so I can't see that we, as parents, should have any objections.   Isn't that so, dear?

RIIS. You understand, I haven't told your mother—[*To his wife*] But don't you think, my dear, that it would be wrong for Frederick to tie himself at this stage?—He ought to keep his heart open to every noble impulse.

MRS. RIIS. I think I should like to know her.

RIIS. [*As he passes in front of* FREDERICK] For heaven's sake! [*To his wife*] I don't think we should mix too deeply into this, mamma.   Now she is leaving the country.

MRS. RIIS. Poor girl!   Where is she going?

RIIS. To America—to some relatives of hers.

MRS. RIIS. But suppose, now, that Frederick's feelings for her are genuine?

RIIS. Let them be tried, then. Don't you think I am right in that?

MRS. RIIS. Yes, you are, dear. Try thy heart, says the Book. Oh, mercy, yes!

FREDERICK. I think I should like to go with you, father, and talk it all over.

RIIS. Why don't you?

FREDERICK. Well, if I may—then I'll get ready also.

RIIS. But—didn't I hear that the Holstes were arranging some kind of excursion? The steamer has been engaged, I know.

MRS. RIIS. The cabinet minister?

RIIS. Yes.

FREDERICK. I haven't the slightest desire——

RIIS. To go with them? Oh, of course, you must!

MRS. RIIS. I think so, too. Young people should be enjoying themselves. Afterward there is so much else.

RIIS. Speaking of parties—when are we going to give that dinner for the engineers?

MRS. RIIS. It was about that I came in—well, and about something else besides. How long will you be gone?

RIIS. Ten days, I should say; under no circumstances more than twelve. What do you think of two weeks from next Friday? Let me see—that will be the eighth.

MRS. RIIS. I met Mrs. Holste at the bazaar yesterday.

RIIS. The minister's wife?

MRS. RIIS. Yes—Magda. They are going to receive communion together, the whole family—that'll be the eighth. Now I thought, couldn't we go that day also?

Riis. That's a good idea. Let us do it! And I hope the children will go with us.

Mrs. Riis. I am sure they will. It is such a beautiful sight to see a whole family together—parents and grown-up children.

Riis. Bear that in mind, Frederick: Friday fortnight.

FREDERICK *makes no reply*.

Riis. But the party?

Mrs. Riis. Well—a few days earlier? On Wednesday? Then we could have the Friday free.

Riis. That's splendid. Then all the arrangements will be made while I am away.

Mrs. Riis. That's just what I had in mind.

Riis. You are a fine housewife, Kamma. Why doesn't Larssen come? [*Looks at his watch*] Oh, there is still time.

FREDERICK. Can I go along?

Riis. Frankly speaking, Frederick—the Holstes have been counting on you. I just happened to recall it.

FREDERICK. So you have been speaking of me?

Riis. Yes. Perhaps somebody else is also counting on you?—Oh, there they are! [*Picks up his field-glasses*] One has to be a little far-sighted. [*Puts them down beside the bag.*

FREDERICK. I'll be at the station to see you off at least.

Riis. All right.

FREDERICK *goes out*.

Mrs. Riis. Dear, it was really about Karen I wanted to speak to you.

Riis. I haven't seen her yet to-day. Is she still unwell?

Mrs. Riis. Haven't you noticed that? She is just as she used to be—pale, without appetite, can't sleep.

Riis. Again? I thought it had passed.

Mrs. Riis. It *had* passed.

Riis. Well, what's the matter now?

MRS. RIIS. I don't know. She won't say anything about it. Couldn't you have a talk with her?

RIIS. Yes—bring her in here.

MRS. RIIS. That's just what I wanted. [*Starts to go out.*

RIIS. Tell me, Kamma—has she seen Hans Kampe again? They have come back from abroad, both he and the father. I see they are having an advertisement in the paper to-day: "Kampe & Son." Has she spoken of them?

MRS. RIIS. No.

RIIS. Well, bring her to me.

MRS. RIIS *goes out.*

SECOND SCENE

A MAN SERVANT *comes in with letters and two packages which he hands to* RIIS.

RIIS. One of the packages is for my daughter?

SERVANT. There was one for Mr. Frederick also, but he received it himself.

RIIS. You can leave that one for my daughter here. Have you taken down my trunk?

SERVANT. Yes, sir.

RIIS. [*Looking at his watch*] I want the carriage in half an hour. And then you can also come for my bag.

SERVANT *goes out.*

THIRD SCENE

RIIS. MRS. RIIS. KAREN.

RIIS. How are you feeling, my girl?

KAREN *leans her head against his shoulder.*

RIIS. All this—oh, that stupid story about the drowning——? [KAREN *nestles closer to him so that her face is hidden.*

RIIS. But there isn't a single soul in the whole city that has even mentioned it.

KAREN. I think the whole city should be talking of nothing else.

RIIS. Now you must be sensible! Will you answer me frankly?

KAREN. Yes.

RIIS. Did Hans Kampe say anything to you that time as he jumped into the boat?

KAREN. No.

RIIS. No? Not a word?

KAREN *shakes her head.*

RIIS. And yet?

KAREN. He only looked at me.   [*Hides her face again.*

RIIS. [*With a glance at his wife*] Have you met him recently—after his return?

MRS. RIIS. I saw old Mr. Kampe yesterday, and he really looked fine.

RIIS. I am not thinking of him. [*To* KAREN] Have you met Hans? [KAREN *turns from him*] And he looked at you again? Reproachfully? Tell me? [KAREN *walks away from him*] Frightful!—Listen, my girl. I have some idea of propriety myself. It has been demanded and developed by my position. So I think myself capable of judging in a matter like this—perhaps even a little better than Messrs. Kampe & Son. And I can assure you—on behalf of our best society, I dare say—that in such a case three young ladies could not do anything but make for the shore, as quickly as possible, in order to bring help. And that's what you did.

KAREN. But suppose he had been drowned——

RIIS. Yes, suppose!

MRS. RIIS. It took the doctor nearly half an hour to bring him back to life.

RIIS. *Suppose* he had been drowned. Whose fault would it have been? His own! We cannot—least of all our young women—save everybody who happens to be dying around here—whether it be on land or sea.

KAREN. I have thought it over a thousand times. Oh, what a lot I have thought of in this one month—and discovered!

RIIS. There now! "Discovered"!

MRS. RIIS. Perhaps this was sent you as a warning from above, Karen?

KAREN. Oh, I have been warned all right. I know now how useless and helpless I am.

RIIS. There! There! Nothing but sentimentality. You should take a horseback ride every day. Don't you remember what a lot of good it did you before? Try it again. You, Karen, useless and helpless? You who are the cleverest of your whole set? Almost all your teachers have said so.

KAREN. Think a moment, papa! Did you ever find any prudishness in a really useful person? No, it's only we, the useless good-for-nothings, who are timid and prudish. We who are always reading and dreaming and—oh, how insincere we are!

RIIS. Well, well! Insincere also!

MRS. RIIS. But there *is* something in that, dear.

RIIS. Oh, please!

MRS. RIIS. Yes, for we go around with a lot of ideals and such things—and then it doesn't mean anything at all. No, indeed!

KAREN. Mamma is right.

RIIS. Of course, your mother is right! Because it is from your mother's crazy family that you have got all these notions. But my patience is coming to an end.

MRS. RIIS. You always run down my family.

Riis. Well, there is much that's fine about it also.—But listen, Karen, I am trying to help you.

Mrs. Riis. I didn't know that my family had ever tried to harm you or anybody else?

Riis. Of course, not; of course, it hasn't.   Listen, Karen! You ought to trust your own father a little.   You don't suppose that I want you to do anything wrong?

Mrs. Riis. No, dear, you have no right to say that my family ever wanted anybody to do wrong.

Riis. But I have said nothing of the kind, my dear. [*To* KAREN] You should resist that weakness in your nature.   It is every one's duty to do so.   And it is nothing but a weakness that you——

Mrs. Riis. You don't mean to say that she has got her weakness from my family?

Riis. On the contrary.

Mrs. Riis. Yes, for that wouldn't be right.   With all the energy, and all the faith, there is——

Riis. Certainly! [*To* KAREN] You don't want to limit yourself to your own concerns.   And so you meet with the clamour of all kinds of things you think should be done, and out of it comes nothing but restlessness and brooding——

Mrs. Riis. But now, dear, there are so many things we ought to do and don't do.   That's really so.

Riis. Of course!

Mrs. Riis. Now, take the poor, for instance.   We don't deal with them as we should.   No, we don't!

Riis. Those who have been placed at the top of society, my dear girl——

Mrs. Riis. —for when we are told we should love our neighbour as ourselves——

> *During the rest of this scene* Riis *and* Mrs. Riis *go on talking at the same time.*

RIIS. —those that have been placed at the top must hold together——

MRS. RIIS. —we don't do it. Oh, we are so very, very far from doing it!

RIIS. —and particularly children and parents.

MRS. RIIS. What we lack most of all is love—yes, love!

RIIS. Now we are on the chapter of love again! I must impress on you, Karen, and with the greatest emphasis, that you don't let yourself go like that——

MRS. RIIS. We live only for ourselves, that's what we do, and we spend small coins and small attentions to escape from what is really wanted of us.

RIIS. —that you don't fly around like a blind bat in the twilight.

MRS. RIIS. It's so bitter to know [*weeping*] that we are not strong enough to be as we should.

RIIS. Now she's weeping! That's what comes from all this nonsense about wanting to help everything and everybody in the whole world.

MRS. RIIS. [*Sings*] "Love alone is the eye of life."

FOURTH SCENE

RIIS. MRS. RIIS. KAREN. FREDERICK.

FREDERICK. [*Comes in with a book in his hand*] Papa!

RIIS. Well, what is it?

FREDERICK. Have you too got the book?

RIIS. The book? Yes, I have received a book. And Karen, too.

FREDERICK. Has he had the impudence to send it to Karen also?

RIIS. [*Reading*] "Hans Kampe, C.E."

KAREN. Hans?

[*Picks up the package addressed to herself and opens it.*

RIIS. [*Reading*] "Concerning the so-called new system for—" Oh, is that what it is?

FREDERICK. I have glanced through it. You cannot imagine what a shameless piece of work it is.

RIIS. Why, that's delightful! Then it will be of great service to us.

FREDERICK. No, it isn't as you think. The book contains a lot of polite admissions and has even an air of fairness about it. That's the worst of it. In this way—by praising you and constantly speaking of you in a tone of respect—he bribes the reader into accepting his line of argument. And before one quite realises what has happened, your system has been picked to pieces. Then he goes on cold-bloodedly—oh, so cold-bloodedly and so logically—to figure out how much the country loses by it annually. And it ends up with some beautiful reflections about the moral effect on our engineers. For they are now compelled to stand by what at bottom they don't believe in, and this becomes possible only by means of calculations and data held to be far from legitimate.

RIIS. Is that what he says?

FREDERICK. He gives illustrations.

RIIS. Well—those we'll have to look over.

FREDERICK. And he is my friend—the best one I ever had. I have looked up to him as—never in my life have I been so deceived. Beside this everything else is as nothing.

RIIS. What was it I always said when you used to praise him so highly: "I suppose he is his father's son."—As a rule that holds good.

FREDERICK. [*After turning and twisting the book in his hands*] Everything is disgusting about it—even the binding!

RIIS. The binding?

FREDERICK. Yes, don't you see that it is bound?   The idea of sending each of us, and Karen too, a bound copy, as if this were something we wanted to preserve very carefully!

RIIS. Now, when I come to think of it, I guess you are right——

FREDERICK. And such a thing to Karen and me—what have we done to him?   And to you, papa, who have stood by his drunkard of a father, although he was a constant cause of scandal.

MRS. RIIS. Not in his work, Frederick.   We must not put any blame on our neighbour that——

FREDERICK. Oh, there is no reason for you to defend *him*——

MRS. RIIS. Yes, Frederick, we should love even our enemies.

FREDERICK. I can't stand that kind of thing!   But I'll——

KAREN. Frederick!

RIIS. [*At the same time*] Sh, sh, sh!—Well, Karen!   Was it not the "look" that "Hans Kampe, C.E.," gave you that made you so dreadfully "sincere"?

KAREN *runs out to the left.*

MRS. RIIS. You shouldn't have said that to Karen.

RIIS. Yes, it will do her good.

FREDERICK. Poor Karen!   But I'll——

RIIS. Look here, my boy, no foolishness!   Now as never before you will have to control your passions.   Or you'll never get anywhere.

MRS. RIIS. But passion for what is right, dear?

FREDERICK. Yes, we have to fight.

RIIS. Yes, that would be lovely!   [*A knock is heard at the door*] Come in!   That must be Larssen.—No, we cannot grant them the honour of fighting them.

FIFTH SCENE

RIIS.   MRS. RIIS.   FREDERICK.   LARSSEN

RIIS. Well? [LARSSEN *shakes hands with him*] Well? [LARSSEN *greets* MRS. RIIS *in the same manner*] Well? [LARSSEN *goes through the same motions with* FREDERICK] Well?

LARSSEN. What is your pleasure, Mr. Riis?

RIIS. The book? What do you say of the book?

LARSSEN. May I ask which book you are referring to?

RIIS. This one, of course.

LARSSEN. May I ask you for a chance to look at it?

FREDERICK. [*Quickly*] Why, Hans Kampe's book about my father's system.

LARSSEN. Oh, that one?

RIIS. What do you think of it?

LARSSEN. Nothing at all.

RIIS. What? Haven't you read it?

FREDERICK. Oh, no, he——

LARSSEN. [*Simultaneously*] Yes, but only twice.

RIIS. And in the course of these first two readings you have not been struck by anything in particular.

LARSSEN. [*Indifferently*] No.

RIIS. You are a solid man, Larssen. There is something about your faith in a cause that does one's very heart good.

FREDERICK. Yes, that's true!

LARSSEN. I do not think that Mr. "Hans Kampe, C.E.," can teach me anything about the new system.

RIIS. No, upon my soul, I don't think so either. He can't teach you or me anything about it. And I was just saying to Frederick here: no excitement, no fighting.

LARSSEN. For heaven's sake!

RIIS. There you see!—And I just thought of something:

[*to* MRS. RIIS, *who comes back after having had a look at* KAREN *in an adjoining room*] we meant to avoid asking old Kampe to the dinner we are giving for the engineers; but now we'll ask both him and the son.

MRS. RIIS. Now I recognise your real self, dear. We should love those that hate us.

LARSSEN. Quite right, Mrs. Riis—that is, if we can.

FREDERICK. [*Bursts into laughter; then to himself*] No, that's more than I can do!

RIIS. Frederick!

FREDERICK. Yes.   [*Turning toward his father.*

RIIS. Don't forget that I am going away.

FREDERICK. That's right! [*Looking at his watch*] I haven't time to get to the station now. So I think I'll ride down with you.

RIIS. Here are a lot of things for you, Larssen. And if you'll accept a seat in my carriage, I can talk over a point or two with you on the way down.

LARSSEN. I shall be honoured, Mr. Riis.

RIIS. [*Hangs the case with the field-glasses around his neck and picks up the book, saying:*] I mustn't forget this one.

LARSSEN. Something to read on the road. He, he! He, he!

RIIS. [*Who has opened the book*] Here I notice some calculations which could only have been made by one on the inside. Well, well!

FREDERICK. That's the old man, of course. Both have had a finger in it.

RIIS. I shall have to study this more closely. [*Puts the book in his pocket*] Could it be possible that the old man wants to cover up something by this manœuvre—what do you think?

LARSSEN. We have no right to suspect anything. But as you have already spoken of it, I must admit that the reading of the book made me think that it might be wise to give Mr. Kampe's accounts a special examination.

MRS. RIIS. Oh, dear, dear! You mustn't be so quick to think badly of your fellow-man, even if he should have erred.

FREDERICK. But this is something you don't understand, mamma!

RIIS. [*To himself*] The mere report of such a measure—it would be worth more than ten replies to the book. Excellent!—Listen, Larssen—let a couple of accountants begin an informal investigation, and afterward we can make an official demand for a more formal procedure. But very quietly! Out of consideration for the man, you know.

LARSSEN. It shall be done, Mr. Riis.

MRS. RIIS. But very quietly—that's right!

RIIS. Well, good-bye then, my dear. Take care of yourself!

MRS. RIIS. Dear, you're so kind-hearted—won't you say a good word to Karen before you leave? She——

RIIS. No, indeed, I won't! Let her think over what it means to believe more in others than in her own father.— Now, that's a sweet little wifie! [*Kissing her*] Good-bye! And don't cry now!

> FREDERICK *has picked up his hand-bag and umbrella.*
> LARSSEN *is at the door, not wanting to go out ahead of*
> *the* DIRECTOR-GENERAL.

RIIS. After you!

LARSSEN. No, after you, Mr. Riis!

RIIS. The idea! In my own house!

LARSSEN. It would be too great an honour! [*To* MRS. RIIS, *whose hand he shakes*] Good-bye, Mrs. Riis!

MRS. RIIS. I'll see you out!

LARSSEN. Permit me anyhow!

MRS. RIIS. And remember now, Larssen, very quietly!

RIIS. Of course, my dear. Have a cigar, Larssen?

LARSSEN. Thousand thanks!

RIIS. And you, Frederick?

FREDERICK. I never refuse your cigars, papa.

RIIS. You rascal! You have been in the box before—I noticed it.

LARSSEN. He, he!—He, he!

MRS. RIIS. [*Reproachfully*] Oh, Frederick!

RIIS. Well—let peace rest on the house!

[*All go out.*

SIXTH SCENE

The scene changes to the same open room at KAMPE'S *as in the first act.*

HANS KAMPE *is working.* KARL RAVN *comes in.*

KARL. Oh, there you are! Will you permit me to thank you?

HANS. So you have read the book?

KARL. If I have read it? I took it along to the Engineers' Club last night. Some of the younger men had arranged to meet. I read the book aloud to them.

HANS. Well?

KARL. We stayed together until two o'clock this morning. I have never experienced anything like it.

HANS. Really?

KARL. Do you know how it is when a large number of people have been oppressed by the same vague sensation of something false, and then one man rises up and gives open expression to their doubts? It puts such courage into us, as if we might make the whole world over.

HANS. You please me very much.

KARL. You may count on the young ones.

HANS. Really?

KARL. For my own part, I feel in duty bound. And my wife quite agrees with me. Well, you don't know my wife?

HANS. I haven't the pleasure yet.

KARL. All this morning we have talked of nothing else. I just *had* to run over to see you.

HANS. Very kind of you!

KARL. Of course, it is nothing new to us.

HANS. If you could only know what encouragement you give me. You are the first one from whom I have heard about my book—a first swallow heralding the spring!

KARL. And its name is *raven*. [*Laughs.*

HANS. Oh, that reminds me. You are not the first one, after all. One person read the book before it was published: your uncle, Frederick Ravn.

KARL. And I suppose he told you not to publish it at all?

HANS. That's exactly what he did. He does not believe in our engineers; not even in the younger ones.

KARL. Of course not. He doesn't believe in anybody. But I wonder if you know—oh, I have to tell you!

HANS. What is it?

KARL. I discovered it myself by a mere accident, so I am not obliged to keep silent. And I have never told it to a single soul before now—my wife excepted, of course; for I tell her everything——

HANS. You make me curious!

KARL. No one but Uncle Frederick is responsible for the introduction of the system, the "new system," both in this and other countries. He was the man who praised it so highly in a number of foreign periodicals.

HANS. Old Ravn? Frederick Ravn? The Canal Inspector?

KARL. Call him anything you please—he was the man!

HANS. All those brilliant articles we read as students in English and German periodicals——?

KARL. And of which we were so frightfully proud when we went abroad!

HANS. Yes! Because finally something strikingly original had come from our own little nation.

KARL. Yes—and he did it!

HANS. I don't think even my father knows of this.

KARL. No, for it is his life's great secret. It was this enormous mistake that made him a broken man.

HANS. But a splendid head like his? How could he——?

KARL. We—ell! Enthusiasts of that kind are by no means an unqualified blessing to a small country, where no strong currents make themselves felt. There they are apt to get caught by all sorts of dreams and abortive projects. For they must be doing something.

HANS. And it is *you* who say this——?

KARL. Oh, I have a wife, and she has saved me.

HANS. But she comes from the same family?

KARL. Mixed blood! Mixed blood! Why, you don't know my mother-in-law?

HANS. I haven't the honour.

KARL. She's a good one. You must come and see us!

HANS. It will be one of the first things I do.

KARL. That's fine! Come to-morrow night—will you? And I'll have some of the younger engineers on hand.

HANS. Thank you!   [*They shake hands.*

KARL. Well, I have to run along. I am frightfully busy.

HANS. I shall never forget this visit of yours.

KARL. I *had* to come. [*Going toward the door*] Just as now I shall *have* to write something.

HANS. But the Director-General is in a way your relative?

KARL. That's one more reason! [*Coming forward again*] It

was from our family he once got the support that made the whole trouble possible.

HANS. Well, how could it happen? For greater contrasts——!

KARL. Never mind! We have got to make up for it now. And we'll do it.

HANS. For which I thank you!

KARL. No, this won't do! I am frightfully busy just now! [*Hastens toward the door, but stops again*] But I simply have to tell you what my wife said. "It is harder to tell the truth in a small country than in a big one," she said. Do you think it's true?

HANS. Beyond all doubt!

KARL. And yet you believe in the small nations?—No, I haven't the time to spare now! You must come and talk it over with my wife and me. Of course, *she* doesn't say much. Probably because her mother says a good deal too much. And I, too! So I have no fault to find! [*Bursts into laughter*] Good-bye! [*Runs out to the right and meets* KAMPE *on the way*] How are you?

KAMPE. Have you got to go?

KARL. I haven't time now! [*Goes out.*

SEVENTH SCENE

KAMPE. HANS.

HANS. If there are many young people like him in this country, dad, it may happen that we shall really get a new system of our own.

KAMPE. He's a fine fellow! But I came in because I saw Frederick Riis headed for the house. You'd better go inside and let me receive him. I have such fine practice in giving and taking abuse.

HANS. Oh, if he's looking for me, I think he had better see me.

KAMPE. You don't want that bother?

HANS. Frederick has a warm heart——

KAMPE. And a hot temper——

HANS. Well, I might wish he hadn't come so soon. But as it couldn't be avoided——

KAMPE. All right!

EIGHTH SCENE

HANS. KAMPE. FREDERICK *enters from the right without greeting anybody.*

KAMPE. Good morning!

FREDERICK *does not reply.*

KAMPE. An extremely polite young man! How are you? And your father? How is he doing?

FREDERICK. [*To* HANS] I wanted to speak with you.

KAMPE. An extremely polite young man!

HANS. Please be quiet, dad!

KAMPE. [*To* HANS] I think you should have let me tackle this job.

HANS. But leave us now!

KAMPE. That last shot told!—Good morning!

[*Goes out through the door to the right.*

FREDERICK. Perhaps you didn't expect me?

HANS. Yes, but I wish you had waited a little.

FREDERICK. If I had not had to go with my father to the railway station, I should have been here before this.

HANS. You ought first to have thought over what I have written.

FREDERICK. I hope you don't imagine yourself able to convince me that my father is an impostor?

HANS. There is nothing said to that effect.

FREDERICK. Yes.

HANS. No.

FREDERICK. Yes, that's what it means.   But you have convinced me of something else—of what kind of fellow you are; and of the fearful—yes, the fearful—mistake I have made in regard to you.

HANS. That's the way I expected you to take it.

FREDERICK. Oh, you did?   But you didn't think it worth while to waste any explanations on me?

HANS. There were reasons for that, too.

FREDERICK. I don't doubt it.   You have proved yourself better versed in the cold art of calculation than I could ever have expected.

HANS. I knew that it must hurt you.   And so I am willing to bear with a whole lot.

FREDERICK. Oh, one who has no heart can bear with anything.—But how could you do it?   To us, who have never done you any harm?   To me—yes, to me who hardly could stay apart from you until you went abroad three years ago? And how I used to revel in the thought that you were at last coming home again!

HANS. Thank you for that, Frederick!

FREDERICK. And when you return, you hardly look at us, don't show yourself at our house—and then you send us this book, which you must have finished before you came home.

HANS. So I had.

FREDERICK. On the basis of your father's data and calculations?

HANS. On the basis of everything that was publicly available.

FREDERICK. And privately?

HANS. That, too.

FREDERICK. And you send the book to us without a word of warning—to my father, my sister, and myself.   It hurts me most for my sister's sake.

HANS. Will you let me answer?

FREDERICK. You should have seen Karen.   If you had, you might have understood what you have done.

HANS. Frederick——

FREDERICK. Could you for a moment overlook the fact that she was the one you would hit hardest?

HANS. I have said to myself that I couldn't look Karen, or you, or your father, in the eyes until I had done this.   I could not come home without having performed my unmistakable duty—no matter what the cost of it might be.

FREDERICK. Have you gone clear out of your mind?   Have you ever dreamt that any one of us would have anything to do with you after this?

HANS. I thought that I should have to give you time, until you saw more clearly what was in my mind—until you saw that I have done nothing wrong.

FREDERICK. Oh, don't put on any airs!

HANS. I saw before me—just as I have put it in my book —an expensive, a disastrous mistake, which it would be a crime to disregard any longer.   Your father has done other things of which he can be truly proud.

FREDERICK. Yes, I notice you say so.   And you think we are going to let that console us after you have taken away from him his life's greatest honour?

HANS. But if it never was an honour, Frederick?

FREDERICK. Oh, that may go down with others, but not with me.   You have an ambitious mind, and it has tempted you until you have lost all other considerations.

HANS. I may have done wrong——

FREDERICK. Indeed, you have!

HANS. But when I came home and saw my father's condition, and when I remembered that you hadn't let me have a single word of warning——

FREDERICK. Of what use would it have been?

HANS. But if it had been *your* father, and I——

FREDERICK. Now see here: don't let us compare your father and mine. That's too ridiculous!

HANS. There you see! And then you will understand, perhaps, that friendship of such a kind is something I don't care to have. And there is another thing besides.

FREDERICK. Oh, there is?

HANS. When we were children, your sister and you and I had a playmate, a little girl belonging to what they call the "lower classes." But she was as pretty a girl as I have ever seen; and she had character, too, for I have heard that she supported her mother.

FREDERICK. Now—all this is none of your concern.

HANS. It must be my concern when I try to decide whether I shall have any further acquaintance with you or not.

FREDERICK. What is that? How dare you——?

HANS. If you had married her——

FREDERICK. That's my own affair.—And it isn't true that I don't want to marry her. But others, and she among them——

HANS. Yes, she's too proud to let you marry her out of charity——

FREDERICK. Drop it! I know all about your moral discourses. And you had better clean up in front of your own door first!

HANS. I am doing my best.

FREDERICK. Oh, you are? Do you know anything about the condition of your father's accounts? They are in such shape that it will probably be necessary to have a special examination made of them.

HANS. What are you saying? My father suspected——?

FREDERICK. Well, now you know how it feels to have unpleasant things said of your father.

HANS. But this is nothing but false and unwarranted gossip!

FREDERICK. Like yours!

HANS. What? Do you mean to say that I am not telling the truth? Prove it!

FREDERICK. The proofs lie in the public documents which you garble.

HANS. Garble, you say?

FREDERICK. And do you know what more they say of your book? That it was written to cover up your father's infamy. He knew an examination would come sooner or later, and so you hurried to get out the book first—in order to make it look as if the examination had been started for the sake of revenge.

HANS. Oh, I see now! So that's the scheme! It's abominable! And it's going to send dad back into worse than madness!

FREDERICK. Did that go home? I should like to know how he gets his living now—without a pension? And I suppose others will also want to know.

HANS. This passes all limits! My father has his faults, I admit, but he is a man of honour.

FREDERICK. Ye–es!

HANS. *My* father has never seduced a poor young girl and then left her in the lurch—for the sake of his career.

FREDERICK. Hans!

HANS. He has not even let a man drown for respectability's sake.

FREDERICK. How dare you——?

HANS. Yes, and he hasn't even been capable of publicly presenting a misleading statement of his system—for honour's sake. There you have *your* family—and its morals.

FREDERICK. [*Leaps at* HANS] You deserved——

> *Silence prevails for a few moments. Then he lets go his hold.*

HANS. [*Straightening out his dress*] So you haven't outgrown those childish tricks!

FREDERICK. I beg you—don't provoke me any further!

HANS. Every time you were told the truth, you acted like that. It has formed a part of my education.

FREDERICK. Then I ought to continue it. Now you prove to me, right here on the spot, that my father publicly has given a misleading statement of his system, or you'll pay for what you said.

HANS. You have the proof of it—in my book. Do you want to see it? [*Picks up a copy of the book.*

FREDERICK. O–oh! You can't find it!

HANS. I might be a little calmer than I am—but—here it is! At the bottom of page 49.

FREDERICK. [*Takes the book*] I don't see anything.

HANS. It has been marked—not by myself, however.

FREDERICK. —A general table showing differences in weight of rails, driving-wheel momentum, dead-weight, wheel diameter——

HANS. Go on! These are the correct figures, mind you.

FREDERICK. And then—report of my father's address before the international railroad congress at Paris. Is there anything wrong about *that* also? Everybody admired him on that occasion, and it seems to me that he was an honour to the whole country.

HANS. So he was, and so I have said. But his figures are not the same as in the other place. Just hold them side by side, and you'll see. This time he had to deal with people who couldn't be fooled, and he knew it. It is clever work!

FREDERICK. Well—and what of it?

HANS. What of it? Two statements that don't tally, made the same year—and by the same man?

FREDERICK. By my father? [*He reads.*

HANS. The report says: "Corrected by the speakers."

FREDERICK. You lie!

HANS. But read for yourself, man!

FREDERICK. [*Reads*] You lie, anyhow! [*Throws the book away*] It's an infernal shameless misconstruction! My father could never be guilty of such a thing. My father is a gentleman. Never! Oh, never! [*Bursting into tears*] Why did I come here? To one like you—who has no heart and no faith! There is nothing so contemptible that your boundless ambition will stop at it. I hate you! I despise you!

[*Runs out to the right.*

HANS. Oh, I shouldn't have let myself go that far—but he goaded me on.—And there comes—? Why, Karen!

KAREN *enters from the left.*

NINTH SCENE

HANS. KAREN

KAREN. Isn't he here?

HANS. Frederick?

KAREN. Isn't he here?

HANS. No—he——

KAREN. Karl Ravn came and told me that I had better hurry up. He saw Frederick going in this direction—and something might have happened.—And hasn't Frederick been here at all?

HANS. Yes, he was here.

KAREN. And did anything happen?

HANS. Nothing that need disturb you.

KAREN. Is it true?

HANS. I assure you.

KAREN. Oh, but I was frightened!

HANS. Don't you want to rest a little?

KAREN. No.—I must ask you not to tell anybody that I have been here.　　　　　　　　　　　　　　[*Starts to go.*

HANS. Karen!

KAREN. I forbid you to speak to me that way.

HANS. I beg your pardon, Miss Riis. But the memory of our childhood came back to me so vividly—how we boys, your brother and I, would fight, and you would step in between us.

KAREN. I cannot understand how you dare to recall our childhood!

HANS. Yes, speak out, and then I can——

KAREN. I have nothing at all to say to you. I only forbid you to say anything further to *me*.　　　[*Starts to leave again.*

HANS. Karen!

KAREN. That is just what I forbid you!

HANS. I am sorry, but—I thought that *you* at least would understand that I had written nothing but what I knew to be true.

KAREN. And I understand only that nothing in the world could have tempted me into a public attack on your father—although he, too, has his faults.

HANS. Dear Karen!

KAREN. Oh, this is revolting!

HANS. But I wanted only to——

KAREN. You may attack my father as much as you please,

if *that* is what you want. But you mustn't at the same time pretend that I mean anything to you.

HANS. And yet——

KAREN. [*Deeply stirred*] Only one question, and then you can settle the matter for yourself. If it had been—not my father, but yours, would you have done it then—and done it publicly?

HANS. How could I? My own father!

KAREN. There, you see! For if—well, it isn't easy to say, but it must be said!—if a woman had been to you what—what I forbid you to speak to me of——

HANS. If she had been very dear to me——

KAREN. Then her father would also have been yours.

HANS. But let me——

KAREN. Oh, don't misunderstand me! I don't say it as a reproach—far from it. I am myself such a useless, insincere creature that it's almost a crime. But I used to look up to you, and that's why it hurts so dreadfully—not that you have attacked my father—but that not even you, Hans—I have lost the last one in whom I could believe! [*Runs out.*

HANS. But Karen! You must listen to me! It isn't kind of you! [*He suddenly stops still.*

Curtain.

ACT III

A room at the DIRECTOR-GENERAL'S.

FIRST SCENE

The hum of an animated social gathering is heard from the outside. Above a conversation carried on mainly by men rises the melody of a humorous song with its piano accompaniment. The song is followed by laughter and loud applause.

KAREN. [*Enters, followed by a maid with a tray laden with refreshments for the ladies*] Put it over there. That's right! Now, you can go in to Mr. Frederick and tell him that everything is ready for the gentlemen in the garden.

HANS *enters in evening dress and holding his hat in his hand.*

KAREN. [*As she catches sight of* HANS] Pardon me, Mr. Kampe, but this room is reserved for the family and the ladies of the house. The men's talk is becoming a little too noisy for them.

HANS. I must have a few words with you.

KAREN. You know that I don't want to listen to you.

HANS. I give you my word that I have nothing to say that you cannot listen to.

KAREN. I don't believe you! The mere fact that you and your father are here to-day implies such a—such audacity, that I am prepared for anything.

HANS. I came here only to speak to you; my father, be-

218

cause he wanted to show himself in response to the invitation
—may I not tell you——?

KAREN. You may, of course. But I may not listen to
you— There, the gentlemen are going down into the garden.

HANS. My appearance frightens you. Well, I have had
a bad time of it since I saw you last!

KAREN. You?

HANS. It is no wonder that you misunderstand me. I
have not understood myself— Yes, you may well look at me!
When I was talking to you the last time, I had not really
thought the thing out, and I gave misleading answers. There
is one point in regard to which I want to set myself right.
Won't you let me do so?

KAREN. Oh, well—if it isn't——

HANS. Don't fear! I said that if it had been my own
father instead of yours—then I should not have attacked him
publicly.

KAREN. Yes?

HANS. Now I have gone to the bottom of the thing. I
have also talked with my father about it, and he agrees with
me. If his fault had been of a public nature, and if it had
had public consequences, so that, for instance, it had caused
the country a loss of many millions, and if nobody else could
or would have stepped forward—then it would have been my
duty, my unavoidable duty, to do so, provided I possessed
the necessary qualifications.

KAREN. What in the world are you saying?

HANS. I am only saying what is right: that it would have
been my unavoidable duty.

KAREN. It's awful! You could attack your own father in
public?

HANS. Don't misunderstand me! It would have been my
duty to do so. But I could not have done it! No—and if this

book had not been written before I came home, and published before I met you again—then it would neither have been written nor published.

KAREN. Do you see now?

HANS. For I have just discovered that my passions are as strong, and my temptations as powerful, as those of my father. They were only waiting to be stirred up. I would have failed as miserably as he did, that time *he* tried to tell the truth. But if I had, it would have gone worse with me than it has gone with him.

KAREN. But, Hans!

HANS. Oh, yes, I know it. My book represented the cumulative determination of several years. To write it was to enter upon my real life-work. If I had let it go, it would have meant that I let everything go. For here lay my gift, my knowledge, my responsibility— I could never have raised my head again!

KAREN. I didn't know that!

HANS. I didn't know it myself. And still less I knew— We grew up together——

KAREN. No, Hans——

HANS. I must finish! To a certain extent I had come to take you for granted—that is, I had to a certain extent forgotten you. But ever since—ever since that moment when you ran away from me—a little while afterward—when I realised the depth of the love bestowed on me——

KAREN. No, Hans!

HANS. To discover a thing like that takes the ground from under a man's feet. I could have burned that book of mine!

KAREN. —Could you?

HANS. I could—I am ashamed to say it! I could have fallen as miserably as my father, or even worse. And you wouldn't want that, Karen?

KAREN. No, no!

HANS. Do you believe me, Karen?

KAREN. Yes.

HANS. For unless *you* believe me— You must believe that I have not betrayed you. For at that time I didn't know what you were to me. You must believe that if I had known it, then, for your sake, I could have——

KAREN. Don't say more, Hans!

HANS. You must let me make this perfectly clear to you. I must lay bare my whole vileness, the utmost extent of my shame! You could have sent me back into cowardly silence; you could have wiped out what is most myself— Oh, it's in my very blood——

KAREN. But, Hans!

HANS. Only it would have gone with me ever so much worse! For I should not have slipped down into it unawares, as my father did; no, I should have plunged into it with open-eyed, conscious surrender of everything. You must know it. Even if you despise me—if you will only believe me!

KAREN. I believe you, I believe you! That is, I believe you are speaking under the influence of a great fear!

HANS. I hope to God it is so!

KAREN. I am sure of it! You have been going around, in the shadow of those dark memories, just frightening yourself!

HANS. Do you think so?

KAREN. I am sure, I am sure! And through all of it I can see only one thing: how strong you are, how wholly yourself! Yes, it is true, Hans, that I love you!

> [*She throws herself into his arms.*

HANS. Karen——!

KAREN. I love you!

HANS. I love you!

KAREN. —Somebody's coming!

> *They slip away from each other and are standing far apart when* MRS. RIIS *opens the door.*

SECOND SCENE

MRS. RIIS. But, Karen, what has become of you? Isn't everything ready yet?

KAREN. Yes, mother, now——   [*Stops short.*

MRS. RIIS. But why don't you come and tell me then?— Have you been disputing with each other? You, too? The whole company is disputing! Have you been saying hard things to each other?—Yes, Hans, I am not pleased with you!

HANS. Mrs. Riis!

KAREN. [*Throwing her arms around her mother's neck*] Mamma!

MRS. RIIS. What is it, Karen?

> KAREN *squeezes her mother time and again.*

MRS. RIIS. But, dear, what's the matter with you? Why, I hope you haven't——?

KAREN. Yes, mamma!

MRS. RIIS. Mercy, Karen!   [*Sits down.*

KAREN. But, mamma! [*She kneels down beside her mother.*

MRS. RIIS. You shouldn't have done it.

HANS. It is my fault, Mrs. Riis.

MRS. RIIS. For it's going to be so hard on me!

> [*Begins to cry.*

KAREN. On you, mamma?

HANS. [*Speaking simultaneously with* KAREN] On you, Mrs. Riis?

MRS. RIIS. Now, he'll say that it is my fault.

HANS. Yours?

MRS. RIIS. And my family's. All my family is disloyal to him. And it's true: they are not loyal to him. But I can't help it.   [*Weeps.*

KAREN. Dear, darling mamma!

MRS. RIIS. And now the children are beginning also—! But this is something you haven't learned from me, Karen!

KAREN. Mamma!

MRS. RIIS. For it isn't fair to him, Karen; no, it isn't!

KAREN *buries her head in her mother's lap.*

MRS. RIIS. [*Patting her daughter's head*] I don't want to make you sorry. But I have to say it.

HANS. Mrs. Riis!

MRS. RIIS. This is something you shouldn't have permitted yourself, Hans. You should have controlled yourself better. And now, children, everything must be as if nothing had happened. For otherwise I should have to tell my husband about it. And, you know, I couldn't lie to him.

HANS. But why shouldn't you tell him?

MRS. RIIS. Yes—and all the blame would be put on me! And I wouldn't mind that, if he could stand it. But it would be more than he could bear. He has enough as it is, already. No, this won't do. Nothing at all has happened—do you hear what I say, children? Nothing at all!

HANS. But, Mrs. Riis?

KAREN. Mamma is right! [*Buries her head again as before.*

MRS. RIIS. Yes, I am right. And you, Hans, you mustn't take the children away from him. That you mustn't do. It isn't right, Hans.

A VOICE. [*Outside*] It's cooler here.

KAREN. [*Leaping to her feet and pointing to the left*] Go! Hurry up!

HANS. But I must talk to you!

KAREN. No, go now! [HANS *goes out, and* KAREN *embraces her mother excitedly*] Mamma!

MRS. RIIS *has got up.* KAREN *runs out to the right.*

THIRD SCENE

MRS. RIIS. MRS. OLE RAVN [*called "Aunt Ole"*]. MRS. PREUSS.

AUNT OLE. Oh, here it is! We come on our own invitation. The garden was no longer endurable, what with heat and disputatiousness.—What's the matter with you, my dear?

MRS. RIIS. Oh——

AUNT OLE. You are the sweetest little girl in the world. But your two mill-races are always going. It's your only fault.—And you, Kamma, who have such a nice husband!

MRS. RIIS. Indeed, I have, Aunt Ole. But other people are not always nice to him. That's the trouble.

AUNT OLE. Yes, Heaven knows! It's a regular scandal. But don't cry on that account. If there is anybody who knows how to manage, it's Riis. He is superior to any situation.

MRS. RIIS. Yes, there is something big about him.

AUNT OLE. Oh! Such cleverness, such tact, such good-humour! Did you notice him during the dinner?

MRS. RIIS. No, I had so much to look after.

AUNT OLE. Only yesterday I was saying to my son-in-law and to Anna: he brings more honour to your family than anybody else has ever done. But you—you peck at him like "ravens." You are what you are!

MRS. RIIS. But there is no bad intention in what they do, Aunt Ole.

AUNT OLE. Well, Heaven only knows what they are really doing.

MRS. RIIS. No, Aunt Ole, they are not bad—not one of them. They mean right.

AUNT OLE. Yes—you admire your family, of course! That's more than I can do. But it's your only fault.—Preserves! Hm! There is none who can beat you at that.

MRS. RIIS. Please, help yourself. I'll get hold of the others.   [*Goes out.*

AUNT OLE. Come on and help yourself. It's delicious! Oh, you have started already!

MRS. PREUSS. Long ago.

AUNT OLE. No, I got tired of all that talk. My ears are still ringing with it.

MRS. PREUSS. I thought it quite amusing, aunt.

AUNT OLE. Amusing? Figures can never be amusing, my girl, unless they relate to our personal affairs. And Heaven knows that often they are not amusing even then. And besides: figures and wheel diameters; figures and curves; figures and track-width, friction, deadweight—ugh! I am so full of it that I think I am going to dream of it.

MRS. PREUSS. But you too were married to an engineer, like all the rest of us.

AUNT OLE. Oh, those engineers! Especially the young ones! They are the scum of the earth!

MRS. PREUSS. But, auntie! Ha, ha, ha!

AUNT OLE. No reverence, no sense of authority! Unbelievers, all of them! And that's the reason why they are not even decent.

MRS. PREUSS. Decent?

AUNT OLE. Well, I don't call it decent to start fighting about the Director-General's system in his own house.

MRS. PREUSS. But that's just what he wanted. That's why he invited them.

AUNT OLE. The deuce he did!

MRS. PREUSS. [*Without letting herself be interrupted*] And at the table he made a speech urging them to discuss the matter to their heart's content.

AUNT OLE. Oh, you talk such an awful lot, my girl.   And if he has tact enough to appear unconcerned, does that mean that they need not show any tact at all?   But they have no upbringing.   I repeat it: they are lacking in common decency.   Those natural studies, I tell you, produce that kind of results.

MRS. PREUSS. No, auntie, that's something I have never heard before—ha, ha, ha!

AUNT OLE. Well, then you haven't heard very much.—Oh, there you are!

FOURTH SCENE

AUNT OLE.   MRS. PREUSS.   MRS. STANGE, MRS. THOMAS.   MRS. KARL RAVN. [*Later*] MRS. RIIS.

AUNT OLE. Here are some wonderful preserves.   This time Kamma has surpassed herself.

MRS. PREUSS. Auntie has got to that point, you know, when she does nothing but push her spectacles up and down.

MRS. STANGE. Are you in a bad humour, auntie?

AUNT OLE. Who?   I?   Oh, I am being driven from one end of the house to the other by all this horrible squabbling. But I told Kamma in advance: you just leave the ladies out when you give your dinner to the engineers this year.   It will be nothing but quarrelling about the new system, I said, and that's not for ladies!

EVERYBODY. Oh, yes, auntie!

MRS. KARL RAVN. [*Simultaneously with the rest*] Oh, yes, mamma!

AUNT OLE. There now! Not one of you deserved to be here!

MRS. PREUSS. But, auntie, it's a public question—and we women have also to consider it.

AUNT OLE. Without understanding a word of it. Yes, that's the way all public questions are dealt with nowadays. They are settled by those who cannot understand them.

MRS. KARL RAVN. [*Helping herself to the preserves*] But you are more excited than anybody else, mamma!

AUNT OLE. Oh, so you are there, too? Well, I'll tell you this much, though you are my daughter, that when I saw you and your husband marching along in this direction, then I felt deeply shocked. Don't you call even *that* indecent? He, who has publicly taken side against his own relative! The rest have done nothing but talk, at least.

MRS. KARL RAVN. I cannot see that this is a family question at all.

> *Gradually, as the ladies have had their fill of the preserves, they produce some kind of handiwork and begin working on it.*

AUNT OLE. Then your husband could just as well stand by the Director-General instead of siding with that drunken American.

SEVERAL OF THE LADIES. American?

AUNT OLE. Oh, well, that's what I call him. He has been out there, and he believes in no authorities. That's American, isn't it?

MRS. KARL RAVN. But the question at issue is just whether they *are* authorities.

AUNT OLE. Will *you* keep still! You and your husband, and your husband and you!

MRS. PREUSS. You are always reviling your son-in-law, auntie. Why did you accept him as such, then?

AUNT OLE. I'll tell you, my girl. When you have stupid daughters, you sometimes get a little stupid yourself. And the young fellow would do well enough, if only he were not such a scatter-brain. But how could he be otherwise? The whole family is the same way. [MRS. RIIS *comes into the room*] Every one of them—that is, with the exception of you, my dear. You are really the only well-balanced person in the whole lot. The rest are not to be endured!

MRS. RIIS. [*Earnestly*] But, auntie, you don't mean to tell us that your husband was not to be endured?

AUNT OLE. Oh, bless him for the honest soul he was! But once he marched up to the Prime Minister in his best clothes and told him that he wanted to quit: he couldn't understand his own time any longer, he said.—Well, that wasn't the only thing he did of the kind.

MRS. PREUSS. Didn't he go up to the King himself once?

AUNT OLE. Yes, he wanted him to make an artisan out of one of the Princes. It would set such a good example, he thought— There was nothing left for me but to stick to reason. All that idealism made me sea-sick.—And this much I want to tell you, my girl, that what little reason you have, you have got from me.

MRS. RIIS. What I came for was to give you my husband's regards. He had to leave with the seven o'clock train.

AUNT OLE. Now, there, so help me God, if they haven't driven him out of his own home!

MRS. RIIS. No, he had entirely forgotten a business engagement.

AUNT OLE. Twaddle! He ran away from all this engineering indecency. Riis is too refined for that kind of thing.

MRS. STANGE. Perhaps he only wanted to give the discussion free scope by keeping out of the way?

AUNT OLE. That would be just like him! Always considerate! And the others? Exactly the opposite!

MRS. RIIS. But Mr. Riis asked them himself, now when they had come together here, to talk the matter over.

AUNT OLE. Oh, you are too tedious with your constant defence of everything and everybody! It's almost impossible to talk when you are present.

MRS. RIIS. But, auntie——!

AUNT OLE. But then it's the only fault you have! Come and give me a kiss! [*They kiss each other*] There! And you are sweet to look at!

[*Pats her on the cheek. MRS. RIIS goes out.*

FIFTH SCENE

The same as before with the exception of MRS. RIIS. KARL RAVN.

KARL RAVN. Are you there?

MRS. PREUSS. Did you think she had run away?

MRS. THOMAS. Or worse?

KARL. [*Smiling*] No. But I lost sight of her entirely. And so I had to find out where she was and how she was doing.

MRS. KARL. Splendidly! That is, I should have enjoyed myself still more if they had stuck more closely to the question in hand, and not gone hunting for——

AUNT OLE. —motives. But that's just what we need to do in this case. For had that old drunkard kept his accounts in proper order, all this would never have been heard of. That's the whole thing!

MRS. KARL. There you can hear how we ladies discuss the question.

AUNT OLE. Oh, it isn't the ladies only that say this, but the whole city, the whole country perhaps.

KARL. Sh, sh, sh, sh!

SIXTH SCENE

The same as before. KAMPE.

KAMPE. Our host doesn't happen to be here?

KARL. No, he has gone away.

KAMPE. Away?   Has he gone away?

KARL. Has anything happened?

KAMPE. Oh, nothing in particular.   His son, Frederick, told me just now that—that——

SEVERAL. What was it?

KAMPE. That a special commission was to be appointed to see if my accounts were—if they were straight.

MRS. KARL. [*Rising*] Oh, they only say that kind of thing because—well, because it has to be said.

KARL. Of course!

KAMPE. He said that everybody believed it, and that everybody was talking of it.   Is it true?   I should like to know if it's true.

MRS. KARL. Oh, you shouldn't mind that kind of gossip.

KAMPE. So it is being talked of, then.   Have you heard it, madam?

AUNT OLE. I can only tell the truth: I have heard it.

KAMPE. So you have also heard it.   The young man was right, then.   So I am to be put on trial.   That, too, had to come.   Of course!

MRS. KARL. But, Mr. Kampe——

KAMPE. Yes, you mean well—with me and with my son. I thank you for it!—So old man Kampe is to be put on trial.

MRS. KARL. If you take it that way, perhaps they may accomplish what they were aiming at.

KAMPE. They will accomplish more than they have aimed at.   [*Goes out.*

MRS. KARL. Go with him, Karl. See that he gets away from here.

KARL. All right.

MRS. KARL. And if he won't—get hold of his son.

KARL. Of course.   [*Goes out.*

MRS. KARL. Oh, this is a plot!

AUNT OLE. A plot? And who has started it?

MRS. KARL RAVN *sits down again.*

MRS. PREUSS. Frederick should not have told him.

MRS. THOMAS. Least of all here!

MRS. STANGE. Frederick is so hot-tempered.

AUNT OLE. Frederick is fond of his father.

MRS. PREUSS. Yes, he is.

AUNT OLE. I don't wonder that his blood begins to boil, especially after a good dinner. He finds his father surrounded by people who envy and abuse him. And, worse yet, he finds his own relatives among those people.

MRS. PREUSS. Have we envied the Director-General?

MRS. THOMAS. Have we abused him?

MRS. PREUSS. You are using such strong terms, auntie.
                                                         [*Laughs.*

AUNT OLE. Well, I cannot call it anything else.

MRS. STANGE. Perhaps I might have a chance to say a word now?

AUNT OLE. Not by any means, my girl. For when you begin, then there is no longer any peace to be had.

MRS. PREUSS *and* MRS. THOMAS. Ha, ha, ha!

MRS. STANGE. What is that you are saying, Aunt Ole? Am I not the one who has always to fight for a little peace among us? For the peace has to be *fought* for—yes, it has, and particularly when you are with us, Aunt Ole.

MRS. PREUSS *and* MRS. THOMAS Ha, ha, ha!

AUNT OLE. Well, the idea! Do you mean to say that one who defends somebody else isn't peaceful?

MRS. STANGE. Yes, I do, for you are so hateful. You say such things behind people's backs—yes, you do, Aunt Ole!

AUNT OLE. My gracious! And here I have been sitting all day defending the Director-General against what people are saying behind his back! What was that you were saying, Anna?

MRS. KARL. [*Who has been sitting perfectly quiet beside her mother*] Nothing, mamma.

MRS. STANGE. You always say such nasty things, and you are so quick with your tongue.

AUNT OLE. Well, I am not slow and solemn as a spook——

MRS. PREUSS *and* MRS. THOMAS. Ha, ha, ha!

AUNT OLE. —but it is just against all kinds of "nastiness," as you call it, that I have been fighting ever since I came to this country.—What was that you were saying, Anna?

MRS. KARL. I? Not a word, mamma!

AUNT OLE. Oh, I can see you all right, back of those glasses of yours. And it is no use to try to hide behind your crocheting.

MRS. KARL. I am near-sighted, mamma. And that I have inherited from you.

MRS. STANGE. Yes, God knows the place is full of jealousy and backbiting. It couldn't be much worse—that's the truth of it. But we women have a part in it, too, and you, Aunt Ole, you are worse than anybody else.

MRS. PREUSS *and* MRS. THOMAS. Ha, ha, ha!

AUNT OLE. Why, you are literally quivering with ill-temper! But now I ask you all whether I am not the one who always has to defend the Director-General against the envy of his own family?

MRS. PREUSS. No, you have no right to say that.

MRS. THOMAS. No, you haven't, Aunt Ole!

MRS. STANGE. But that's the sort of thing she says all the time.

AUNT OLE. Well, well, what a stir in the hennery, just because I dare to mention the family. The miraculous family, which has patent rights on all the virtue in this country!— What was that you were saying, Anna?

MRS. KARL. Ha, ha, ha!

MRS. PREUSS. Why, Aunt Ole, you know very well that without our family the Director-General would never have reached his present high position.

AUNT OLE. Of course not! You have picked us out of the gutter, every one of us! Good gracious, that I didn't know it before I ever came here! It makes me mad to think of it. [MRS. RIIS *enters*] Oh, there you are! Well, you are the only well-behaved person in the whole lot.

MRS. RIIS. What were you talking of?

AUNT OLE. The same thing as usual, of course. I say that the family ought to be ashamed of its behaviour toward your husband. And then they reply that without the miraculous qualities of the Ravn family your husband wouldn't be anything at all.

MRS. RIIS. Oh, no, auntie; that's not what they meant.

AUNT OLE. Yes, it was! Just ask them! For on one thing they all agree—although they differ on everything else —and that is that the Ravn family alone is good for anything. —What was that you were saying?

MRS. KARL. I? It seems to me *you* were saying something.

AUNT OLE. Now, don't provoke me! I have looked over

the family carefully since this noise against the Director-General began. And I can tell you a few things about it.

MRS. PREUSS *and* MRS. THOMAS. Oh, please do, Aunt Ole!

MRS. STANGE. You are perfectly welcome.

MRS. RIIS. Dear, dear, let us keep peace in the family!

MRS. STANGE. So we do—the rest of us.

AUNT OLE. Yes, because all of you agree when it is a question of abusing him.

MRS. KARL. Then there is one more thing on which we can agree.

MRS. PREUSS. Ha, ha, ha!

AUNT OLE. And the reason is that all of you are a little cracked.

MRS. KARL. Ha, ha, ha!

MRS. STANGE *and* MRS. THOMAS. [*At the same time*] That's right, auntie!

MRS. PREUSS. Well, what else? It isn't the first time you say *that!*

AUNT OLE. Oh, isn't it?

MRS. RIIS. But, auntie, now I think you are going too far!

AUNT OLE. One goes mad with dreaming, another with doubting and brooding, a third with everlasting business speculations— Yes, you know whom I have in mind.

MRS. STANGE. Now, Aunt Ole, you had better stop!

AUNT OLE. You are not going to fight me, are you? It would be the only thing wanting!—A fourth one goes mad with inventions and all sorts of similar tomfoolery. And the fifth——

MRS. KARL. Ha, ha, ha!

MRS. PREUSS *and* MRS. THOMAS. [*Together*] No, please, let us have the fifth one also.

MRS. STANGE. [*At the same time as the other two*] I know whom you mean, and it isn't nice of you!

AUNT OLE. The fifth one does missionary work for peace and love.

MRS. RIIS. Yes, love, Aunt Ole—you should abide in love.

AUNT OLE. Oh, don't bother me with your love nonsense! You are just the fifth kind. And the most tedious of the whole lot at that.

MRS. KARL, MRS. PREUSS, MRS. THOMAS. Ha, ha, ha!

MRS. STANGE. [*At the same time*] But a little while ago you said——

AUNT OLE. You, too—imp that you are!

ALL. [*except* MRS. RIIS] Ha, ha, ha!
  Loud talking is heard from the outside.

AUNT OLE. Mercy me, here they come—even here! Where in the world càn we turn to get a moment's peace? [*Everybody rises*] How about the bedrooms—I suppose they keep out of them?

ALL. [*except* MRS. RIIS] Ha, ha, ha! [AUNT OLE *laughs also.*

MRS. KARL. [*As they are going out*] Yes, that's the way *we* discuss this railroad question!

ALL. [*including* AUNT OLE] Ha, ha, ha, ha!
                        [*They go out to the left.*

SEVENTH SCENE

KAHRS *and* PREUSS *appear on one side of the* CHAIR-
MAN OF THE RAILROAD COMMITTEE; *on the other
side of him are* LANGE *and* KRAFT.

KAHRS. But it's the proofs that have to be weighed.

LANGE. But when proof is put against proof?

PREUSS. Figures! I want figures! For figures cannot lie.

KRAFT. But when there are figures on both sides?

KAHRS. Why, it is just your proofs and your figures that Hans Kampe has turned upside down.

LANGE. Not one of them! His premises are wrong.

PREUSS. His premises are in the official documents.

LANGE. But it's no good as evidence. The peculiarity of the country——

KRAFT. And of the traffic, too.

PREUSS. Well, let's take the Southern Railroad. There Kampe has proved——

LANGE. But that's just where Larssen has proved——

CHAIRMAN. Gentlemen!

KAHRS. A calculation made by old Kampe is not the same thing as one made by a man in Larssen's position——

PREUSS *and* KRAFT. What is that you say?

LANGE. I believe in the accuracy of Larssen as I believe in——

PREUSS. In God, I suppose?

LANGE. —in a mathematical demonstration. That's what I do!

EIGHTH SCENE

Those already on the stage are joined by LARSSEN, CANAL INSPECTOR RAVN, *and* KARL RAVN. *Two conversations are carried on simultaneously: one by the previous group, gathered on one side in the foreground and speaking in lowered voices; the other by the newcomers, who pass slowly down the stage toward the footlights.*

[*First group.*]

KAHRS. No, you had better place your trust in the reports of the operating engineers.

KRAFT. What of them?

PREUSS. Those reports have now been analysed in a way that leaves no loophole.

KRAFT. Yes, and the man who has done it is that shrewd fellow over there, the brother-in-law of the Director-General.

LANGE. That's another piece of falsehood, I tell you!

PREUSS. And I tell you that you no longer know what you are saying!

CHAIRMAN OF THE RAILROAD COMMITTEE. Gentlemen!

LANGE. Nobody doubts that we are now confronted by a plot which is directed by a drunkard and secretly nursed by family dissensions.

[*Second group, speaking more loudly.*]

RAVN. Why don't you come to me some day and have a look at it? I have made a compilation of the reports by the operating engineers.

LARSSEN. So have we.

RAVN. But not in the same way. Come and look at it.

LARSSEN. I will, since you permit me.

RAVN. I know you care for nothing but the truth of the matter.

LARSSEN. I hope so, Mr. Ravn.

> KARL RAVN *has gradually approached the whispering
> group.*

KARL. [*Jocularly*] Family dissensions? Above all, speak up!

LANGE. [*Aloud*] Well, I am not afraid of doing so. Every matter has to be searched down to its moral ramifications. Our small circumstances permit this—and it is a great advantage.

KARL. It's thoroughly national, at least.

PREUSS. Apparently it is part of our patriotic feelings.

LANGE. Don't mention such a thing! If there were any

patriotic feelings among us, we would at least stick up for what is known to belong to ourselves.

RAVN. That is to say, for our mistakes?

LANGE. And what are you sticking up for?   The delirious ravings of a drunkard!

CHAIRMAN OF RAILROAD COMMITTEE. Pardon me, but my work in the Diet has accustomed me to insist on a certain parliamentary moderation.

LANGE. But even in the Diet you can tell the truth.

CHAIRMAN. [Smilingly] No, that's exactly what you cannot do in the Diet.

SEVERAL. Ha, ha, ha!

KRAFT. Speaking of the Diet—how do they feel about it there?   What do you think they will decide on?

CHAIRMAN. Well, it isn't easy for the Diet to decide as long as the experts remain divided among themselves.

PREUSS. So you regard those who are directly connected with the railroads as experts?

KAHRS. That's an abominable piece of rudeness!

KRAFT. Yes, it's "abominable," indeed!—But what do you think will be the decision of the Diet?

RAVN. Why, that's easy to foretell.   The Diet has two roads to deal with.   They will vote on one of them according to the new system, and on the other according to the old.

CHAIRMAN. Then the principle of the matter would still remain undetermined.

RAVN. Exactly!   What the devil is ever settled on principle among us?

KARL. O-oh—now you're "seeing black" again, Father Ravn!

LARSSEN. [Who has approached the CHAIRMAN] But, if you permit me to say so: two diametrically opposed things cannot be true at one and the same time?

NINTH SCENE

The same as before. KAMPE.

KAMPE. Here's a merry old bird for you!

KARL. Why, is he still here?

PREUSS. And drunk?—They said he had straightened up?

KAHRS. He didn't touch his glass during the dinner.

KAMPE. [*Singing*] Gaudeamus igitur, juvenes dum sumus——

LANGE. [*Speaking simultaneously with* KAMPE *to the* CHAIRMAN] Permit me to introduce the man who is at the bottom of this whole thing.

CHAIRMAN. Has he fallen as deep as that?

LANGE. Yes, he has made good headway in a few years.

KAMPE. Gaudeamus igitur, juvenes dum sumus——

RAVN. What does this mean?

KAMPE. It's me, old man! Magnus Holm Kampe.

> RAVN *is seen to whisper to* KARL, *who leaves the room hurriedly.*

LARSSEN. [*Who has again approached the* CHAIRMAN] If you'll excuse me, two diametrically opposed things cannot be true at one and the same time.

KAMPE. Well, if it isn't—(*mimicking* LARSSEN] His Excellency the Principle is here also—ye-es!

LANGE. [*To* KRAFT] Oh, please, get the whole railroad committee in here, won't you!

KRAFT. In a moment. That's a good idea.

LANGE. And ask Frederick Riis to give you a hand.

KRAFT. I will!

> *Goes out; in the meantime* FREDERICK RAVN *has tried to pull* KAMPE *aside and to whisper to him.*

KAMPE. Nonsense! [RAVN *whispers to him again;* KAMPE

bursts into laughter] All of you are nothing but a lot of school-boys compared with my son. [RAVN *is whispering to him again*] Harm? No harm can come to him. He'll be director-general and minister, too, no matter what you cook up. Ha, ha! Gaudeamus igitur——

LANGE. [*To the* CHAIRMAN] Do you hear what they are aiming at?

CHAIRMAN. I do.

RAVN. Oh, he's spoiling everything! What has become of Hans?

PREUSS. I will——

RAVN. I have sent Karl after him. But you might try also.

PREUSS. [*Hurrying out, meets in the doorway some men who are trying to get in*] Nobody can get in here! There is nothing to see!

FREDERICK RIIS. [*Appearing from the outside*] What do you mean? Do you want to stop us from going in?

PREUSS *hurries off.   The others come into the room.*

KAMPE. [*Who in the meantime has been surveying the company with a smiling face*] All of you look so sour. Do as I do: put on a little night-cap, and then the world becomes livable—ye-es!

FREDERICK. Good!

KAMPE. Isn't it true, Lange? Oh, you're a stiff one, you are. You're the personified wheel-and-axle friction, that's what you are. You're equal to 0 multiplied by f-one plus f-two-r divided by R.

ALL. Bravo!   [*They applaud.*

KAMPE. Why should we engineers get angry? What's the use of having a state, if it doesn't pay for our stupidities? [*He laughs; some laugh with him*] Isn't that so, you—Mr. Principle? [*He pokes at* LARSSEN] Brrrr!

FREDERICK. But the Diet, Father Kampe, hasn't that to control——?

KAMPE. The Diet? What does the cat know about mustard? Are those who sit in it engineers, do you think? Chatterboxes, that's what they are. [*Laughs.*

SEVERAL ENGINEERS. Bravo, bravo!

RAVN. Shame on you, Kampe!

KAMPE. Shame? Did anybody say shame?

RAVN. Come along with me now!

KAMPE. If this were a big country—then I would be minister of public works—and you? My secretary! [*Laughs.*

ONE OF THE ENGINEERS. Listen to him!

SEVERAL. Bravo, bravo!

KAMPE. And do you know what you would be then?

SEVERAL. No.

KAMPE. Nice little boys—nothing at all.

SEVERAL. Bravo, Kampe!

KAREN. [*Has entered and pushes through to the front*] What is it? Oh, can't you get him away?

RAVN. Impossible!

KAMPE. [*Who has been looking for something in his notebook*] Now, you'll hear something—or perhaps you have heard it before?

SEVERAL. No!

LANGE. [*To the* CHAIRMAN] Twenty times at least. He always reads it when he gets drunk.

KAMPE. [*Reading*]

> "Wide horizons, small conditions:
> There your gifts will lift you upward.
> Small conditions, close horizons:
> There your faults will drag you downward."

[*Speaking*] I won't have anybody laugh at that.

KAREN. But can't you speak to him?

RAVN. Oh, I have tried it!

KAREN. Frederick!

FREDERICK *doesn't hear.*

KAMPE. [*Reading*]

"Greatest ship in windless waters
　　Rots until it falls to pieces."

SEVERAL. [*Laughing*] Bravo!

RAVN. There is Hans now!

HANS, KARL RAVN, *and* PREUSS *come into the room.*

KAREN. [*Meeting* HANS] Hans!

KAMPE. Hans?—Oh, come here, my boy! Look at him! Get out of the way for him.

HANS. But, dad!

KAMPE. Ye-es——?

HANS. But, dad!

KAMPE. Yes, what's the matter! Won't you look happy, please? I am so happy when I look at you!

HANS. Don't you remember what you have promised me?

KAMPE. I? Promised you?

HANS. Don't you remember?

KAMPE. [*A cry escapes him. Then he whispers*] That's so!

[*He has to be supported by several of those around him.*

RAVN. Give him some water!

KAREN. [*Who has hurried over to the ladies' table, where she finds a water-bottle and glasses*] Here it is.

HANS. Thank you, Karen!

KAREN. Drink a little.

KAMPE. No—I don't need it—it was only——

RAVN. Now he's sober again.

HANS. What was it?

KAMPE. It was only my memory that came back.

HANS. But what has happened? When I saw you last, you seemed so happy and satisfied.

SEVERAL. Yes.

KAMPE. Well, you see, it was Frederick Riis——

KAREN. You?

KAMPE. He told me—that my accounts were to be—that there was to be a special commission——

KAREN. But, Frederick!

KAMPE. A special commission to examine my accounts. Ordinary examination was not enough.

KAREN. [*Whispering*] Oh, Frederick!

KAMPE. Well—and that was too much for me. And so I forgot you, Hans—and what I had promised you. A wretch like me shouldn't give any promises.

HANS. There is such a crowd here. Come, now, and let us——

KAMPE. No, let them hear! They have witnessed my shame. I have been a traitor to you. Let them hear me say so.

HANS. But, dad!

KAMPE. To-morrow, it will be all over the city. I, your father, have spoiled everything for you.

HANS. Dad!

KAMPE. I can't be helped. You go your way. Don't stay here any longer.

HANS. [*Close to him*] Yes, I will.

KAMPE. Sh—don't say that!

HANS. Yes, I'll never leave you!

KAMPE. You won't, Hans? You won't?

HANS. Not for anything in the world!

CHAIRMAN. There's character in those two fellows!

KAMPE. Hans, do you dare to trust me once more?

HANS. Now more than ever.

KAMPE. Then I'll promise you—No, I'll promise nothing. But I'll beg of you: please, stay by me!—And what had become of you anyhow?

HANS. I had my own sorrow.

KAMPE. You?—Who dares to cause you any sorrow?

HANS. Come now and let us go home.

KAMPE. All right.   Can you forgive me?

HANS. That I forgot you for a moment!—Come, now!

> [*They go out arm in arm.*

Curtain.

ACT IV

A living-room at the Director-General's.

FIRST SCENE

*Riis is dressed in black and wears a number of decora-
tions. Mrs. Riis wears a rich dress, but all black.*

Mrs. Riis. [*Reading*] "For it is upon your own hearts
that you must keep watch. This is neglected by the children
of the world. They have so many things that take them out
of themselves. And if a reminder should reach them, they
seek diversion, or, if forced into a reckoning, they try to put
the fault on some one else. At the best, they strive to set
themselves right, although we can accomplish nothing by our
own powers."

Riis. Quite right! By our own powers we can accomplish
nothing, indeed! See here, Kamma, it's late already, and
the services will last for some time—hadn't we better have
a bite before we start?

Mrs. Riis. But you know, dear, that we never eat before
we receive communion. It seems as if we were a little more
ready for it, then.

Riis. Well, as you say—Yes, yes! How would it be if we
could not find religious consolation against the inconstancy
and treachery of the world!—I suppose the debate in the Diet
is at its hottest just now.

Mrs. Riis. Don't let us be thinking of the Diet, dear.
245

These decisions that are nothing but human devices, what do they amount to?

Riis. You are right, dear girl, you are right! That was an extremely comforting book, out of which you were reading to me. Nothing that we human creatures devise is good for anything. Oh, if it were possible to rid oneself of it altogether, to get away from it entirely!

Mrs. Riis. Are you now thinking of the life that comes after death, dear?

Riis. Well, not death exactly—but peace, rest.

Mrs. Riis. Yes, you certainly need a little rest, you who have worked so hard.—But why, then, don't you resign?

Riis. What makes you think of it? Who has been talking of it?

Mrs. Riis. Nobody, as far as I can remember.

Riis. Yes, it must have been somebody. Try to remember. —Frederick?

Mrs. Riis. Oh, Frederick is saying so many things these days. He isn't himself any longer.

Riis. He is no longer wholly loyal to his father. That's what's the matter with Frederick, my dear.

Mrs. Riis. Don't say so, dear! Frederick is having a struggle of his own, now.

Riis. Well, don't let us talk of it just now. Let us fix our minds on something that brings peace with it.

Mrs. Riis. Do you want me to read a little more?

Riis. Oh, no! Although it's an excellent book.

Mrs. Riis. Perhaps you want to read it yourself?

Riis. Oh, no! Hadn't we better start soon?

[*Looks at his watch.*

Mrs. Riis. Why, it won't begin for an hour yet.

Riis. But isn't it customary to get there a little early?

Mrs. Riis. Yes.

RIIS. It is as if one could manage one's thoughts better in the church—I can't keep it out of my mind: after all, it's my life-work they are discussing in the Diet now.

MRS. RIIS. I think what shows your greatness, dear, is just that while they are persecuting and tormenting you, you pursue your way calmly toward the only thing that can bring you peace.

RIIS. But it's hard to bear the thought that our children will not be with us.   Holste is a fortunate man, he is.   He will be surrounded by all that belong to him.   It is as if I had built up nothing, brought nothing together.

MRS. RIIS. How can you talk like that?   As for the Holstes, it is her work more than his.   Magda is so much stronger and more capable than I am.

RIIS. Don't let it worry you, my dear.   I am sure you have done all you could.   But I really think the children ought to have gone along for *your* sake.

MRS. RIIS. Oh, they are not accustomed to pay much attention to me.

RIIS. Don't say that!   Don't say that!

MRS. RIIS. I can't say how it hurts me that I cannot make them stay by you just now.

RIIS. You're loyal, Kamma!   But don't cry now!   It will show!

MRS. RIIS. I have no such gifts as you and the children.

RIIS. But you have a heart—that's what you have!   Much will be different hereafter.   I have thought it all over.   And I have not always been what I ought to have been.

[*Gives her his hand.*

MRS. RIIS. Dearest dear!

RIIS. But don't cry now!   People will misunderstand.— Couldn't we talk of something else now?

MRS. RIIS. Yes, but there are the children now.

SECOND SCENE

RIIS.   MRS. RIIS.   FREDERICK.   KAREN.

RIIS. That's right, children! You are coming with us, after all?

MRS. RIIS. I knew they would! But you don't look well, Karen!

RIIS. I suppose you have been unable to sleep again? But how is it going to end, child, if you don't get any sleep? Tell me!

MRS. RIIS. Come with us to-day. *That* will bring you the peace you are looking for.

KAREN. I should like to. But I cannot. Not just now.

RIIS. What is the matter with you? Have you two heard anything? They can't have come to a decision in the Diet yet?

FREDERICK. In the Diet? I haven't been near it.

RIIS. Oh, you haven't?

MRS. RIIS. It is much better that Frederick should stay with *us*. You must stand by your father in days like these, Frederick.

RIIS. Oh, there's no reason why he should consider me at all! If his own heart doesn't make him find out what is happening to his father——

MRS. RIIS. Say rather: if it doesn't make him go to church with his father.

RIIS. You are right—rather that!

MRS. RIIS. One has to make some sacrifice for one's own father.

RIIS. Not at all! I have already declared that nobody need do anything for me. He has his full freedom.

MRS. RIIS. That's splendid of you, dear—but children may have a little too much freedom.

RIIS. Love must be free, unconditional.

KAREN. That's just what Frederick wanted to talk with you about, papa.

RIIS. [*Surprised*] About what?

KAREN. About his love—for Anna.

RIIS. I think both of you——!

MRS. RIIS. But Karen, dear—don't!

RIIS. And that's what you are coming with *now!*

MRS. RIIS. Really, you shouldn't!

FREDERICK. We thought, Karen and I——

MRS. RIIS. Hush!

FREDERICK. We thought that to-day, when you have both prepared yourself and are going to——

RIIS. Then we are to be upset, of course!

MRS. RIIS. Now you are really tormenting your father!

RIIS. Don't you think I have enough as it is? Do you think it is so very easy, my dear Frederick, to keep my thoughts on higher matters just now—in the midst of a persecution which at this time, perhaps at this very moment——

MRS. RIIS. Haven't you common sense, Frederick? You must show some consideration!

RIIS. Oh, oh!

FREDERICK. I thought that on a day like this your minds might be more open to what is stirring me most deeply.

RIIS. So that's what's stirring you?

MRS. RIIS. And not the thought of your father?

RIIS. Oh, my dear, don't mention *me!*

FREDERICK. Papa, if I am to be good for anything, I have to begin with this. I see that now.

RIIS. Oh, with this!

MRS. RIIS. You should begin with your father, with love and trust for him!

RIIS. Oh, *that's* of no importance!—But this other thing! Then I am sure you'll go far! Merciful heavens, then *nothing* will become of you! You'll spoil your career, waste your whole future! Why—a seamstress!

KAREN. Yes, but a good girl, papa!

RIIS. Good? She? I am astonished at you, Karen. How could she be good, who— [*With a glance at his wife, in a low voice*] Oh, that's right!—[*Aloud*] Nobody can be called good who wants to force herself upon a respectable family.

FREDERICK. But she doesn't want to.

KAREN. [*Simultaneously*] No, that's just what she doesn't want. She is determined to go to her relatives in America. She doesn't want us to do anything out of pity. She *is* a good girl!

RIIS. So much the better! Then it's all settled. When she herself doesn't want it?

MRS. RIIS. I think so, too. Since she is going anyhow.

FREDERICK. Yes, but *I* want it! And in order to win her around, I must be able to say: My parents have nothing against you; my parents are kind and good.—If you could only understand—I can't put it in words!

RIIS. No, you had better control yourself, Frederick.

KAREN. But I, who have seen them together, I understand.

RIIS. You are feverish, Karen. I think you ought really to be in bed.—Now, don't let us do anything quickly in this matter. If it is possible, children, let us choose some other time.

MRS. RIIS. Your father and I are going to church. [*She goes over to her husband*] But for that matter, dearest, I think that when they really love each other, then— Why, bless your heart, it's love that is the greatest thing of all.

RIIS. Yes, Frederick *says* he loves her. But then Frederick says also he loves us.

MRS. RIIS. So he does.

RIIS. And he hasn't even thought of going up to the Diet to find out what is becoming of his father's life-work. That shows how great his love is!

FREDERICK. Papa!

RIIS. I don't think, my dear, that we need to be alarmed by his declarations of love—not even when they concern others than ourselves.

FREDERICK. Papa!

KAREN. Oh, don't take it that way!

RIIS. How am I to take it, then? Perhaps I should respect an affair like this last one of Frederick's?

FREDERICK. Papa!

RIIS. Oh, you may as well hear the truth!

FREDERICK. If it only were the truth!

RIIS. What was that you said?   [*General silence follows.*

MRS. RIIS. Go away, now, Frederick.

KAREN. No, papa, I cannot bear this thing any longer.

RIIS. You cannot? Oh, you are sick—that's what is the matter with you.

KAREN. Yes, I am sick. But I am sick because it is impossible for us to deal truthfully with each other——

RIIS. Oh, are we back there again?

MRS. RIIS. Now, dearest!

RIIS. Yes, I'll try not to lose my patience!—I assure you, Karen, that all this talk about sincerity and truth is nothing but phrases.

KAREN. Phrases? That?

MRS. RIIS. But, dear——

Riis. Well, now don't misunderstand me. I don't know exactly how to put it— But you see, don't you, that I have made some headway in the world after all? Haven't I? Well, don't you think I have some idea of how it has happened?

Mrs. Riis. Of course, dear!

Riis. But do you think I have made my way as far as I have by going around to all sorts of people and telling them the truth? No; had I done that, I shouldn't have gone very far.

Karen. That isn't what I mean either.

Riis. Well, what *do* you mean?—Oh, is there never going to be an end to this?

Karen. I mean that among ourselves, to ourselves——

Riis. Well, what's the matter with ourselves?

Karen. Why, I am not sure I can tell—not now. I am so—I am so kind of——

Mrs. Riis. But I can, dear. It is true—yes, it is—that our life is not given to truth and love. No, it isn't!

Riis. Yes, when everything gets mixed up, then *you* have to take a hand. Then it's your chance.

Mrs. Riis. Dear!

Riis. I beg your pardon—all I meant was that, as far as the truth is concerned, we don't know what we are talking of.

Mrs. Riis. Yes, we do.

Riis. Wait a moment. I am a mathematician, and I am accustomed to exactness. Do you think anybody is absolutely truthful?

Mrs. Riis. Yes, dear.

Riis. Why, where's your head?—Oh, I beg your pardon— but let us consider any kind of relationship you please. Let us turn to the very highest—to the highest of all—to the King and our relation to him. He makes speeches to us, and

we make speeches to him. Suppose he should tell us just
what he thinks of us, or we were to let him know all we happen to think of him? Why, the law won't permit it even!
We would be punished for doing it. And rightly, too. And
as for him? If he won't be satisfied with paying us compliments, he has to speak through his ministers—and they are
not the kind of people that say too much. Or let us consider
another relationship—with the church.

MRS. RIIS. Why, that's sincere, isn't it?

RIIS. Of course. So is everything else. But suppose our
minister, instead of telling us what the Bible and his oath of
office prescribe, should begin to talk of his own doubts—
and who is entirely free from them? Wouldn't that make a
nice little rumpus?—although, of course, it would be nothing
but the truth! And we, too, if we should begin to vent our
doubts, one more loudly than the other? Why, the result
would be such a Babel that nobody in the whole world could
hear himself think! No, the only way is to let the world
run in accordance with custom and law—here a little more,
there a little less. The main thing is that it does run. And
if you want order in it—why, then it *is* in order.

KAREN. But, papa——

RIIS. Oh, you are sick! But am I not right? Now, look
at us here, for instance.

MRS. RIIS. But really, dear, we tell each other the truth.

RIIS. Oh, we do, do we? Suppose I were to tell you the
truth, the whole, unqualified truth—why, we shouldn't be
living together another day——

MRS. RIIS. But now, dear!

KAREN. [*Speaking simultaneously with Mrs. Riis*] You
don't mean it, papa!

RIIS. ——in peace, I mean. And vice versa also. Not
because you or I are worse than others. Perhaps we are bet-

ter than most. But if everything is to be blurted out, then it all goes to pieces—family, society, nation, church, everything would go to pieces. Yes, we should be reduced to mere animals—for as a rule it would be nothing but the animal in us that spoke.

KAREN. But listen to me—all that is not what I am thinking of.

MRS. RIIS. No, it is not what we are thinking of.

RIIS. No, that is not what you are thinking of, when it is placed before you in its proper light. I knew that, of course. But now perhaps you can perceive what lies hidden beneath those insidious phrases.—Life is so far from being based on truth that, instead, all its fundamental relations are based on a tacit agreement never to let the whole truth out. To be more truthful than custom demands is nonsensical, unmannerly, stupid—perhaps even dangerous.

KAREN. But just let me answer——

RIIS. Wait a moment. The art of life, the great art of living, is a question of balance, of strategy—no, strategy is so often misused: let me stick to balance.

MRS. RIIS. But, dear!

RIIS. Oh, lord, haven't I for so many years been dealing with people both above and below myself? I ought to know how the thing is to be managed. Now, *this—is—the—thing:* not to "queer" yourself. Of course, you shouldn't do anything that is wrong either. It is a great foolishness to do anything wrong. And then, of course, it is against the law——

MRS. RIIS. And against what we were taught in our childhood.

RIIS. And what we were taught in our childhood also, of course. But *this—is—the—thing:* to get out of everything in an easy, proper, gentlemanly way.—Prrrr!

FREDERICK. And may I ask what is the meaning of all this? The application?

RIIS. This is the meaning and the application: you have been guilty of a piece of foolishness— [*Coming closer to* FREDERICK] and I suppose it was "sincere" enough of its kind.

FREDERICK. Papa!

RIIS. And undoubtedly your marrying her would also be "sincere"—I have not the slightest doubt!

FREDERICK. Oh, papa, please!

RIIS. But it would only be another piece of foolishness. Which means that it wouldn't lead anywhere in particular— except up into the air, into the blue. And there it's very hard to keep one's balance.

MRS. RIIS. I think it's time for us to start now, dear.

RIIS. Right you are!—Well, this was not what ought to have been occupying our minds, but I suppose it will prove useful in some way. And it has helped to take my mind off other things. Yes, yes!—Oh, Frederick, help me on with my coat, please!—and go up to the Diet and find how soon they are likely to come to a decision.—I shouldn't won- der if my friends proved to be in the majority, after all. And, speaking quite frankly, do you think that would be the case if I had begun life as you now want to begin it?—Pull down the coat a little behind—that's it.

MRS. RIIS. Now, dear, you must come.

RIIS. Yes, yes. Oh, well, there is no time to prepare oneself as one ought to. Good-bye, children. May God be with you!

[KAREN *breaks into hysterical laughter.*

RIIS. What is it?

MRS. RIIS. [*Speaking simultaneously with Riis*] Karen!

FREDERICK. I expected it!

KAREN. Ha, ha, ha, ha, ha, ha, ha!

The scene changes to the room at KAMPE's *as before in Act I.*

THIRD SCENE

Hans is working at the table. Larssen comes in.

Larssen. I beg your pardon!

Hans. Glad to see you! [*Rising*] You look hot. Perhaps you'll let me——

Larssen. Nothing at all, thank you.

Hans. But won't you——?

Larssen. No, thank you.

Hans. Won't you sit down?

Larssen. Thank you, I will in a moment——   [*Pause.*

Hans. Perhaps it's my father you are looking for, Mr. Larssen.

Larssen. No.   [*Pause.*

Hans. Have you been listening to the debate in the Diet?

Larssen. [*After a moment's hesitation*] Yes.

Hans. Nothing has been settled yet?

Larssen. No——

Hans. But I cannot do anything about that, can I?

Larssen. Oh, you cannot?—Will you let me have a look at the French—at the verified French report of the speech made by the Director-General before the Railroad Congress?

Hans. It is quoted in my book.

Larssen. I know. But in this case it is a question of the authentic document. That is to say, in so far as *that* can prove anything.

Hans. Why, as it happens, I have just been using the publication in question——   [*Goes over to the table.*

Larssen. [*Following him*] Would you let me look at it?

Hans. You're welcome.

Larssen. Will you permit me to sit down?

Hans. Of course.

LARSSEN. Thank you. [*Sits down*] Oh, this is the publication? [*Examining the outside of it carefully*] French? Yes. Paris. Hm!

> *He studies the imprint, the list of contents, the date of publication, and finally he reads a little here and a little there, frequently comparing one passage with another.*

HANS. [*To himself*] I think he is making a comparison of the print—as if he believed I might have inserted something. [*Aloud*] You see that marked passage——?

LARSSEN. Yes, I see.

HANS. Perhaps you would like to see how I have translated it. [*Picks up a copy of his book.*

LARSSEN. Thank you.

HANS. Page 49, farthest down—the marked passage.

LARSSEN. I have it. [*Begins to compare.*

HANS. Have you found any mistakes?

LARSSEN. Not yet.

HANS. Well, I don't think you will.

> LARSSEN *puts away the book with a sigh and buries himself in the French publication again.*

HANS. Well, I don't think you will find it necessary to read the rest. It's only the marked place that counts. But it is enough.

LARSSEN. If it were correct—it would be enough.

HANS. If it were correct?—Don't you believe it?

LARSSEN. No.

HANS. But, my dear Mr. Larssen, don't you see that the report was taken down on the spot and approved by the speaker himself?

LARSSEN. So it says.

HANS. And still you do not believe?

LARSSEN. No.

HANS. Do you think that the publication, as a whole or in part, has been tampered with? Do you think the report is forged?

LARSSEN. I don't know— But I have perfect faith in the Director-General.

HANS. You're welcome to it!

LARSSEN. I might say that he is too moral a man, too respectable, too trustworthy, to do such a thing. But employed in such a manner, my words would imply an insult. I am satisfied with saying that he is too clever a man—by far too clever—to do such a thing. He is the cleverest man I have ever met.

HANS. Yes, he's clever. But if you——

LARSSEN. I have no intention of entering upon any argument. Neither with you, nor with anybody else. I believe what I believe.

HANS. And not what you see?

LARSSEN. I have seen nothing.

HANS. Why, that beats everything! When his own words —words authorized by himself——

LARSSEN. I have not seen them. For I dare not say that I have seen a thing until that thing has been *investigated.*— Will you let me borrow this publication?

HANS. With pleasure.

LARSSEN. Thank you!   [*Takes the publication.*

HANS. But—only on one condition——

LARSSEN. N-n-no. I will not be entangled by any kind of condition. I will promise nothing.

                    [*Puts the publication back on the table.*

HANS. It is not a difficult promise. Only that you are to acknowledge it openly if you find what I have found.

LARSSEN. [*Picking up the publication again*] I don't promise what is a foregone conclusion.   I have no desire to deceive anybody.   Neither anybody else nor myself.   Good-bye.

> [*He takes his hat.*

HANS. I believe that of you, Mr. Larssen.

LARSSEN. I am not at all in need of such an expression on your part.   [*Turns to go and runs into* FREDERICK RAVN.

FOURTH SCENE

HANS. LARSSEN. RAVN.

RAVN. Why, I declare!   This is a collision of two principles.

LARSSEN. [*Returning*] I must protest against any kind of insulting remarks—particularly from you!

RAVN. What's the matter with you?   Insulting remarks?

LARSSEN. I am no principle.   Even if I possess sufficient self-control to observe certain established rules, I am no principle.   I am a living human being.

RAVN. Well, if you say so yourself, I suppose we must believe it.

LARSSEN. [*Returning once more*] So you haven't known before that I was a living human being?

RAVN. Oh, yes, yes, yes!

LARSSEN. Oh, you really have!   [*Goes out.*

RAVN *and* HANS. [*Simultaneously*] Ha, ha, ha!

RAVN. What has happened?

HANS. I have to ask that!   For he was excited before he came here.   He came from the Diet.

RAVN. I saw him.   What did he come for?

HANS. For that French publication which——

RAVN. Oh-h!   Then I understand.

HANS. What?

RAVN. A speech by the Chairman of the Railroad Committee.

HANS. Oh, is that so? But, dear man, why are *you* here? Now? When they are in session?

RAVN. Oh, we have adjourned for an hour. Give me a glass of water!

HANS. There you are! Nothing else?

RAVN. No, thank you.

HANS. Have you spoken?

RAVN. The Chairman of the Railroad Committee has spoken.

HANS. Yes, of course.

RAVN. You don't understand. He is almost on your side. He has changed front.

HANS. Changed front? The Chairman of the Railroad Committee?

RAVN. That is to say, to some extent. I don't think we can get him beyond that point. But it is an event as it is.

HANS. I should say so! And what has caused it? The campaign in the press?

RAVN. Do you call it a campaign? Then you must be easily satisfied. No, in our conditions that kind of thing is entirely the result of casual personal contacts and impressions. His change of heart dates back to the dinner which the Director-General gave to the engineers.

HANS. But how can that be?

RAVN. There he saw your father and yourself together, and what he saw made him trust you. That's what he hadn't done before.

HANS. There now!

RAVN. Don't cry victory yet, my boy.

HANS. But then you will speak also?

RAVN. The Chairman has, in the main, said all I should have to say.

HANS. But nevertheless?

RAVN. Frankly speaking, Hans, I don't care to appear publicly in opposition to my brother-in-law.

HANS. What do you mean?

RAVN. Nobody should be driven into doing what is against his nature. And I don't like to stir up scandal— Your drinking water is very good.

HANS. But you must vote at least?

RAVN. I think I shall stay away. It was to tell you that I came here.—Have you a cigar to give me?—Thanks.—What's the use of your standing there making eyes at me? Privately I can very well be against him, and I am. Publicly I keep my mouth shut—just because I am against him. This is the more dignified way, or rather, it's the only one.

HANS. And the country?

RAVN. The country, the country? Are there, then, no private circumstances within it? Even stupidities involve the honour and welfare of numerous families. And such things are more important than money.

HANS. But back of the money we find——

RAVN. —the taxpayers. A very distant relationship, which they themselves often don't realise— Oh, of course, I don't mean that the stupidities are to be preserved for all eternity. All I mean is that we shouldn't delve too much in everything, and thereby make the trouble still worse. It comes out all right in the end, if we only give it time. I am growing tired of the whole job.

HANS. They tell me that you are brother-in-law to the stupidities——

RAVN. What is that you are saying?

HANS. —and also their godfather.

RAVN. I?

HANS. You were the man who got them praised abroad.

For from abroad must come whatever is to succeed here. And in this case the success was so marked that it made even you hesitate. But you kept silent. And your silence was very expensive—to yourself and to the country alike.

RAVN. How the devil did you get hold of that?—Oh, this cigar is too damned strong!   [*Throws it away.*

HANS. Now I expect nothing less of you than that you return to the Diet and confess your own share in the mischief made——

RAVN. Well, I'll be——

HANS. —that you confess yourself ashamed at not having spoken up before——

RAVN. But, Hans?

HANS. —and that you ask the others to do the same—that is, confess that they have made a mistake, and that they have waited too long to say so.

RAVN. In other words, we are to strip ourselves naked? Oh, you arch-sentimentalist, you king of all phrase-mongers! Will you please accept my most subservient compliments? So this is "the new system of the new generation"? Is it?

HANS. Jesting is of no use. It will have to begin with confessions——

RAVN. Suit yourself.

HANS. And if *you* won't, I shall assist you.

RAVN. In what way—if I may ask Your Profundity?

HANS. I shall reprint the articles you wrote that time. They are in my possession, and I have made a historical study of the influence they exerted. This I shall set forth—as well as the author's name.—Now, you have your choice!

RAVN. I think you have lost your reason! Oh—you are the biggest fool the world ever saw!

KAMPE. [*Enters*] My, but you're looking glum! What's up? I thought you were in the Diet.

RAVN. We have adjourned for an hour.

KAMPE. Has anything happened, as you——   [Stops.

HANS. I'll tell you.

RAVN. No.

HANS. Yes. Do you know that it was Father Ravn here who, in his day——

RAVN. Stop that nonsense now! It's my concern, and not yours.

KAMPE. What is it?

RAVN. Oh, it's a confounded story, that's what it is—and that fellow over there is a regular lunatic, a scatter-brained idealist, an inveterate scandal-maker, a chatterbox—in a word, your son! Good-bye!   [Takes up his hat.

KAMPE. Well, well?

HANS. He was the man who once got the system praised abroad and who started the whole mischief in that way.

KAMPE. What did you say?

HANS. It was he—none but he! And he has nicely managed to keep it covered up all these years. And now, when there is a chance to make up for it, he wants to dodge the voting.

RAVN. [Coming back into the room again] Well, don't you know that a speech or a vote more or less doesn't matter at present? For the system is not going to be dispensed with just yet—not this time. So, why don't you leave me alone?

HANS. It's the proceedings in the matter that are the main thing. Every issue must be dealt with in such a manner that through it we get ahead a step or two, morally and intellectually. [RAVN starts to go; HANS follows him] Go back to the Diet. There is only one way for us to get out of the mud in which we are sticking: let us stand up and confess!

KAMPE. Ravn—you have got to do it.

RAVN. Oh, go to Hades with your idiotic talk!

HANS. Don't then! And I'll do it for you.

RAVN. [*Going up to* KAMPE] Did you ever hear anything like it? What kind of generation is this?

KAMPE. We were too easy-going in our day. Now these young ones are a little too keen, perhaps.

RAVN. He will ruin himself, just as you ruined yourself, only in a different fashion.—Well, now I must go. Any cigars?—Oh, that's right, they're too strong for me.

KAMPE. Good-bye.

HANS. [*Simultaneously*] Are you going to speak?

RAVN. Oh, I am not proclaiming in advance what I am going to do.—Lunatic! [*Goes out to the left.*

KAMPE. I never thought that he—— [*Stops.*

HANS. Well, there you are. Even those who are held particularly outspoken among us, are as cowardly as the rest. They only feel differently about it.

KAMPE. Well, well!

HANS. Look—who's coming there?

KAMPE. What? Karen——!

HANS. And the way she looks.——

KAMPE. I think something——

HANS. Oh, what can it mean? Step aside a little, will you? —Karen! [*She appears in the doorway on the right side.*

FIFTH SCENE

HANS. KAMPE. KAREN *has no hat on and appears just as she was when she rose from the bed or couch on which* FREDERICK *had laid her after her attack of hysterics.*

KAREN. No one must see me. I have stolen out of the house. Mamma thought I was sleeping. Hans, let us make haste!

HANS. Where?

KAREN. Away—very far away. Come now!

HANS. Yes.

KAREN. For I can't stay at home any longer. No, I won't!

HANS. No?

>KAMPE *signals to* HANS, *pointing first to* KAREN, *then to himself; then in direction of* KAREN'S *home; then he hurries out.*

HANS. You are sick?

KAREN. Yes, I am sick—for I have such a pain here—especially in here—oh, such a pain, such a pain—oh, this struggle!

HANS. But you should wait till you are well again.

KAREN. No, I'll never get well at home. No!—They say that I don't sleep enough. But it isn't that! No—I have known a long time what it was. But I haven't wanted to speak of it. I can tell it to you, but nobody else must hear it.

HANS. Nobody will!

KAREN. Do you remember when we were children and went out rowing together?

HANS. Yes.

KAREN. Why can't we do that now? Come!

HANS. Karen!

KAREN. Oh, how nice it is to feel your hand about mine! How good it feels! Just as when we were children. I think of it every day. Don't you do that also?

HANS. Karen!

KAREN. If you'll only row me far, far away, then everything will be as it used to be.

HANS. But hadn't you better rest a little first? You are so tired.

KAREN. Not at all. It's only my head—oh, that feels good, so good! Now I feel quiet, Hans!

HANS. Do you?

KAREN. Yes. For I have had a hard time. Oh, this struggle, this struggle!

HANS. But hadn't you better rest?

KAREN. I am resting now.

HANS. Sit down here, and you'll rest still better.

KAREN. But remember, we must go away.

HANS. At once!—Now sit down here.

KAREN. No, you must sit down first.

HANS. All right.   [*He sits down.*

KAREN. And I'll sit here.   [*Sits down on the sofa.*

HANS. That's it.   [*He keeps her hand in his.*

KAREN. Poor little mamma!

HANS. Should we let your mother know?

KAREN. No.—Poor, poor mamma!

HANS. Yes, she is kind.

KAREN. Do you like me?

HANS. I have never liked anybody else.

KAREN. Why did you start all this struggle then?

HANS. But you agreed with me about it before?

KAREN. We women have to bear the worst of it.

HANS. Dearest!

KAREN. It wasn't nice of you, Hans.

HANS. Karen!

KAREN. No, not nice—not nice at all——

HANS. She's sleeping.

> FREDERICK *appears in the background, approaching hurriedly.* HANS *waves him back.*

KAREN. What is it, Hans?

HANS. Oh, I thought you were asleep? Are you not all right now?

KAREN. Yes—it's all right. [*Silence*

FREDERICK. Is she asleep?

HANS *nods affirmation.*

FREDERICK. That's good!

Comes nearer on tiptoe; holds out both hands to HANS, *who gives him the one hand that's free.*

KARL RAVN. [*In from the left*] Come up to the Diet! Uncle Frederick is going to——

FREDERICK *and* HANS. [*Turning toward* KARL] Hush!

KARL. [*Who has stopped on seeing* FREDERICK] Oh, are you here? What's up?

BOTH. Hush!

Curtain.

A C T   V

The private office of the Director-General in his home by the sea.

FIRST SCENE

When the curtain rises, Riis *is seen escorting a gentleman to the door and beyond it with the utmost courtesy.
Then he comes slowly back into the room and takes up
a position in the middle of it.   There he stands for a
few moments with his feet far apart.*

Riis. So His Excellency is in doubt! I have been sus-
pecting it.   There was an unmistakable question in his eyes—
whether, at bottom, I was not in doubt myself. [*Brings his
feet together and walks around a few steps, but soon he resumes,
as if unconsciously, his previous position*] Doubt—yes, yes,
doubt?—What is there in this world that cannot be doubted?
—And it is the same thing in the office.   Exactly the same
kind of eyes.   They have been vouching for the system, those
fellows.   And now they are in a dilemma.   They have lost
their own faith—and now they are drawing on mine.   Except
Larssen.   He has faith!—But when a firmly founded, wholesome nature like Larssen can have faith in it, then I am sure
there must be something to it.   There must!—I had my
doubts in the beginning—yes, I had!   The whole thing
seemed too good to be true—but by that time the others
were convinced—and they restored my own conviction—
At bottom it is entirely their fault—indeed, it is!—Of course,
it is!   There is no question about it.   The whole thing had
been turned into a national cause before anybody knew what

was happening. To believe became a habit, and all the
doubters were laughed into silence.—Those were beautiful
days! Oh, my!—And then—then a young fellow comes back
from America and joins hands with an old drunkard—and
that's all that's needed! It's almost like a fairy tale! No
amount of chloroform will help any longer—it has to be
fought out—and when it's all over, I find myself left behind
like "a bridge across dry land." [*Bringing his feet together
again*] That's an infernal habit I have got into!—But what
am I to do now? Act as if nothing had happened? Impossible! Those confounded eyes are pursuing me. If I only
had faith myself—! Larssen has! But when Larssen believes, there must be something to believe in. And haven't
I proved that there is? Yes, I have—and there can be no
question about it.—Larssen is so complete. Larssen believes
in himself—and that's the real trick. Yes, that's what all
hangs on!—Why the deuce can't I believe in myself? I am
the man who has furnished Larssen with all the proofs—those
very proofs on which his faith is founded!—Yes, but *I* don't
believe in them any longer— No—yes—no—I don't believe—not quite. There is something—Now, there I am
with my legs the old way again!—"A bridge across dry land!"
—It seems to me as if everybody was staring at my legs ever
since that thing was printed in the paper. [*Brings his feet
together nervously and begins to walk again*] If I had anybody
—anybody that really believed in me!—Kamma?—Of course,
—she means well—[*with a sigh*] but—Marie? Yes, *you*
would have been the right one now! And much I would
have bothered about the rest then! You were so wise and
strong—you would have kept me firm—and it would never
have come to this!—Oh, it's nothing but that family, that
confounded family! God preserve a poor human creature
from falling into the hands of enthusiasts! Of all people

they are the most treacherous—and to make it worse, they call that honesty! Even my own children—Frederick! Oh, Frederick! He is always looking at me with a pair of eyes like those of a sick animal. He has his doubts, he, too—and I cannot help him! They have poisoned him, for their blood is in him also—the traitors, the thieves! [*A knock at the door is heard*] Thank heaven, somebody is coming! It's simply dreadful to be left alone in this way. Come in!

SECOND SCENE

LARSSEN. INSPECTOR RAVN. RIIS.

RIIS. Oh, it's you, Larssen? That's nice of you! You are just the man I want!—So, the Diet has partly decided against us, but—not in principle, Larssen.

LARSSEN. Not in principle.

RIIS. A man who does things has always strong allies, and then, when you have a cause—a cause in which you have *faith*——

LARSSEN. Well—it's on that it depends——

RIIS. On *that?* [*He discovers* RAVN, *who has entered behind* LARSSEN] Oh, you?— Are you there, too?

RAVN. Yes, why not?

RIIS. And you ask that? You, who publicly—oh, this is carrying it a little too far!

RAVN. Oh, is it? To me it seems as if I had a great deal better right to come here than I had before.

RIIS. Indeed? No——

RAVN. Our relationship is much more truthful now. But, of course, if you want to be solemn about it, I can leave.

LARSSEN. It is I who permitted myself to ask the Canal Inspector to accompany me here.

Riis. You, Larssen? How can that be?

Ravn. Larssen and I have had a consultation—perhaps you may guess about what.

Riis. No.

Ravn. Oh, you cannot?— Well, let's get out the documents then. There is doubt in the air, as you probably know —and we wanted you to settle the matter. May we be seated? [*Is about to spread out some papers on the table.*

Riis. In other words, you mean to put me on trial?

Ravn. Didn't I tell you, Larssen, that he would take it in that way?

Riis. What does that mean?

Larssen. I relied on the kindness—on the generosity you have always shown, Mr. Riis—and your impartiality——

Riis. What is it all about? If it's something that you, especially *you*, my dear Larssen, want to find out—then you know where to look for me.

Ravn. There is a point on which we differ, don't you understand?

Riis. I should like to have Mr. Larssen's explanation.

Ravn. Does that mean that you want me to go?

Riis. [*After a moment's hesitation*] You are my wife's brother—and if you have forgotten it, then it behooves me, for her sake, to remember it.

Ravn. How very considerate of you!

Larssen. Now that's what I expected of you, Mr. Riis. That's the way I have always seen you. And it is for that reason I venture to speak openly to you.

Riis. By all means, Larssen. We two have always stood together.

Larssen. So we have, Mr. Riis. It has been the pride of my life. For in you—if you will permit me to say so—I have beheld a man—a man standing in the very front rank of what we may call the engineering science of our own day.

RIIS. You have always over-estimated me, Larssen.

LARSSEN. And nevertheless you have been generous enough— Well, I have—if you will permit me to say so—for I am immensely—I don't know how to express it—I have been carried beyond my usual—that is, I have entertained boundless confidence in you, Mr. Riis!

RIIS. And I in you, my dear Larssen.

LARSSEN. I thank you, sir—but it is wholly undeserved on my part.

RIIS. Not at all.

LARSSEN. Pardon me. I know better. No, indeed! I am not a strong soul. I have always needed a support. You, in your tremendous superiority, cannot realise what that means.

RIIS. Don't say that, Larssen!

LARSSEN. Yes. If I have ever admired anything in this world, it has been the lofty equanimity always preserved by you when my own soul was undermined by doubt.

RIIS. Your——?

LARSSEN. What a thing to be able, as you have been, to concentrate the opposition within your own house, so to speak! This smiling self-assurance—yes, smiling, literally smiling! That's what it means to have faith, I have often said to myself.

RIIS. But tell me, Larssen—you believe, don't you?

LARSSEN. I want to be frank, Mr. Riis.

RIIS. You always are, Larssen.

LARSSEN. Yes—that is, in so far as it lies in me to be so. For frequently I have not known where I stood—whether I believed or not.

RIIS. *You*, Larssen?

LARSSEN. But in such moments I drew strength from watching you, Mr. Riis.

RIIS. You watched me? [*Quite forgetting himself*] That's something you should not have done, Larssen.

LARSSEN. But heavens, why not, Mr. Riis?

RIIS. [*Forgetting himself still further*] No—because I put my faith in you, Larssen.

LARSSEN. [*Horror-stricken*] In me?— You!

RAVN. This is becoming quite amusing.

RIIS. No—oh, no—this is the worst I ever—! [*Running back and forth*] Are you, then, nothing but an impostor?

LARSSEN. Wha—wha—what's that you are saying?

RIIS. Well, what do you want to call it that you have made people, that you have made me, believe that you believed what you did *not* believe?

LARSSEN. Didn't I believe? Of course I believed!

RIIS. The deuce you did! You only believed in me.

LARSSEN. It means that one thing went with the other—as it usually does in this world.

RIIS. It means that one lie went with another! Oh, how could I let myself be fooled in such a way?

LARSSEN. Fooled? Yes, one of us has been fooled. That new system of yours——

RIIS. Mine? It isn't mine!

LARSSEN. Whose can it be, if not yours?

RIIS. It was in practical use long before me.

RAVN. That's a fact.

LARSSEN. And yet it was you who introduced it?

RIIS. I? Am I the government? Am I the Diet? Have I the power to introduce anything?

RAVN. Hear, hear!

LARSSEN. But nevertheless—all the same—why, it was done by the Commissions, of which you——

RIIS. Do you think I appointed the Commissions? Or that they were made up of me alone?

LARSSEN. Well—this is the end of it!

RAVN. That's the stuff! Bravo!

LARSSEN. And yet—why, it was—*the estimates* were misleading.

RIIS. That's too bad! For the estimates were made by you, Larssen—by yourself and the rest of the office. Have you forgotten that this fact was mentioned in every report?

LARSSEN. F—f—finally, it's *me* who—who is to blame for the whole thing?

RIIS. Well, I'll be hanged if I am!

LARSSEN. And I who have relied so completely on you!

RIIS. Well, I never asked you to do anything of the kind.

LARSSEN. And this language! This tone!

RIIS. Well, you may be sure *that's* "true"—there's no deceit in that! If this kind of thing is in fashion, I can be fashionable, too. Now, Larssen, you'd better go, or I might become "truthful" to the extent of throwing you out.

LARSSEN. Good-bye, M—M—Mr. Riis!   [*Goes out.*

RAVN. I might as well take away the papers again—I don't suppose we'll have any use for them.

                              [*Puts the papers in order.*

RIIS. Oh, go to the devil with the whole outfit!

RAVN. Why, this is lovely! It's a real joy to strike the bottom of a man's character for once.

RIIS. [*Comes to a standstill, as if struck by the remark just made*] I have long enough been the patient one. What would be the use of it in this case?

RAVN. Oh, is that how you feel? Then you had better follow my example.

RIIS. [*Stopping again*] In what way?

RAVN. Confess everything.

RIIS. I have nothing to confess.

RAVN. Oh, you haven't!— Good-bye! [*Goes out.*

RIIS. Confess?— Why? Is the man crazy!— Who's that? Oh, you! [MRS. RIIS *enters.*

THIRD SCENE

RIIS. MRS. RIIS. FREDERICK *a little later.*

RIIS. You also?— What are you crying for? What's the matter, now? I haven't time, and I'm in no mood for it.

MRS. RIIS. [*Weeping*] Fred-er-ick——

RIIS. Well? What about him? What about him?

MRS. RIIS. —has told me all. [*Still weeping.*

RIIS. All of what? [FREDERICK *comes in*] What's all this?

FREDERICK. About Anna, papa.

RIIS. There now! Do bring out everything at once! You have just hit on the right moment for it.

MRS. RIIS. There is nothing for it, dear, but that Frederick must start after her at once.

RIIS. Well, if this doesn't beat everything! He sha'n't move from the spot! Do you think Frederick has duties to every possible kind of human being but me? I might overlook his disloyalty——

FREDERICK. What do you mean?

MRS. RIIS. [*Speaking simultaneously with* FREDERICK] Dear!

RIIS. Yes, to-day I have become "sincere" also. I can overlook it as long as it is known only to myself. But for him to leave now—it would seem as if he fled from a sinking ship. I'll never in the world permit it.

FREDERICK. Then I shall have to leave without your permission.

MRS. RIIS. But, Frederick!

Riis. Yes, you just try!— Did anybody ever experience anything like it before?

Mrs. Riis. Be loving now, dear!

Riis. Oh, leave me alone with your babblings about love!

Frederick. No, now I have to——

Riis. Are you two in a conspiracy? And all this comes from that miserable family of yours!

Mrs. Riis. You are always saying unpleasant things about my family!

Riis. Well, isn't it responsible for the whole disaster?— Oh, what a misfortune to be tied to that kind of company! What haven't I done to maintain some kind of balance! To preserve *outward* propriety at least!— And now—! When everything is tumbling down about me, then my own children turn on me, led by their mother. One of them throws herself into the arms of my worst enemy——

Mrs. Riis. But she didn't know what she was doing!

Riis. The other one into the arms of a strumpet.

Frederick. Now, you had better go, mamma!

Mrs. Riis. Oh, Frederick! Forgive him! He has suffered so much!—Dear, I have never seen you like this!

Riis. No, you haven't. But when a man has spent all his life patiently listening to all sorts of unendurable twaddle —then—just for once—perhaps I may also say what I think!

Mrs. Riis. No, this is not what you think, dear. I know it.

Riis. Yes, it is! I think that you have taken the children away from me——

Mrs. Riis. I?

Riis. You and yours—in a way, that is—before they were born even.

Mrs. Riis. Dearest, I cannot help that the children take after my family. [*She begins to weep.*

RIIS. Oh, if you hadn't thought more of the family than of me, I guess those cubs of yours would have resembled me a little more.

FREDERICK. Now, mamma, you mustn't stay any longer! Come now!

MRS. RIIS. You can't speak to your father without me.

FREDERICK. Oh, yes, I can.   [*Leading her to the door.*

MRS. RIIS. But Karen? I was to——

FREDERICK. I'll speak about Karen also.

MRS. RIIS. Please remember what he has had to bear!

FREDERICK. Mamma!

> *Embraces and kisses her; then he leads her out and returns alone.*

FOURTH SCENE

RIIS. FREDERICK.

RIIS. I don't want any further conversation.

FREDERICK. No, but *I* do.   [*Takes out a letter.*

RIIS. I hope you'll understand that my patience is at an end.

FREDERICK. And so is mine.

                [*Takes another letter out of the first one.*

RIIS. Go.

FREDERICK. Here is something from a person named Marie.

RIIS. Marie?

FREDERICK. *You* know her, don't you? [*Reads*] "Your mother writes to me, dear Anna, that you love Frederick Riis, the son of the Director-General, and that he is offering to marry you." [*Stops reading to say*] Pardon me—but I must! [*Reads again*] "Once his father offered to marry me. Yet he left me to marry for money and advancement. Such things are in the blood, my girl. You had better look out for the son." [*Speaking*] Perhaps *you* would like to read the rest?

RIIS. No.

FREDERICK. "Such things are in the blood."—To my misfortune, I have been made aware of it. But, fortunately enough, what I have got from my mother is stronger still— I am going to follow Anna. I don't care for a career at such a price. It might so easily end in another fallacious system.

RIIS. My boy!

FREDERICK. I know that—until a short while ago—I should rather have given my life than let myself be forced into saying such things as these. Now I must leave—and one more reason is that I could never bear to say them again.

RIIS. Frederick——!

FREDERICK. Don't be cruel to mamma!

RIIS. [*In a whisper*] What are you saying?

FREDERICK. Don't be cruel to mamma!—You have begun by deceiving her.

RIIS. But, Frederick!

FREDERICK. She doesn't know. Mamma asks for so little. She thinks well of everybody.—Oh, what might not have become of her! In her innocence, in her very lack of development, she is sweeter than anything else I can think of. [RIIS *shows emotion*] Be good to mamma! Please be good to her!

> RIIS *goes over to* FREDERICK *and they fall into each other's arms.*

FREDERICK. Thank you for what you have done for me! To me you have been good.

RIIS. I meant to do the best I could.   [*Deeply moved.*

FREDERICK. I know it.—But do it some other way hereafter— Why don't you begin with Karen?

RIIS. I will.

> *They draw away a little but continue to hold each other's*
> *hands.*

FREDERICK. Thank you!—I think the memory of this
moment will bring me home again some time. [*They embrace
again. Silence. When they have torn themselves away,* FRED-
ERICK *says*] Now, I must first of all try to make something
out of myself.

RIIS. You are not leaving at once?

FREDERICK. Not at once. Papa, may I bring Karen to
you?

RIIS. Yes.

> FREDERICK *opens the door for* KAREN *and goes out him-*
> *self.*

FIFTH SCENE

RIIS. KAREN.

KAREN. Don't get angry with me, papa—I wanted only
to ask you—May I go away also?

RIIS. You, too, Karen?

KAREN. I have applied for a position as a teacher—and
I think I'll get it.

RIIS. You teach? Why?

KAREN. Because it is the only thing I can do—if I can do
that.

RIIS. But are you not just as free here? Don't we let you
do what you will?

KAREN. I do nothing at all— And then—— [*She hesitates.*

RIIS. And then?

KAREN. I need the work.

RIIS. But you can work at home.

KAREN. Yes—but—— [*Hesitates again.*

RIIS. What is it, Karen?

KAREN. I cannot stay here. [*She bursts into tears.*

RIIS. Things will change. I promise you they shall.

KAREN. Papa, let me go!

RIIS. Do as you will. [*He sits down*] So you are leaving me also.

KAREN. [*Kneeling beside him*] Nobody is leaving *you*. We are only leaving what is wrong.

RIIS. Oh, Karen!

KAREN. I can do a great deal for your sake. Mamma has taught me.

RIIS. Are you then also to be unhappy for my sake?

KAREN. As the years go by, we shall see.

RIIS. As the years go by— Then there will not be much left of me.

KAREN. As the years go by, you will, perhaps, see things differently.

RIIS. I understand. You don't believe in me.

KAREN. Don't get angry, papa—but do you believe in yourself?

RIIS. [*Rising*] Yes! [KAREN *gets up;* RIIS *sits down again*] Leave me now, Karen!

KAREN *goes out.*

SIXTH SCENE

MRS. RIIS. [*Puts in her head through the door on the right*] Are you alone now?

RIIS. Yes, my dear.

MRS. RIIS. [*Comes into the room*] Don't let that dishearten you, my own dear! It's what happens to every great and noble man. It means that his faith has to be tried, don't you know—and his love also.

Riis. Oh, no, no, no, no!

Mrs. Riis. Is it as bad as that? If I only knew how to help you! But a wife is merely what the man has made out of her, and sometimes that isn't quite enough.

Riis. You say such things at times—well, don't let us talk of it now.—Oh, Lord!—Yes, yes, yes!

Mrs. Riis. It's such a queer time, too. Nothing remains secure any longer.

Riis. It's a time of doubt, of transition.

Mrs. Riis. But isn't every time one of transition? For every time has its own system——

Riis. [*Jumps up*] Don't mention the word!—I beg your pardon! Please be patient with me. Things will grow better, I assure you.

Mrs. Riis. Dear, you mustn't think that I don't understand you.

Riis. No, *you*, for one, believe! You are the only one.

Mrs. Riis. And how about yourself, dear? As long as you feel sure of yourself, nobody else can touch you. That's a true word.—What is it, dearest?

Riis. I want to go—I should like—but I don't know where? There seems to be no place for me to go to.

Mrs. Riis. How about the shore? The sea? There is a sense of infinity about the sea. Don't you think so, dear?

Riis. Yes—yes, of course. Well, let us go down to the shore, then.

Mrs. Riis. Yes, I am going with you. [*Takes his arm.*
Riis. Well, then—we're going then!

Curtain.